The
Creative Writing
Coursebook

EDITED BY JULIA BELL
AND PAUL MAGRS

Julia Bell is a novelist and lecturer in Creative Writing at Birkbeck, University College of London. Her novels *Massive* and *Dirty Work* are widely translated and published in the US. She has edited many short fiction anthologies and is also the founder of Birkbeck's literary magazine *The Mechanics' Institute Review*. Before moving to London she taught at the University of East Anglia, which is where she wrote *The Creative Writing Coursebook*. She has just completed a third novel – *Wise Up!*

Paul Magrs is a lecturer in English Literature and Creative Writing at the University of East Anglia. He has published a collection of short stories and seven novels, including *Modern Love* (Allison and Busby, 2000) and *All the Rage* (Allison and Busby, 2001).

The
Creative Writing
Coursebook

Forty Writers
Share Advice and Exercises
for Poetry and Prose

EDITED BY JULIA BELL
AND PAUL MAGRS

MACMILLAN

First published 2001 by Macmillan
an imprint of Pan Macmillan, a division of Macmillan Publishers Limited
Pan Macmillan, 20 New Wharf Road, London N1 9RR
Basingstoke and Oxford
Associated companies throughout the world
www.panmacmillan.com

ISBN 978-0-333-78225-5

23 25 27 29 28 26 24 22

A CIP catalogue record for this book is available from
the British Library.

Typeset by SX Composing DTP, Rayleigh, Essex
Printed and bound by CPI Group (UK) Ltd, Croydon, CR0 4YY

Visit **www.panmacmillan.com** to read more about all our books and to buy
them. You will also find features, author interviews and news of any author
events, and you can sign up for e-newsletters so that you're always first to hear
about our new releases.

Contents

12 Off the Page

Conclusion

Acknowledgements

Big thanks are due to the following people for their help in preparing this book:

Julian Jackson at UEA, Emma Hargrave and Penny Rendall at Tindal Street Press and our very patient editor at Macmillan, Catherine Whitaker. Also thanks to Jeremy Hoad, Joy Foster, Stuart and Pru Bell. Many thanks to all the contributors for being so generous with their own work and experience.

Foreword
Andrew Motion

This coursebook grew out of the Creative Writing programme at the University of East Anglia. The MA course at the university, founded thirty years ago by Malcolm Bradbury and Angus Wilson, is one of the best known in the country, due largely to the fact that many of its graduates have made famous names for themselves.

But as those who have taken the course often testify, its main purpose is not to discover ways of achieving wordly success – welcome as that might be. The real value of the MA lies in its presenting students with a chance to concentrate on their work in an atmosphere that is at once intense and supportive: to develop their skills, to search more deeply into their selves and their imaginations, to experiment and to diversify. It is first and foremost a writing course – and if this emphasis eventually leads to graduates seeing their names in lights, all well and good.

In this respect the MA resembles the creative writing component of the undergraduate course at UEA. At this earlier stage there is a similar value attached to commitment and adventure, and a similar combination of openness and rigour in the teaching. This is what the coursebook celebrates – and, as it celebrates, elaborates.

Although the coursebook reflects the mood and method of undergraduate creative writing teaching at UEA, it embraces notions of similar practice elsewhere. This is its great strength: it is at once particular and general, solidly based and outward looking. Because of this, and because it so ably mixes good sense with distinguished example, the book is a vital asset for writers and teachers alike. It represents an important contribution to the emerging debate about how criticizing and creating can be combined in English studies everywhere.

Introduction
Julia Bell

There remains in circulation a myth that writing can't be taught. That despite the proliferation of writing courses, creative writing is something esoteric, unpindownable, something inspired by muses and shaped by genius. You've either got it or you haven't, so there's little point in trying to teach it. The success of the writing courses at UEA and elsewhere belies this myth. Under the pressure of sustained practice, criticism and exercise, we see, every year, students emerging from our courses who will go on to become successful writers. But it is not only the success stories who validate our belief that writing can be taught. There are plenty of students who will write good stories or poems, maybe even get them published, who won't go on to enter the world of writing, but in learning how to generate and shape a successful piece of creative work they have added something important to their repertoire of life skills, something that will go on to give them pleasure throughout their lives.

This coursebook loosely follows the structure that we use at UEA on our undergraduate Creative Writing programme. The aim is to take you through a series of exercises from the first words you will write on the page, to shaping your piece of work into something coherent, to practical advice on what to do with your work once it is finished. We hope that this book will be useful to writers of both poetry and prose and that the sound practice which it contains will be of help to writers, from beginners to experienced professionals, who are looking for ideas for their own writing workshops.

This book won't teach you how to be instantly successful; indeed, if this is your motive for buying this book, the chances are you won't progress a great deal. Neither can we legislate for perspective or personality or an openness to self-investigation. What we can do is provide you with the tools through which you can begin to create a piece of imaginative writing. Here are exercises and essays that will make you think about how a piece of work is shaped once it is written, and that try to offer distinctions between good and bad practice. This book can offer you advice that on your own may take years to learn.

Writing and academia have not always sat comfortably together. The literary food chain from writer to critic does not always create a happy environment within which to work. Increasingly, however, as creative writing becomes embedded within many university English curriculums, the relationship has changed. Many of the critical questions more often associated with literature seminars are now being asked in writing seminars, as students investigate the process of writing a text. Questions, for example, about the nature of character, narrative, point of view, landscape and ambiguity. Asking students to investigate these issues through the production of their own piece of writing increases their understanding and confidence in their critical abilities. They become more articulate, more flexible, more engaged with their texts.

Perhaps the real question is not whether writing has a positive effect on criticism, but whether such close proximity to one's own dissection has anything useful to offer a writer. This book, we believe, is proof that it does. Here are writers who can anatomize and explain their own practice, who can offer rigorous advice and examples. This is more than simple common sense; it is a product of the relationship between a critical and creative discourse.

The book is split into three sections: Gathering, Shaping and Finishing. There are exercises and activities to try throughout; and to help you navigate the book you will see that they are marked with a symbol in the margins. In Gathering we start off with encouragement and simple exercises to get you started; the essays move through issues of detail and abstraction to the uses of autobiography in your own work. Following that, Shaping is the section where the creative/critical crossover is most obviously addressed. Academics and writers explain plotting and narrative construction, the uses and effects of point of view, the nature of characterization and the employment of landscape in writing. Finishing, the final section, offers pragmatic advice on how to edit and refine your work. It contains essays by editors and publishers on how to prepare manuscripts for submission, how to publish your own work and how to find editorial guidance. A chapter on workshops features different perspectives on the nature and uses of writing workshops.

This book is really a gift. It is a unique and generous pool of information, one that contains the condensed experience and expertise of over forty different writers and editors from around the UK and abroad. Here you will find writers elucidating their own practice and sharing the pitfalls and triumphs they have encountered over the course of their professional lives.

This book may well have a strange effect on your life: you may find yourself sat at midnight scribbling into a notebook, or muttering to yourself on a long walk as you try to figure out the next stage of your poem or story, or you may find yourself sending off stories or poems to small magazines or big publishing houses. We hope you will be as encouraged and delighted by this book as we have been in editing it. But be warned, the practice of writing, once initiated, is very hard to stop.

Gathering

1 Getting Started

Introduction
Julia Bell

Clearing Your Throat

Good writing depends on practice, like sports; the more limbered up you are, the better you perform. But how do you pass through that first, often terrifying, encounter with the blank page and find a voice that will carry your thoughts and feelings with eloquence and flair? You have lots of ideas, but little confidence in your ability to express them. What if it comes out wrong? What if it makes you look childish or naive? What if you can't do it? The blank page seems to taunt you with your own underconfidence; it points to all the great works that have gone before and says, You can't do that, or, What's the point? It's all been said already. The reams of sentences, the characters, the ideas that drove you to the page in the first place wither into nothing. Suddenly the whole project becomes impossible and your desire to write remains just that.

The only way to overcome this problem is to write. Get some material down on paper, however rough and ready. Start off with notes, fragments, half sentences, until the stuttering stops and you find yourself writing whole sentences, paragraphs, pages. Often the first hurdle is the writer's own self-consciousness about the act of writing itself. And that hurdle might well take a few pages to clear, like an old car with a dirty petrol tank; the first few miles will be a juddering, stop-start journey. Be prepared for this. You are engaging with something unfamiliar to you, don't expect to produce a masterpiece in your first attempt. Start off with what you had for tea, the last phone call you made, the colour of your lover's eyes, your

3

favourite CD. Give yourself a subject and write about it, without stopping or correcting yourself, for five minutes. Just generate some pages, a body of work.

Then read it back to yourself.

This will be hard: a first-time encounter with your own work is not dissimilar to watching yourself on TV or hearing your recorded voice for the first time – Do I really sound like that? Oh no, I never knew I looked like that. You might well be embarrassed or disappointed. Don't stop. This is a rite of passage. Good radio presenters listen to their own voices over and over so they can control and improve their pitch and delivery. In the same way, good writers will read through their own writing, looking for sentences that can be improved, pushed further, expanded, cut. It is only when you have developed a sense of your own fictional voice that you will really have the confidence to jump in and write a story. However, paradoxically, it is only through writing that you will develop a sense of what your voice really is.

Your fictional voice is not a million miles away from how you speak. A good storytelling voice is a more honed and structured version of speech, and it is as individual to you as your fingerprints. Look at the books you read. What kinds of voices are clamouring for your attention on your bookshelf? You are likely to find lots of disparate voices talking, all with different accents, references, cadences, obsessions.

Voice in fiction or poetry can be interpreted as perspective or personality. It is different from style, which is something that you can develop later to create effects. A poem I wrote when I was thirteen still sounds like me in my thirties. Perhaps it's a sad reflection on my continuing juvenility or, more seriously, it is the thread of me-ness that runs through my work, the personality that inhabits all the words I write.

✍ *Try the following exercise either by yourself or in a group.*

Write down five sounds that you can hear. Then list the things that you associate with those sounds. A car engine may remind you of being picked up after school, clanking crockery of that summer you worked at Pizza Pie, an aeroplane of your holiday to Ibiza.

This exercise is especially effective in class because in the institutional hush of university buildings there are very few sounds to be heard: air con, buzzing strip lights, heels down the corridor outside, the droning of the lecturer next door. Everyone in the group hears the same or similar things, but they all use different words to express what they have heard, and the sounds have very different associations for them. These associations are unique, born out of individual experience; no one else has these particular stories to tell with these words. These associations and words are, very embryonically, the writer's voice.

If you have done this exercise on your own, look at the words you have chosen to describe the things you have heard and the associations you have made with those sounds. These are your stories, this is your language, this is the beginning of your fictional voice.

Getting into the Groove

'I have to start to write to have ideas.'

FRANÇOISE SAGAN

Write every day. Even if it's only a letter. Now you've put pen to paper, you want to try to write something every day. Set yourself some achievable targets. Try to write that story you've always meant to write about the mad woman with orange hair who lives down the road or that poem about your cat.

Choose concrete subjects: draw some word sketches of your living room, your backyard, the fish tank. Get into the habit of looking for the telling details, and don't waste adjectives – when you qualify a noun make it interesting, pertinent, unusual.

You want to have words at your fingertips, so read like mad. Everything and anything: dictionaries, cookery books, novels, poetry, biographies, textbooks, car manuals, football programmes, magazines. Write lists of words and keep them near you; if you get stuck, write five hundred words using a new word in every sentence.

Buy a notebook and a few good-quality pens and take yourself out for the day. Go and sit in a café, get an extra-large cup of coffee and write for a few hours. When I lived by the sea I used to sit and write on the beach, right up at the end by the cliffs where no one could disturb me. With my writing class, one of the first exercises I ask them to do is to go and sit in a café or a pub and write a few character sketches of the people they see around them.

Good writing practice is about discipline. You want to be limbered up, supple, articulate, but this will only happen when you are locked into a groove. If you find it hard to pick up the beat day after day, trick yourself. I find it helpful when I stop for the day to leave the last sentence unfinished or the last paragraph only lightly sketched out, so that when I start again I can pick up where I left off the day before.

Writing creatively takes a peculiar kind of concentration. A concentration that develops its own little habits and tripwires to help set it off. We always want to know *how* authors write, as if their behavioural patterns might be an indicator of how to do it ourselves. But these habits are as idiosyncratic as the writer: Keats could only write if he put on a clean shirt, Virginia Woolf only in the mornings, Douglas Coupland likes to write in bed, longhand, between the hours of midnight and 2 a.m., and if he's mulling over a problem, he'll go out for a long drive and play the car stereo really loud.

Don't expect to write a whole story in one breath. If you get stuck halfway through a piece, be prepared to go back and start again. Make notes on your story, your character, your setting. Though it may feel like treading water, like the notes aren't 'proper' writing, they are essential to the process of developing a sense of what you want to say and of finding the added layers of character and setting that will make the narrative convincing.

Notebooks
Paul Magrs

I write in the same kind of exercise books that I used as a child. At any given moment I have a book on the go. I always carry one with me and each of them soon gets filled up with what I'm thinking about or descriptions of scenes I've witnessed or made up: irresistible snatches of dialogue from bus stops and shops. Little drawings, too. The books are my place to file things away.

The earliest notebooks I remember having and using in this way were from when I was about four. I remember an old-fashioned stationer's in South Shields, which smelled of crayons and had scratched glass counters. I would insist on being taken there and I would spend all my pocket money on drawing books.

I think you can still get those Silvine books. I always had to have books with blank pages. I still don't like writing on lines. That's like ploughing, not writing. And where do you draw when you've got all those lines? Maybe I was fussy like that even at four, and I can see my dad hot and exasperated in the shop as I checked out their stock.

Their very biggest books had covers the colour of mushed-up bananas. Huge creamy pages, and only a few of them, so that after a few large drawings and a bit of writing the whole thing was used up. This was part of the excitement; using books up and getting to the last page. Considering the book as an aesthetic whole. (At four? But I do remember looking through and being pleased.) And having all the finished books in a pile, going through them now and then to remind myself where I'd been and who I'd been looking at and earwigging on.

The smaller books were the size of ordinary school exercise books and these were pillar-box red. I had even more of these.

I'd been set off on this whole writing and drawing business by my infants school teacher, Mrs Payne. She was large and hearty with a shock of silver hair and thick black eyebrows. She made me think she was a more famous version of my own Big Nanna. (Do all little kids think of their teachers as being famous? Whenever I saw a teacher of mine in the town precinct I felt horrible and thrilled; I thought them famous and no one else apparently did.)

Mrs Payne instigated this rule in her infants class that if we were good and industrious enough we would be allowed to have a Busy Book. She gave out new, fresh books and she explained what she meant. She ripped reams of brown paper off the parcels of books and slapped them down, one by one, on our desks. They were blue-covered Silvine books, the intermediate size. She told us that these books were for any spare time we might find. We had complete carte blanche and we need never show anyone what we did on these pages if we didn't want to. The pages were wide, half lined, half blank. Perfect. What we weren't to do, she told us, was to waste time. Fill up any spare time with Busy Books.

After that I made sure I learned everything fast: numbers, spellings, the names of trees. Just to get a chance to get back to the Busy Book. Everything went into those books; I built up quite a stack. After that, I had to have them at home as well.

The book you could put anything into, the book you never had to show anyone.

Mrs Payne had a burglar once and my dad was the copper sent round to take her statement. When he came home, he said he'd been surprised that her place wasn't that posh. They had Venetian blinds up in the living-room window, and he didn't think that was very nice. I was busy writing all this down in my book and, when I'd finished it, I realized for the first time that I'd written something Mrs Payne wouldn't be pleased to read. She wouldn't want to know what my dad had said about her shabby Venetian blinds.

The most important time for writing in these books was, of course, the weekend. Especially at the end of the seventies, when Mam and Dad had split up and he went off to live in Durham in the flat that smelled of new carpets. We stayed with him every weekend, and we would go to see matinees of films like *Battlestar Galactica* and *The*

Wilderness Family. Then, before going up to South Shields to stay with my Little Nanna, we would sit in an ice-cream parlour and have milkshakes. I would start writing immediately, saving the last frothy glugs of strawberry milkshake till afterwards. My brother would have his own book, but he was only three or so, and he'd be filling the pages with vivid, laborious swirls of colour.

I don't have any of the books I used then. With each successive house move everything went out. The oldest writing of mine I now have is from when I was twenty. Those first two hidden novels. A bunch of stories.

Recently I discovered that a friend of mine has kept Busy Books of her own. I've known her novels since I was sixteen; it was her writing that made me think I had every right to write about the people and things I knew about. I was staying with her in London and we talked about having Busy Books, and it turns out she'd kept them consistently since 1959. Little drawings and bits of dialogue, all that stuff.

I thought about how many hundreds of thousands of miles those biro lines would cover and it was exhilarating. That, to me, suddenly represented the real work that a writer does; the white heat of actual composition.

The things a writer publishes are just postcards; extended cards sent back from the distance they've reached. With all the lines she'd written in her Busy Books over the years, my friend had travelled immense distances, even though she's lived mostly in South London.

What I also liked about what she was saying was that she used her notebooks and journals as a kind of anchor. She knew they were always there. When she looked back through different volumes – at 1987, 1976, 1962, whenever – she found that she could put herself back into that moment and into the person she was just then. She could familiarize herself with events and details that she, as a person, had forgotten, but that would always be there in her notebooks.

Some of those moments had made it into her published fiction. They had escaped and been distilled; the notebooks were never a very tight corral. There were fascinating overlaps between life and work if she wanted to find them. But to her the work in her own private books seemed more stabilizing and permanent than the writing that she had actually published.

Think of your notebooks as a way of capturing the things that go through your head. Think of them as yourself, your memory and everything you witness; all of it distilled. In notebooks and journals we see writers in mid-flight.

In my friend's sunny kitchen, she explained to me that she needed the books to remind her of the smallest, most telling details; the things that she saw that rang true to her. These details were small nudges, she said, and you need them to make you feel confident and brave in your writing. You have to be ready to see them; you have to be watching and listening all the time.

'I feel like I'm a pond creature,' she said, 'worrying at plants and busying about, seeing what's going on underwater. And sometimes it's hard. But it's interesting. Very, very interesting. I need to live somewhere that's raw and in the thick of things, but where I can pretend that it's village life, too. And I like to go out in the morning and see wild animals. All of that is important to me.'

I thought: You have to stay open to everything. You have to take notice of everything. The purple in the cornflowers we bought at the tube station; the tea bags curiously left behind on the pub table being scooped into the ashtray and brushed away with the butts. You have to be alert to the twists and tangents of the myriad stories around you, even when they don't seem directly pertinent to the main thrust of the plot you are living inside.

My friend was right. Immersing yourself in the tangents and detail really is like being underwater, and it is hard work. You have to make notes while you are in there. But if you skim over the surface, and if you don't leave yourself prey to distractions and random preoccupations and observations, then what you write will be too composed and artificial. You have to stay open to the surprise of everything.

I end up meeting so many people who want to get their work 'out there'. By which I suppose they mean into the public domain, into publication. And, of course, they want that special reader to get the point of what they're saying. They want to make that connection with strangers. They want to leave a record of their own private view. Many of the writers I meet these days want to make that connection with millions of strangers. They want to be Stars.

To do that, I imagine, they would have to lose some of the privacy of writing. They'd need a microphone rather than a notebook. A writer who becomes a Star, I think, loses a little or a lot of their equilibrium and the stability their notebooks once gave them. They're too concerned with divining what their massive public desires of them. They become genies in lamps. They aren't writing for themselves any more. How can they love what they do? Everything becomes a deadline and it has to be what people expect. Everyone's lamp-rubbing. They have to write books to fit a contract and a jacket that has been designed before they have even written a first line. No more Busy Books; there isn't any time.

But that's what some people want. It's tempting to tell them, So why write? Go and be a Star. Go and be Shirley Bassey. How much time does Shirley Bassey get to experiment and produce the work she really wants to do? Where does a Star keep her private, sketchy work?

When I was staying in London, my friend gave me directions to an old-fashioned stationer's on the King's Road, opposite a cinema. I bought a new book there and walked into town, looking for a café, maybe in Soho, to sit in.

On Keeping a Diary
Nicole Ward Jouve

I have been keeping a diary since I was ten. I am now sixty. Half a century of diary-keeping, fifty-odd notebooks, are now lined up on a bookshelf, close to my bed. There have been years in which I wrote almost nothing. Others that filled up several notebooks. Roughly one per year.

What can I draw from that experience that could be of help to others – at least to some of the readers of this book? Everyone is different: keeping a diary does not suit everybody. Some very good writers have kept them, others, also very good, wouldn't have dreamt of it. The thing is to find out what's right for oneself. What is offered below, however enthusiastic and admonishing, is written in that spirit.

So, what diaries have been for me:

1 A source of tactile and visual pleasure. I like the activity of writing, somewhat under threat in the computer age. I enjoy writing as an act, a craft. Something material, in which the whole body can be involved. I have used notebooks large and tiny, rough and handsome, whatever was at hand when the need to write was upon me. But now I think about it, the sensuousness of paper and cover seems important. I love strong bindings – I feel protected; I'm in business inside strong bindings. I love paper which my travelling, spiralling hand can glide over, can stroke, but also the rough grain of some copybooks. I want rules wide enough for me not to have to squeeze myself to fit in between. And if the cover is silky, shiny, beautifully patterned – well! It follows I'll have to try for something of beauty, won't I?

2 A trusted friend. Especially at adolescence: I could pour it all out, rave and swear at the adults around me, satirize them in poems or devise tragic tales of romantic passion, safe from prying and judgemental eyes. I could be anybody, hold any opinion. There was a space where I was totally wanted. Unconditionally loved. A diary was a kind of permanent transitional object: when one was finished there was a brand-new one between the safe covers of which I could reinvent the wheel. I had a future.

3 The beginning of a voice of my own. When I eventually made it to the world of learning, of academia, where everybody seemed to know better than me and I seemed not to be entitled to my own opinion, it was because I had behind me a long practice of diary-

writing that I could hang on to a sense of self. Something whispered that whatever was valuable about me was who I was. I did not need to dance to the world's tune.

4   A writerly gymnastics. It's like being a dancer or a musician. Unless you practise, you don't develop the muscles, or the suppleness, or the nimbleness of fingers. There are of course geniuses who don't need the practice, some who – like Stendhal, 'raturant le vif', correct the script of life, not the textual script. Yet when I think about it, even Stendhal wrote a great many books (on painting, music, politics and love) before the mere six weeks it took him to pen *The Charterhouse of Parma*. Baudelaire wrote Latin verse at school, and Rimbaud, the lightning genius, began with pastiches of Victor Hugo. Some friends of mine, who were not writers, who wrote clumsily or naively in a magazine we edit together, started the practice of writing for twenty minutes every morning on waking. Anything that came into their heads, any which way, without any care for style, etc. I was doubtful: but I have found that their magazine writing has improved out of all recognition. It is not naive or clumsy any more. It has a flow, a sharpness, an inventiveness that was not there before. The diary-keeping has triggered their creativity.

5   The key to freedom, but also to a sense of the infinite richness of life. If one writes about the day – what's been going on, inside and outside – it soon becomes clear that the choices are endless, and that through the choices one makes one is structuring one's world, inventing oneself. Do I write about what happened in this conversation with a friend, the way the first crescent of moon rose above me in the startlingly black night when I walked out of the doctor's surgery this winter evening, being told on the telephone how my nephew miraculously escaped being injured in a terrible car crash, the memory I had of reading *Anna Karenina* when I was sixteen, the sweet smell of Guinness in the pub yard as I walk past and the memories that summons, or the grief I've been trying to repress? It soon becomes clear that it would take many days to

write down what's been happening during the day – during one hour. It might take the whole of life. That is what books like *Ulysses* or *Mrs Dalloway* or *Remembrance of Things Past* are about. Writing and time. Writing and life. In the choices one makes to write this or that in one's diary, year after year, out of the flow, the shape of who one is appears.

6 The means of transformation, of managing emotions. A friend told me that when an emotional crisis was upon her, especially at nights, she would go into her kitchen, take a large sheet of paper and some paints, and let rip. Paint with her fingers, her hands, her face, anything that she felt like. When she was done, she would find peace. It made me reflect that at times this is how I have used notebooks. When an unbearable climax was upon me, I would write – let rip – dare anything. Or I would vent my rage on to a tape. A grown-up version of the adolescent 'pouring it out'. Then the fit of passion loses its grip. It becomes bearable. One can sleep. When one comes across these outpourings, years later, they can make you wince, they are so raw. But some will have the making of something. There is a shape to be carved out of them, a distinctive voice to be released. Rough drafts, after all, of something that was struggling to be born. Throes of a long drawn-out, yet distant parturition.

7 A tool for inner growth. If one is interested in that sort of thing, of course. Not all diarists are, at least not consciously. But I am, and have been writing down my dreams whenever they seemed important for a great many years. For a long time I could see little meaning in them, or only bits of meaning, or only the bleakest, scariest meaning. If one is a fiction writer these recorded dreams can be an enormous asset, helping one find the inner logic or evolution of a character. But with time, and work, and practice, and the help of people who are gifted in the elucidation of dreams, not only do dreams evolve, new patterns of dreaming appear, but dreams – some of them at least – begin to make more and more sense. A friend of a friend in France wrote a book about her

dreams over a long period of time and called it *Letters from the Night*. That they are messages our unconscious sends us, ever elusive, ever shifting, and yet at times extraordinarily helpful, I do not doubt. One has to keep up the practice of diary-writing over a long period even to begin to decipher some of these messages, but what a treasure trove. It is well worth it.

I could go on for a long time. But seven is a good number. And here I'll stop.

Clearing Some Space
Paul Magrs

I'm always interested to know when people first started writing. Lots of the students I interview to come on the Creative Writing course at UEA tell me that they have 'always written'. They can't exactly remember the moment that they first wrote for themselves. This strikes a chord with me because I'm the same and, like them, it always seemed natural to keep notebooks, journals, to invent stories and poems and make sense of the world, alone, with a pen and a book.

The students do remember a certain time, though, when they took seriously to writing. Often it was the first time that they decided to make something public. They typed up a story, or copied it out neatly, lifted it from the private notebook and attempted to turn it into a shape that someone else could appreciate. Maybe they gave it to a relative or a friend and maybe the reaction was pleasure, surprise, encouragement. From then on a new urgency came into the young writer. They had become aware of an audience out there, that would perhaps consist of just one person, but was there nevertheless. There could be a recipient of the writing that had previously been private and produced naturally as simply an offshoot of their personality. Now they would have to learn to craft their work.

Writers start writing at different stages in life. For every one who has 'always written', and started to learn the techniques of making their work audience-worthy early on, there are others who don't start until much later in life. Perhaps they had all of their confidence knocked out of them by the educational process or their adult life since. Maybe they haven't had the time to spend on an activity that is, in the end, a rather selfish one. They could well have decided that they weren't clever enough or skilled enough when they read the work of other published writers. They might have become convinced that they had nothing to say. All sorts of thoughts put people off from doing the things they really want to do.

When I meet these people, whose confidence has been knocked or who haven't had the chance to try their hand yet, it's often apparent that, whatever reasons they give for not having written yet, they still really want to do it. It's still the thing they would most like to do.

They need to clear some space for themselves. Complicated things like guilt, underconfidence, ambition, pride, and the rest of everyday life – these need to be set aside for a little while. They need to get to know themselves all over again, I think, and get some words down on paper.

Writers at all stages of their career talk about the terror of the white, empty page and that horrid sagging feeling – the hopelessness of ever being able to fill it with anything worthwhile. I think that in order to be able to write well eventually, we have to allow ourselves to write quite badly en route. What tends to hold people up in the first place is their determination that the first line they write down be brilliant. You can wait a long time for that first brilliant line to turn up.

We're used to reading published fiction and poems and, of course, their first lines often are brilliant. They're designed to be like that, in order to seduce us and draw us in. But you have to remind yourself – you have to be told – that these first lines were most probably not what the author first wrote. There could have been hundreds of pages of nonsense they wrote beforehand as they worked themselves up into a position where they knew what they wanted to write about.

So don't aim at brilliance straight away. Nothing is more guaranteed to freeze you up and stop you writing altogether. What a writer publishes is generally only the tip of the iceberg of what they've actually worked through. For every one of my published novels and stories there's another one that I wasn't happy with or that didn't quite work out in the end. There are scores of experiments and half-finished things. There is a lot of waste involved in writing. You could see it as a waste if you were only thinking about finished product. In the process, though, there is an awful lot to learn. I like to tell students that there's often more to be learned from an interesting failed piece of writing than there is to be learned from something that arrives, all in a rush, and seems tidy and perfect on first or second draft.

In this coursebook you won't hear many of these authors talking about muses, flashes of inspiration, or the powerful overflow of emotion. None of us are much given to producing perfect works of art in a blinding crash of lightning. There is a lot of talk about craftsmanship and training yourself, and how that apprenticeship really goes on through the whole of a writer's life. You never stop learning new things about this whole business. A writer wants to go on and on learning. That is, I think, why they do it. It's a discipline with no end, no finite goal in sight.

Which is why people starting out – at any age, at any stage in their lives – shouldn't be scared of not knowing the ropes yet. They shouldn't be so scared that they prevent themselves from broaching that first white page. You have to remember that no one can write exactly as you do. You are the unique product of a unique life history. Even if you had an identical twin, they could never write precisely the poems, plays, stories that you will. So if you don't write this text and in your own particular way, then no one else ever will. No one can ever do it for you. (The best illustration of this comes in the form of ghostwritten autobiographies. Usually they are of celebrity foot-ballers, singers, actors. Have you noticed? In hiring someone to write up their lives for them, these reluctant autobiographers wind up with a blandly unexciting text, full of clichés and second-hand experience, something that just anyone could have written. Even the most exciting life story can be killed stone dead like this.)

Tell yourself that you are writing now because no one else can ever do it for you. It's important for that reason alone. No one has to see the first attempts and experiments you make. Remind yourself that anyone learning a craft has to practise and waste materials as they learn. But our materials are relatively cheap – paper and pens. At least we're not cutting diamonds or stained glass. One slip of the pen and you haven't blown a fortune.

Also, remind yourself that writing practice isn't something only novices do. All writers, at all stages in their careers, have to do it, and you can bet your life that even the most wonderful poets and novelists write wild unpublishable nonsense some of the time, just to get themselves going again.

✍ *Set yourself the following task:*

> You are going to write a page about each of the following topics. Don't let anything intrude on this exercise. No distractions. Don't even think about it too deeply or try to make much sense.
>
> Write down (in five minutes or so for each topic) what you know about:
>
> 1 Garden furniture
> 2 Marilyn Monroe
> 3 The Earth's core
> 4 Eagles
> 5 Fireworks

When you read back what you've written on these subjects, you might find that you've got a mess. A whole list of associations, maybe descriptions, maybe some clichés and commonplace observations. But in the reading back you will also find something you've written that will surprise you. There will be some reminiscence you've forgotten – some spark of memory that the process of writing has unearthed. Or maybe you've made some bizarre leap in logic and lateral thinking, which makes you laugh out loud upon reading back, so that your page of notes on Marilyn Monroe begins with you thinking about her singing 'Happy Birthday' to John F. Kennedy and ends with a recollection of a holiday to Lake Ullswater when you were six and you ate boiled eggs for breakfast on the rocky shore.

These leaps sideways – the moments in which you take yourself by surprise – these are the moments to capitalize on. These are the ones that make the rest of writing worthwhile, because they remind you that no one else could have made the connection that you just have in quite that way.

Allow your pen to wander, just now, on this range of subjects. Spend time afterwards on seeing what associations and connections you have made. Then set down these further associations as a list – 'boiled eggs', 'Lake Ullswater', etc, and see how far another blast and burst of writing can take you.

It's endless. There's an awful lot of ready-made material inside you that you haven't even started to tap.

2 Training the Eye

Introduction
Julia Bell

'There are very few human beings who receive the truth,
complete and staggering, by instant illumination. Most of them
acquire it fragment by fragment, on a small scale, by successive
developments, cellularly, like a laborious mosaic.'

ANAÏS NIN, *The Diaries of Anaïs Nin*

Beginning to write is a process of learning to look at the world differently. To be able to construct vivid, believable narratives a writer needs to develop a sharp eye for the details in the world around them, details that are often easy to miss in the hustle and bustle of everyday living.

The details of a story are the point at which character and setting begin to take on their shape, where the story starts to come alive in the mind of the reader. It is here, in the cement of a text, that a story will stand or fall.

It's not just any detail that a writer looks for, it's the telling detail like that moment when the woman in the chip shop, ordering double egg and chips, dropped her purse and her Weight Watchers membership card fell out. Or the second-hand wedding dresses in the window of the Relate charity shop. The small ironies that most of us encounter in our everyday lives can provide a writer with some of the best material for fiction. But we have to unpeel our eyes, re-sensitize ourselves to our environment. How many of us could write an exact verbal description of our journey to work? How often have you passed that crumbling warehouse and not noticed the graffiti: 'Elvis Lives'? Or realized that they've changed the supermarket on the ring road from Tesco to Kwik Save?

Describe your world to yourself as you move around it. What best describes your living room? Your street? Your town? Who lives here? Write lists of words and phrases and try to be as precise as possible in your observations. Get used to knowing and understanding the meanings of words, buy a good dictionary and read it. The broader your vocabulary, the more ideas you will be able to express.

When constructing a narrative you need to think quite carefully about how you are presenting details to the reader. What kinds of details are important to the narrative? What type of world are you trying to create? Focusing too much on irrelevancies will throw the reader off the scent: Do we really need to know what your character's had for tea, what colour their bath mat is? (If, of course, the tea is poisoned or the bath mat has a revealing stain then these might be your moments of telling detail.) In many ways it is what you filter out that focuses the reader's eye on the important details.

Next time you read, slow yourself down, tick off the sentences that create a strong visual image of the story in your imagination. You will find that a series of complex visual and textual prompts have created an image of the story in your mind. Take this example from F. Scott Fitzgerald:

> He took out a pile of shirts and began throwing them, one by one, before us, shirts of sheer linen and thick silk and fine flannel, which lost their folds as they fell and covered the table in many coloured disarray. While we admired he brought more and the soft rich heap mounted higher – shirts with stripes and scrolls and plaid in coral and apple-green and lavender and faint orange, with monograms of indian blue. Suddenly, with a strained sound, Daisy bent her head into the shirts and began to cry stormily.
>
> 'They're such beautiful shirts,' she sobbed, her

voice muffled in the thick folds. 'It makes me sad because I've never seen such – such beautiful shirts before.'

F. SCOTT FITZGERALD, *The Great Gatsby*

This scene comes from a moment where Gatsby – reunited with his lost love, Daisy – is showing off his opulent house and possessions. Consider the effect of the detail in this passage. The 'thick folds', the 'sheer linen', the 'fine flannel', the 'soft rich heap', the 'coral and apple-green'. There is an extravagance that borders on mania in the way that the pile of shirts becomes suffocatingly larger. And Daisy's dramatic response fits the mood and tone of the wealthy New York set that Fitzgerald is satirizing. What does such an opulent wardrobe suggest about Gatsby's character? He is the enigma at the centre of the book, the man whom no one has ever met but everyone claims to know. Why is he showing Daisy all his possessions? 'While we admired he brought more' hints that the shirts only have value for Gatsby when others are admiring them. Certainly, Gatsby displays more shirts than he could ever wear.

Pinning your writing down to specific detail is the first way to develop good practice. Learn from reading other writers. Don't settle for bland or vague adjectives. Words such as 'nice', 'good', 'dark', 'bad' are so general as to be insipid. Only use metaphor if it is pertinent and surprising. Develop a sensory understanding of the world, how perfumes, sounds, textures and tastes reveal character and place.

Consider the stories and the characters that might lie behind these sketches:

1 *A butter-yellow Ford Cortina, key scratches on the bonnet, spelling out a word or a signature, can't tell which. A peeling Canaries sticker on the bumper, green and yellow seat covers. Magic tree air freshener hanging off the mirror. Crumpled McDonald's bags on the backseat.*

2 *He's wearing a shirt the colour of ectoplasm, vile*
fluorescent green. He's on his second can of Red Bull,
which smells worse than his aftershave, and he's laughing
out loud at a copy of Loaded. *Oh God, he's trying to catch*
my eye.

When you write, take time to draw a few quick verbal sketches, which describe where you are, where you've been, who you've been with. What are the key details that define your environment? Writers develop the ability to take a moment and split it into its component parts – what he or she was wearing, how he or she looked, how he or she gestured.

Consider how you can subvert expectations. The owner of the car in the first example is most likely to be a man, but what if it's a woman? What does this say about our cultural expectations? Details are always loaded with significance, use them precisely, don't go for the obvious or the stereotypical.

In *Camera Lucida* Roland Barthes talks about detail as that which impacts upon the memory when an image is out of sight. When you try to remember an image or a scene, what is it that most sticks in your mind? Look at a photograph, close your eyes and try to recall the image. What is it that you remember? Is it the red of her shoes? The shape of the tree? The way he's smiling? The yellow chairs? Try to describe the photograph. Break up your gaze into jigsaw bits, then fit it back together on the page.

If you were to give one hundred people the same photo to describe, they would all write it down differently. They would pick different details, use different adjectives, have different cultural references. Training the eye is about learning to articulate your own perspective clearly. It's a cliché, but no less pertinent, that writing is a journey of self-discovery, of finding and defining things you didn't know you thought about yourself, about the world, about your place in the world. The keen eye that picks out all the telling detail has to be aware of the angle and the object of its own gaze.

The infamous narcissist Anaïs Nin said that the world only became real when she wrote about it. To this end she kept copious diaries in which she recorded and constructed the story of her life. She created herself on the page as a character in a world where everything was heightened, more romantic, more passionate, more extravagant. She created herself as a character that she would go on to use in her novels. She knew that writing was indulgent, and she revelled in it.

Get to know yourself. Write a few essays, express your opinions. What do you really think about that film you went to see last week? For me, one of the great joys of writing is articulating something I have felt but never expressed before. The phrase 'coming to terms with' means precisely that: finding words to express experience. At this stage it's complete self-indulgence, you can say what you like; there are no witnesses, no audience, just you and the page.

Creative Writing Workshy
Ali Smith

Writing, from day to day, is like dealing in a series of controlled explosions that vary in speed, in size and in stretch; can stop, hang mid-air like Cornelia Parker's sculptures of exploded things suspended at the point of impact. Writing – writing anything at all – is to invite a dynamic meld of anarchy and discipline, to leave our prints in the fizzing, fuse-lit possible places between order and chaos. Did you know that our hearts hang between order and chaos with every beat? That every heartbeat is subtly different from the last, and that too much order, conversely too much disorder, will explode or implode a heart?

I always think that the act of writing, strung as it is between instinct and edit, is an occupation best done in solitude, at least in the first instance. Teaching creative writing workshops gives me irritable bowel syndrome. Something about the concept (and about how I can say yes and then regret it and worry about it for weeks) inflames my gut in what might be called an explosive, sometimes an implosive, manner. I can't make up my mind whether this is a commonsensical and protective physical urge from the notion that writing is always best done alone in a room with a pencil and nobody watching, or a perverse and antisocial response, the response of the lazy and the vanity-ridden person, who uses something like Cocteau's comment – that asking an artist to talk about art is a bit like asking a plant to discuss horticulture – as a lame excuse for not wanting to articulate. Then again, I'm drawn to Cocteau's suggestion. Here's the fact: I'm green, I've got roots, I need water. Give me a pencil, some paper, an empty room; I really don't want to talk about it, I want to do it. Talking about it is just another way of putting off doing it.

All of which is a cunning cop-out kind of inarticulate thing with which to preface this piece, since workshops offer exactly one of those possible lit spaces, exactly the anarchy-discipline dynamic I began this section with.

Most of the following exercises are things that were made up on the spot in workshops and for workshops or culled from other people's workshops, in other words made up by other writers less fearful than I am of talking about it.

✍ 1 A Useful Exercise Called Image-Music-Text

This is an exercise best done quickly. It can double as a poem in its own right, and could maybe also benefit from being set to music.

Write down the first image that comes into your head.
Write down the first emotion that comes into your head.
Write down the first line that comes into your head.

It can be the first line for a story.
It can be the first line for a poem.
It can be the first line for anything.

Write down a different emotion.
Write down a different first line.
Write down a different image.

Write down another first line.
Write down another emotion.
Write down another image.

Write down an image that is an emotion (i.e. that will act as one).
Write down a first line that is an emotion (i.e. that will act as one).
Write down an image that is a first line (i.e. that will act as one).

Write down an emotion without mentioning the emotion.
Write down a first line that's nothing but image.
Now remove the image (so that its absence can be felt).

Can emotion ever be removed from image?
Can image ever be removed from emotion?
Can you have a first line of a story, poem, anything, without emotion or image?

Choose your preferred first line. Now. Start.

✍ 2 *Some Useful Three-Word Lists for One of Those Here-Are-Three-Words-Now-Write-a-Paragraph-that-Uses-All-Three Exercises*

inveracity	gowan	vulsella
cribble	durmast	obovate
flux	zedoary	sauba
dag	monophobia	isthmus
parergon	sockdologer	bort
fractal	incarnadine	deodand
cat	dog	rain

NOTE: Is it necessary to know what words mean? Or is it necessary to invent meanings for words?

✍ 3 *Workshop Exercise Instruction in Haiku*

Write a short story.
Very short. One hundred words.
You have ten minutes.

✍ 4 *Gendercise*

Have the workshop participants read out their hundred-word stories created under the haiku method above. Now ask everybody to change the gender of one of the characters in their stories, without changing anything else, and read them out again alongside the originals. What happens? How much of the story can stay the same? How much of it changes or shifts and why? This is an excellent way to bring preconceptions to the surface or to spot them in prose.

✍ 5 *Tense?*

Now choose just one of the stories the class has been working on. Copy it on to the board or photocopy it, so that everybody has a copy of it to work from. Then assign everybody in the room a different tense into which to put the story. The comparisons are / will be / would be / could have been / might be fruitful. Ask some people to choose a mix of tenses to see what happens to the story then. Ask one person to use a different tense each time a verb is used.

✍ 6 *Editcise*

Choose a good full-blown sentence from somewhere. One of my personal favourites is the first line of an Alan Warner story, called 'Car Hung, Upside Down', which goes: 'The car hung, upside down high above the earth, in the leafless sycamore tree.'

Minutely edit. Start with almost nothing, the impact of
The car was in the tree.
Compare it to the impact of
The car was upside down, in the tree.
Then compare the impact of
The car hung upside down, in the tree.
And so on, with
The car hung, upside down, in the tree.
The car hung, upside down in the tree.
The car hung upside down, in the tree.

27

The car hung upside down in the sycamore tree.
The car hung upside down in the leafless tree.
The car hung upside down in the leafless sycamore tree.
The car hung upside down, in the leafless sycamore tree.
The car hung upside down high above the earth in the leafless sycamore tree.
The car hung, upside down high above the earth, in the leafless sycamore tree.
The car hung, upside down high above the earth.
The car hung in the leafless sycamore tree.
The car hung in the leafless tree.
The car hung in the sycamore tree.
The car hung in the tree.

And all the variations I've left out. This should lead to a discussion: e.g. Which is the perfect sentence for which occasion? It could lead to sleep or trance state. These, in turn, could lead to

✍ 7 *Thinking of Nothing*

Try this. Try thinking of nothing.
This is an excellent exercise for clearing the head.

Keeping Your Eyes Open
Alicia Stubbersfield

When I'm making notes which may end up as material for a poem, I think of that perfect note-maker Dorothy Wordsworth, tramping along with brother William, recording description and comment so that he could 'recollect in tranquillity'.

Unfortunately, I don't have a Dorothy. I don't have much time either, so my notes are scrappy things written in a little book I keep in my handbag. I often wonder where male poets keep their notebooks but have never asked. These notes, though, are important despite their brevity and allow me to trawl back through my responses to experience and to make connections.

My connection, as a woman poet in the year 2000, with William Wordsworth comes from recording those scraps at all. It also comes from the development of the scrap. After days and nights of Welsh rain, the field across the road from my house was flooded so badly that two swans took up temporary residence. I recorded the fact and the way their necks made a perfect heart shape in the instant I was watching them. There's plenty of serendipity involved in being a writer. The important thing is to see the heart shape, write it down in your notebook and then go back to it later.

Swans mate for life and make a wonderful metaphor for enduring love. I'm more interested in what goes wrong in relationships. The temporary quality of the lake on the flooded field offset by that fleeting glimpse of the swans' necks forming a conventional symbol for love made the kind of contrast I'm interested in. I find an image that is essentially visual and then subvert it, develop it, make it resonate in a new way. Faithful swans washed up on a flooded field allow me to tap into what we know as well as what we don't expect.

Developing an image needs the other four senses. And this is the simplest element of writing and the one we forget most easily. Think of the importance of smell. That wet-dog-drying smell of small schoolchildren, the smell of pavements after summer rain, the smell of the person you lust after. A familiar smell can transport us back to childhood in an instant. Smell, like taste, is difficult to describe but will work hard for you in a poem. The reader will be transported without scratch and sniff, by the power of your description. In a poem about a lover going away with someone else I have the girl sleeping in his shirt so she will 'wake smelling of you'. Smell becomes a metaphor for her loss as well as a strong physical detail in the poem.

Taste, too, allows another layer of physicality and abstraction: 'the cigarette-and-wine taste of you' or 'how desire tastes in someone else's mouth'. These are clear enough and open enough for the reader to fill in the absolutes.

Texture and sound are equally important in letting the reader imagine the scene clearly. In a poem written in the voice of a human cannonball I wanted to make the inside of the cannon as real as possible, so I used the sounds of the circus, which she can hear outside the cannon, and the feel of the metal on her skin. 'I hear tigers roar in the distance' and 'Cold touching my skin, seeping into me.' The sound of tigers emphasizes her isolation and the cold 'seeping' into her becomes a metaphorical cold and represents her relationship with her father.

Physical details become metaphorical in the writing and so allow the poem to take on another layer: the physical becomes metaphorical and allows the reader to connect in a more profound way. The choice we make about the physical details, the use we make of the senses, allows us to have control over our material, to direct our readers and to allow the reader to make the poem their own. Leaving room for the reader is important but not so that we edit what we want to say to appease some imagined person. Many of the women writers I have as students have great difficulty finding their own, confident voice. Speaking out above the noise of our mothers and grandmothers can be almost impossible and I certainly found, and find, it difficult, although the way women talk to each other can be the beginning of writing.

My mother was my first audience. I learned to tell stories to keep her entertained, to describe exactly where I'd been, who I'd seen, who had said what to whom. 'And what colour were her shoes?' she'd ask, pursing her lips at the unsuitability of white shoes in winter. 'How common.'

I learned to edit my experiences. If I didn't want my friends to appear common, and I didn't, I changed the colour of their shoes to black patent, which were 'plain fancy' and, thus, acceptable. I rehearsed the amusing bits of an evening out, the quasi-tragic highlighting the elements that would entertain. The most important thing, however, was the detail. What kind of clothes was she wearing? What colour? What cut? What does that say about her?

My mother maintained that she knew what I was thinking, and I don't think I ever fully accepted that she didn't. But she didn't. No one ever does know what someone else is thinking and that's what makes the job of the writer interesting. We, somehow, have to communicate our thoughts, whether speaking or writing, and that takes us back to the five senses.

The elements of my social life that I remembered and edited for the benefit of my mother were usually visual. I've already mentioned the clothes people wore but, as a writer, I am interested in more than that. The exact colour of the shirt he wore the night he dumped you tells us about him, about your mood, about his place in the world. That rip in the sleeve matters. In my poem 'Letters Home', which is about the versions of our lives we choose to tell others, I list the things the girl in the poem can tell her mother and the things she can't, creating contrasting images inside the head of the reader. She can describe 'the books / snack-bars with plastic cups / lads playing football' but not '. . . coffee / or waiting in the kitchen for a kettle, your back against the fridge / then green mugs, a bottle of red wine'.

Each of the things on the list resonates beyond just what it is. The details carry much of the emotional weight of the poem.

Making connections between the different aspects of our lives is important. Sharon Olds writes about the death of her children's gerbil, and all of us who are parents know how important those little deaths are. We can write about the effects of the bigger deaths by reducing them. Shortly after my mother died I found myself writing about the deaths of animals: the pet sheep, a hen that curiously laid an egg as she died, which was a gift of a metaphor. So much so that a friend who is also a poet accused me of making it up. The trick is to spot the metaphor and use the simple event of the dead hen and her egg to reflect feelings about the death of a parent and that which is left after such a death.

I live in the country and am very conscious of the turning of the seasons. The leaving and returning of the swallows or curlews gives a structure to life that makes sense to me. The advent of spring with the gradual colouring in of the hedges and lambs hiccuping round the field may sound romantic but is juxtaposed with the blood and death we encounter in the poetry of Ted Hughes. Once in a poetry workshop I brought a poem that was set very much where I live; lush countryside full of wild flowers, particularly poppies, which I used symbolically to show the disintegration of a relationship. In the poem the woman rescues a wounded swallow from the cat and cups it in her hand, aware of its incredible smoothness. I was fictionalizing experience, using the place with which I was familiar, describing an incident with a wounded swallow as it had happened to me but giving these to fictionalized characters and making the elements significant within the narrative. A member of the group work-shopping the poem was disdainful of its authenticity because of the setting, thinking that it was too 'Laura Ashley', believing ironically that I had made up the setting and the relationship was real.

The temptation to respond with 'But that's what it's like' or 'That's what happened' is often a strong one, but literal truth is not important to the emotional truth of the poem. I may have a strong idea of an image I want to pursue, or want to write about an incident that happened, capturing a particular moment, but when I have started to write, something else takes over and the poem begins to have its own energy and dynamic. At that point I feel it's important to follow that energy and see where the poem takes you. That's not to say I'm not controlling the line lengths, the stanzas, maybe even the rhyme, but there is something more there, and it is that which gives the poem its emotional truth and the indefinable charge that makes a poem work.

Writers have to be alert to everything around them, to the strange little connections and contrasts that become symbols for the way life is. The making of the poem comes afterwards. We dig out our own clay and then shape the pot of the poem later. The possibilities are endless, from the fine porcelain of a villanelle to experimental pieces that barely look like poems at all. Each one will come from expe-rience and will be transformed by imagination.

✍ *Try the following exercise, which will mimic the process of note-making and the establishing of connections.*

First choose an object of some kind and place it in front of you. It can be the blue vase you bought in Greece, full of Greek sea and sky, or it might be the pink pebble you found on the beach at Llandudno, or something as simple as an item of clothing. Pamela Gillilan has written of the shape of her dead husband's feet in his shoes and Tess Gallagher of two women smoothing out a man's black silk vest so that the vest almost becomes the dead person.

Once you have the object, describe it in as close detail as possible, including all the five senses without forcing it. Taste might just be the remnants of that morning's toothpaste, rather than anything directly associated with your object. And that leads me to the important part. As you write, let your mind wander and call up any associations at all, then write those down, too. You might include the weather outside as well. Try, after a while, to bring yourself back to the object.

You will now have plenty of notes to work on. These can be shaped any way you choose but an excellent model is Ted Hughes' 'View of a Pig', where he moves from a description of the pig to musings on death, back to the dead pig and musings on its life and then to other experiences he has had with pigs before coming back to the dead pig again. The important element is to allow the connections between the object and your other ideas to be shaped by the poem. In this way the object can become metaphorical and add a layer of significance to the description. Like swans touching their beaks on a temporary lake in a Welsh field.

Articles of Faith – Using Objects in Poetry
Esther Morgan

'It [poetry] creates anew the universe, after it
has been annihilated in our minds by the recurrence of
impressions blunted by reiteration.'

SHELLEY, A Defence of Poetry

'Description is itself a kind of travel.'

MARK DOTY, 'Two Ruined Boats' from Atlantis

I start with Doubting Thomas. In the New Testament, Thomas is famous as the disciple who is only convinced in the risen Christ when he sees the crucifixion wounds for himself, when his fingers can actually touch them. Christ's riposte is to tell him 'blessed are they that have not seen, and yet have believed'.

This is all very well for a religion. Religions require faith. Poetry is not a religion. I ask my students to imagine that Doubting Thomas is reading their poems. He is not prepared to take anything on faith; so what if you are happy or sad or angry, why should he believe you? The only way you can convince him of the truth of what you are saying is by making him feel it; with his eyes, his ears and, yes, his fingers.

I have found that using objects early on in a poetry course helps students to begin writing in a way that will satisfy the most doubting of Thomases. Focusing on an object sensitizes us again to the physical world, an alertness that tends to diminish once we've left childhood behind. By using objects I am trying to help students (and myself) recapture a sense of wonder, which in turn helps us rediscover or strengthens an excitement in the possibilities of language. The two are closely connected; just as we tend to use language in a formulaic way in ordinary life, so we can be lazy in the way we encounter the world physically. We spend a great deal of time editing out our environment, not noticing its richness as we tick off our tasks for the day.

There are other reasons, too, which make working with objects of particular value in the writing of poetry. One of the differences between poetry and prose is, I think, a question of focus. Whilst acknowledging that there are areas where the two genres do overlap, in general, poetry is more tightly and intensely focused than prose. An analogy I've developed is that reading prose is like walking into a room and switching on an overhead light: you can see everything in the room at once. Poetry, on the other hand, is more like walking into the same room and switching on a torch: although you don't see all that's there, what you do see appears with greater intensity by virtue of that single beam.

The first exercise that I bring to class is designed, therefore, with two aims in view: to encourage this intensity of focus and to bring the senses back into writing. I ask the students to forget about meaning and messages, and to become like children again, exploring the world with a child's curiosity and immediacy.

I bring to the class a selection of household objects, which might include, for instance, a candlestick, cheese grater, light bulb, scarf, corkscrew, pepper grinder, etc. Before distributing these to the students to write about I ask them to close their eyes. I tell them to explore their object purely with their hands for a couple of minutes. Touch is a sense that it's easy to neglect in writing, dominated as we are by the visual. Asking them to explore their object through touch in the first instance is a good way to start the defamiliarization process. When they are ready, they can open their eyes and make notes on what they have just experienced. They then explore their object further using their other senses, making notes on the appearance of their object, any sound it might make, taste, smell, etc. I then tell them to widen their writing to include any memories or other thoughts triggered by their objects. At this stage they shouldn't be worrying about poetry with a capital 'P' or shaping this raw material. I give them plenty of time for this exercise, so that they are forced to keep going, to keep noticing more and more detail.

What becomes evident as they read out their pieces is the extent to which this exercise helps them to re-imagine their object. In the same way that a word repeated over and over begins to sound bizarre, so an object scrutinized with such attention will start to shed its everyday invisibility. So pepper grinders become armless women who scream when their heads are twisted and rain bitterness, a cheesegrater becomes a steel wall of tears, or a light bulb the lost eye of a Cyclops. The exercise shows how a description of external reality can lead to an exploration of emotional and intellectual territories; the kind of journey suggested in Mark Doty's definition of description at the head of this chapter. With this discovery comes the pleasure in knowing that (theoretically at least) writers should never be stuck for something to write about. If a simple object can be so extraordinary, can yield several pages of notes, then surely there should be no such thing as writer's block! It also distracts students from the perceived need for Poetry to be Profound (lots of capital 'Ps'). This desire to say something important from the start, as opposed to discovering whether a poem has something to say in the course of writing it, can often cramp the student new to poetry.

I often use this exercise myself in my own writing practice and find it helpful in focusing and intensifying my writing even if I don't then go on to develop the material it triggers. Sometimes a finished piece has been the result as in the following poem, 'Avocados':

> I like the way they fit the palm,
> their plump Buddha weight,
> the slight squeeze for ripeness,
> the clean slit of the knife,
> the soft suck as you twist the halves apart,
> the thick skin peeling easily.
> Naked they're slippery as soap.
>
> I serve them for myself

sliced and fanned on white bone china
glistening with olive oil
or I fill the smooth hollow
with sharp vinaigrette
scooping out
the pale buttery flesh.

Every diet you've ever read
strictly forbids them.

I follow up the initial exercise described above by asking students
to extend their imaginative engagement with their object by giving it
a voice, that is writing a piece in the first person from their object's
perspective. To help them find a way in, I suggest thinking about a
'Day in the Life' of their object, visualizing where it spends its time,
how it is used, etc. I ask them to consider whether their object has all
the senses or whether it is deaf or blind and what kind of 'character'
their object has, for instance if it is aggressive, friendly or lonely. The
surreal aspect of this exercise is also useful in creating 'anew the
universe'. A useful poem to discuss, which shows the possibilities of
this technique, is Sylvia Plath's 'Mushrooms', which interestingly
was itself written as an exercise. I leave them with the question as to
how Plath manages to create a voice for the mushrooms that sounds
convincing, and also ask them to consider what else the poem might
be about.

This two-step object exercise is particularly helpful early on in a
course as it seems not to ask the students to be too revealing of
themselves. I say 'seems' as it often does provide a personal insight
into a writer's concerns, but it nevertheless offers new writers a
fictional veil. Asking them to write on something that is both
arbitrary and ordinary can also free students up to experiment in
ways which they might be reluctant to do faced with the task of
writing that difficult poem about their mother. On both counts, this
can be liberating for students who have not yet got to know each
other (in a British context at least!).

By the third week of a course I tend to move on to more personal exercises, which nevertheless still use objects as a point of entry. One in particular I've found useful in helping students develop a distinctive voice, by which I mean a use of language which is uniquely their own. This involves using objects as a way of prompting memory. I'm aware that the topic of memory is examined elsewhere in this book, so I won't go into detail here, except to say why I think the use of memory can be key in the discovery of voice.

In his essay 'Feeling into Words', Seamus Heaney lists the various influences that have helped shape his own language: the catechism, the shipping forecast, Irish folk songs and legend, the accent of his particular part of Ireland. Significantly, the first poem in which he felt he was successful in getting his 'feel into words' is 'Digging', a poem which is based on memory and the idea of writing as a kind of retrieval, an excavation of the past. This was the first time he felt he had managed to speak with his own voice, instead of ventriloquizing the mannerisms of other writers.

It is because our memories are unique to each of us that using memory in writing can be so constructive in developing an awareness of our own voice. But how can we access our memories in a way that is vivid and detailed? Famously, a madeleine did it for Proust's narrator in *Remembrance of Things Past*, and taking this as an example, I encourage students to find their madeleine equivalent, their trigger that will release the past.

One method of achieving this is to ask them to think of someone they know well and to write a list of possessions that they associate with that particular person, taking care to be as precise in their description of these objects as possible. I then ask them to choose one of these objects, the one that seems most resonant to them, and to write for a further ten minutes or so, introducing any specific memories which the object triggers. The resulting pieces are often very powerful; one student wrote about the jacket her dead father used to wear, another on a miniature writing table which once belonged to an ancestor who died young, another on his grandfather's violin. Each time the exercise seems to produce memorable work, often of an intensely emotional kind. A similar exercise asks students to write about the object they would save from a fire. In these exercises, the objects become icons, part of a personal vocabulary of experience and remembrance. I'm not advocating that all poetry should be based on memory and the personal; there is an equally important place for fantasy and fiction in poetry. But as a way of accessing a living spring of language (in the same essay Heaney talks about poetry as an act of divination), as opposed to the kind of language students *think* is poetic, these exercises can provide a valuable starting point.

Speaking personally, one of the delights of writing and reading poetry has been the way it enriches my experience of the sensual world, alerting me to things that would otherwise go unobserved. For me every poem is an act of retrieval, an attempt to record the transient. Some may fail, but the very fact an attempt has been made seems to me a positive to set against mortality. With this observation I seem to be moving into the realm of general meanings myself, but perhaps that's because I believe that Poetry is important enough to deserve its capital P after all.

What Are You Looking At?
Paul Magrs

I once saw a terrifying medical documentary in which a patient was blindfolded and his brain was hooked up to some kind of scanning device. The medics could watch his mind on a screen and in it they could see flashes of the guinea pig's thoughts. They were like solar flares, passing from one side of his skull to the other; all crimson and gold. And that, the voice-over told us, was in a quiet room with his eyes covered. When visual and aural stimuli were returned to him, the invisible activity inside his head was greatly increased. It looked like fireworks going off.

I wish I'd taped the documentary to show my students. This is how much is going through your mind, even when you are not even thinking about much. The world crams itself into us through all our senses and even when we think we're having a lazy time of it we're mulling things over, making connections, trying to see sense.

Do this now. Write down, in list form, the next ten things that pop into your head. Can you unscramble them?

Some people claim that they can clear their minds and think of nothing. I never believe them, really.

When we come to write then, no wonder it's difficult to get a handle on our thoughts or the world and learn to control and shape them. It's hard to select. In this section Julia Bell talked about fixing on the telling detail and Esther Morgan wrote about renewing your engagement with everyday objects. Both are strategies for seeing the world anew; for stripping away the layers of conditioned reflexes and habitual behaviour. Defamiliarization is the game Esther Morgan's playing with her exercises; making us look at quite ordinary things in new, extraordinary ways. It's like that parlour game where you have to put your hand inside a bag and, without looking, guess at the object inside.

✍ *Here's an exercise along similar lines.*

> Remember those photographs you used to get in puzzle books and comics? The ones where they showed an everyday object from a strange angle or in extreme close-up? Play this trick on yourself. Pick some objects and go into extreme close-up. A shower head becomes a UFO, the bottom of a fish tank becomes a drowned city.

See what an alteration of scale can do to your writing. By seizing on the tiny details and expanding them, by exaggerating them, you are making them into something much grander and exciting.

By looking at the familiar in an unfamiliar way, we are slowing down the process of observation. This is a good thing; slowing yourself down in writing can be extremely productive. It makes you aware of your decisions and selections at every turn.

There is no way we can ever get down everything that goes through your mind. In that medical documentary the solar flares were far too quick ever to be recorded. They were before language, it seemed; they were faster than the speed of words. This is probably a good thing. I can think of two novels that try to set down everything that goes through one character's busy mind, Dorothy Richardson's *Pilgrimage* and Nicholson Baker's *The Mezzanine*. Both bored me in the end, and I think, in a way, they were meant to. In both the reader is swamped by the myriad solar flares.

We need to sift through experience and observation and seize upon what Julia Bell very properly calls the 'telling detail'. Some people have this knack straight off. You can hear it in their conversation, as they gossip or tell some shaggy-dog tale or reminiscence. I've been lucky enough to know quite a few extremely funny, engaging talkers and often they are people who would never think of writing. They can't seem to believe that their talent as witty, vivid conversationalists would translate to the page. Yet I think the skill involved in making a verbal anecdote come to life involves the selection of the right, telling details and, together with a knack for suspense, punchlines, revelations, mimicry, what we have here is the makings of a writer.

Think about the stories you already tell about your life; about your past and your family. How do you remember them? Usually, it's through vivid hooks and memories, and that's how you explain them to others. If I think about a particular teacher at school, it's because the first time I saw her she had purple hair and glasses like a visor. If I think of another one, it's because her clothes looked as if she'd made them by hand out of curtains and carpet. These are the things that stick in your mind and that will stick in your reader's mind.

Our eyes will always flick to the most interesting part of any scene we enter. We're so used, now, to so much input, to receiving so much information, minute by minute, in our hyper-technical world, that we flick ever faster to the most interesting thing in front of us. We're ultra literate in reading signs and absorbing information. As writers, we need to slow down a little, take stock, and really think about why our eye is drawn in this direction or that. Adverts, both in magazines and on TV are interesting here. Great skill is employed in catching our attention and passing on a host of messages to us. Much of this selling is done subconsciously, or the messages we are meant to receive are inferred somehow, through association and other related seductive means. It's good to be sceptical about adverts; to stop and wonder – what are they really trying to say to us here? How is this collection of images meant to pique my interest? What am I supposed to be looking at?

Take a number of adverts from magazines, newspapers, the television. Which details in their imagery stand out? Describe them. Do you think you are looking at what you are supposed to?

Now do the same with some paintings, from postcards or an art book. Which details leap out at you? The obvious ones? The more obscure ones? Are you looking where you are supposed to?

In many ways, writers are often the kid in the back of the class. The one who should be watching and listening to the teacher at the front. Often they're looking out of the window, staring at the patterns in the cloud, the football team on the field, the pedestrians going past outside in the rain. They are looking where everyone else isn't looking, and that is why, at school, they were the one that the teacher threw a piece of chalk at.

Everyone is drawn to look at different details. You have to learn to be confident in your own view. Let your eye wander and take down what it is you've picked out. There's nothing more compelling for a reader than seeing the world through the unique view of somebody else.

A writer friend of mine came round to our house one night recently, and on the doorstep she turned and I caught her staring up at the window of the baker's opposite. I followed her glance, knowing that she would have found something interesting to look at. And, indeed, up in that lit window one of the bakers was, without a scrap of self-consciousness, taking off all his clothes for the street to see. He wasn't doing it on purpose, I don't think, and he wasn't making himself that conspicuous, but this writer's eye had gone straight to him.

Let yourself be nosy. As people, we are trained not to stare too long. If you watch a streetful of people out shopping on a Saturday they don't look around them much. Commuters are the worst. People heading home on buses and trains keep their eyes straight ahead and you'd think they hardly saw anything at all.

Go into town. Stand in a crowd or sit on a bench. Look up at the roofs of buildings. Stare at the gutters. Watch who goes into and out of shops. Watch what other people do when they don't think they're being observed.

I once saw the writer and actor Dirk Bogarde standing alone in the middle of a busy street in Manchester. He had an extremely famous face, but no one recognized him. He stood still as they swept past and he was grinning, staring all around him, up to the tops of the buildings and at everything about him. He looked so happy to be taking it all in.

3 Abstracts

Introduction
Julia Bell

The French writer and critic Hélène Cixous interprets writing as a process of explaining yourself to yourself, of pushing into the places of your experience where you have no articulated understanding of the world. She suggests that when we are presented with a gap in our knowledge of our lives, some of us are compelled to fill it with words. To write stories to explain ourselves to ourselves. We are aware that experience will always be more than can ever be written and still we feel a need to create narratives about it.

Maybe it's the satisfaction of wrapping something external to ourselves up in words that drives us to sit for hours creating extended verbal universes. These mental structures are dramatized explorations of the emotional turbulence we all experience: anger, love, hate, guilt, paranoia, jealousy, betrayal, fear, joy. But it is only in the *art* of these narrative constructions that we have the power to make abstract concepts appear concrete on the page.

Take this paragraph, for example:

> *She curled up on the bed. From deep down inside her came a pitiful cry for a love that wasn't there. It was lost to her. She thrashed herself about, trying to prevent herself from being engulfed.*

The emotion being described is vague: what is she being engulfed by? What does this mean? What is the writer trying to say? We can't really get a handle on the character because the emotion is being told to us in a way that is hard to visualize.

If we replace description with metaphor we might write instead:

She lay on the bed and curled up like a caterpillar.

Or we could suggest her emotion through a description of her physical actions:

She lay on the bed and curled up so tight her knees were pressing into her eye sockets.

A combination of metaphor and suggestion makes it possible to show what the abstracts mean in the first example. The image grounds the concept, making it easier for the reader to understand how the emotion is affecting character. As a reader I have more empathy with a girl who feels like a caterpillar than with one who feels as if she's being engulfed.

✍ *Use your sensory understanding of the world to consider how abstracts can be made concrete.*

Try this exercise: list abstract words and then describe them through the senses. What colour is love? What does it smell like? What does it taste like? What does it feel like? What does it sound like? One of my students said 'love tastes like Fizzy Chewits', another claimed it felt like 'watching the last-ever episode of *Dallas*'.

Be surprising. Love doesn't always have to be imagined as sunsets, hearts and flowers. Avoid clichés. If you've seen it somewhere before, scrub it out. Personalize your metaphors, think about your associations, your memories. The *Dallas* metaphor came about, my student explained, because he had been watching the last-ever episode of *Dallas* when a girl he really liked rang him up and asked him out. One of the joys of new writing is that it presents the world to us in a different way. Strong metaphors are the ones that make the reader and the writer alike tingle with the pleasure of articulacy.

Take this example from Chekhov:

Ryabovitch stopped, undecided what to do. Just then

he was astonished to hear hurried footsteps, the rustle of a dress and a female voice whispering breathlessly, 'At last!' Two soft, sweet-smelling arms (undoubtedly a woman's) encircled his neck, a burning cheek pressed against his and at the same time there was the sound of a kiss. But immediately after the kiss the woman gave a faint cry and shrank backwards in disgust – that was how it seemed to Ryabovitch . . .

His heart pounded away when he was back in the hall and his hands trembled so obviously that he hastily hid them behind his back. At first he was tormented by shame and he feared everyone there knew he had just been embraced and kissed . . . But when he had convinced himself that everyone was dancing and gossiping just as peacefully as before, he gave himself up to a totally new kind of sensation, one he had never experienced before in all his life. Something strange was happening to him, his neck, which a few moments ago had been embraced by sweet-smelling hands seemed anointed with oil. And on his left cheek, just by his moustache, there was a faint, pleasant, cold, tingling sensation, the kind you get from peppermint drops and the more he rubbed the spot the stronger the tingling became.

ANTON CHEKHOV, *The Kiss*

Ideas of loneliness, desire, love, disappointment are all conveyed in this story through metaphor and suggestion. Ryabovitch, the shy, embarrassed staff-captain, falls in love with the strange woman who kisses him in the library. The story examines how this small incident awakens him to his own loneliness. Before this moment Ryabovitch doesn't question his life: afterwards, he finds himself craving physical contact and believes himself to be in love.

What Ryabovitch feels like physically is the best way to suggest to the reader what he might be feeling emotionally. Think about how we might change the paragraph to create more sinister or less pleasurable inferences. What if it stings? Or burns? The connotations of 'peppermint drops' are ambiguous. As sweets they suggest childhood, naivety; but as aftershave or smelling salts, they hint at something vital and arousing. Ryabovitch's rubbing of the spot mirrors the way he turns the incident over in his mind, the way it becomes more meaningful the more he thinks of it. The art of this story is the way it shows the effects of unarticulated emotion on character. It is precisely the interplay of abstract idea and concrete image that makes the text spark with energy and expression.

To write in a way that just lists abstract terms instead of investigating them is too telling. 'Show, don't tell' is one of the most common catchphrases in writing classes, but students are often perplexed by the notion of telling. 'I don't know what you mean. I'm writing, so I'm telling a story, aren't I?' In this context to tell is to over-explain, to burden your writing with unnecessary exposition. Chekhov could have written a paragraph telling how the kiss made Ryabovitch recognize his own loneliness, but this would have read more like notes or an essay. It would make the story shorter, too, more like precis.

Take this example:

> She was devastated; it was all too much. She felt terribly sad. It had been such a long time since she'd seen them. Years in fact. They had been so happy that summer in Cornwall, they were all so glad to be a family again. It was so terrible, being ripped apart like this. But Sofia knew she'd manage somehow. She was a survivor, always had been.

All these sentences are statements about character, they are telling you what to think about how the character thinks and feels. Abstract words are too big conceptually to mean much without descriptive associations, and if we never get to watch how the character behaves in action and dialogue, we won't really feel as if we've got to know them properly. If writing is a dialogue between a reader and a writer, then narratives that are too telling are a one-way conversation: there is no room for a reader to project their own imagination into a narrative that is telling them very bluntly what to think.

Margaret Atwood compares the process of writing to 'wrestling a greased pig in the dark', suggesting that the meaning of a text is always somehow very slippery for a writer. While a text is under construction it is impossible to see the whole picture. Even when a piece is finished, the writer can have a certain sense of astonishment at what they have created. For all the notes and forward planning and reading a writer might do, the finished product will always be different to the original idea because it has become a tangible body of work not just an abstract idea. This is the point where a writer can begin to draw links, see the hidden meanings, smooth down the writing into something more coherent.

On a day-to-day level, the writer is engaged with minutiae, not big ideas. The practice of writing is a succession of small choices – finding the right adjectives, getting the character from A to B, deciding on the progress of the next scene. Writers who start with a manifesto, instead of a character, usually become unstuck very quickly.

Political ideas in fiction are best explored through character or metaphor, take Émile Zola's *Germinal*, for instance. *Germinal* is a great, angry, blockbuster of a novel about the struggle between the labourers and the owners of a coal mine in northern France during the Second Empire. The environment of the mines is imagined in graphic, physical detail as a strange, labyrinthine underworld, where men work in terrible, inhuman conditions:

> Not a word was exchanged. They all hacked away, and all that could be heard was their irregular tapping, which sounded distant and muffled, for in this dead air sounds raised no echo but took on harsh sonority. The darkness was mysterious in its blackness, thick with flying coal-dust and heavy with

gases that pressed down upon the eyes. Only reddish points of light could be seen through the gauze cover of the lamps. The coal face was scarcely discernible; it went up slantwise like a broad, flat, sloping chimney, blackened with the impenetrable night of ten winters of soot, and in it ghostly forms moved about and an occasional gleam threw into momentary relief the shape of a man's haunch, a sinewy arm, a wild, dirty criminal-looking face. Now and then blocks of coal shimmered as they came loose, their surfaces or edges glinted suddenly like crystal, and then all went black again, the picks tapped on dully, and the only other sounds were panting breath and groans of discomfort and fatigue in the heavy air and dripping water.

ÉMILE ZOLA, *Germinal*

What stops this novel being a political tract is characterization and description. No one, on either side of the debate, is 'good' or 'bad' but all the characters are shown to be battling within a system that is beyond their control. Political struggle is illustrated though the characters' emotional and physical struggle while the mine continually heaves and shifts around them, a living, monstrous beast that feeds on human flesh.

The fumbling, half-realized nature of work-in-progress is an inevitable part of the writing process: no text arrives to a writer fully formed. We tend to forget that a good novel or story is the product of endless redrafting. Writers must free themselves up, allow themselves to make mistakes, write whole scenes they might end up cutting. Only by letting themselves loose on the page will a writer ever stand a chance of wrapping their abstract demons up in words.

Deconstructing Beds . . .
Alison Fell

I generally use this collage exercise early on with students – perhaps in the third or fourth session of the term – because it does seem to open eyes, hearts and minds to some of the essentials of poetry. Also, it encourages students to relax their control of language in order to allow a lighter and fuller control to emerge. And introduces the notion of abstract or concept words (e.g. 'health' or 'jealousy' or 'dissatisfaction'), versus concrete words (anything you can perceive with the five senses, e.g. 'fence post', 'lightning', 'growl'), and what happens when they link in metaphor. (Abstract lifts and expands concrete, while concrete grounds and particularizes abstract.) But to the exercise:

1 Write 100 words prose description of a bed you slept in as a child. It needn't be perfect Virginia Woolf-type prose, as it is only raw material, but write in sentences rather than in note form, as the verbs will be important later.

2 When you've done that, write another 100 words on the bed you currently occupy, what's in it, what surrounds it, what you do in it, etc. We spend one third of our lives in bed but no one seems to write about it!

3 Write a final 100 words on a fantasy bed, a bed where money is no object, a bed that can be made of anything you like. (When I was working out this exercise initially, I found myself inventing a bed made of meringue and chocolate.) You may find this more difficult than the previous two sections, so let yourself go to town on it.

4 It's interesting to read back at this stage, and sometimes in workshops I even get students to pair up and read their work to

each other, partly to loosen up the class, and partly because of the interest involved in deciphering common strands that exist in some cases between the past, present and fantasy bed. Another point that can be made is that this preliminary stage of the exercise may help them with characterization in novel or story . . . To imagine what sort of bed your fictional character slept/sleeps/ would like to sleep in brings you in quite close, I think, and is a tactic I've used myself when in difficulty.

All this will take up to two hours. I usually go on with the second stage in the next session. Their homework is to type up the three 100-word pieces (preserving the originals), and cut them up into very short phrases and single words, put the cut-up words in an envelope, and bring them back next week – with scissors and glue if necessary. It's as well to have scissors around, as some students will cling to favourite or fancy phrases and have to be encouraged to dismember them, and many will have left predictable or clichéd phrases intact. I always ask people to separate 'books', for example, from 'shelves', and 'chest' from 'drawers', to open up the possibilities for, say, 'a chest of tortoises'. I also ask them to fracture subject from object and noun from verb, so that as many elements as possible can be set free to play their part – and play *is* the operative word – in what is, after all, a completely new composition.

Now they have to lay out all their words so that they can be scanned easily. Next they can begin to assemble short sequences, intuitively, without worrying about commonsensical things like meaning or narrative. At this point the rationalists in the class will object that the results of such a process can only be random nonsense, but you can counter this by pointing out that this would be true only if the words were assembled face down! I think it's important to make the point that words don't need to be whipped into shape all the time by a big boss writer (in fact they hate it, and will probably dig in their heels and refuse to be of any service). Given a little space, they will play together creatively. Given a little love, they will love you back. They like to co-operate, with themselves and with you, and will do so, if you let them. By the way, this is an excellent exercise for anyone who is suffering from blocks or general stodginess in their writing.

The one thing I do stress at this point is to use normal syntax in the reassemblage, for syntax provides a holding frame for the new, non-realist images and meanings. Otherwise students should be encouraged to keep an open mind and allow their themes to emerge, rather than attempt to reproduce their original pieces in any way. It's important that the unconscious be given permission to play its part. Which indeed it does, judging by the reactions of surprise, recognition, even illumination, when the writer sees what kinds of motif are emerging.

The reassembly takes a long time – at least a two-hour session. The short sequences should be put to one side or written down. Later they can be rearranged, verb-tenses unified if necessary, etc. I do urge people to use all the words if possible – at least if this is their first encounter with collage. When they are more confident they will scan more fluently and very quickly take what they need from the selection of words in front of them, and disregard the rest.

In the next session the finished pieces can be read out. Those will be very open texts that, compared to naturalistic prose, make big demands on the listener. (However, it's always good for students to be aware that the reader is willing to *work*. How *hard* is another question, of course!) I ask everyone to make notes during the readings, to see if there is a consensus about which images and sequences resonate, and why they do. Then we can begin to put our minds to uncovering some of the deep structures that are operating within the text.

I'm sure that every tutor will focus on different aspects, according to their own aesthetic tendencies, for it seems to me that there is so much to be discovered. For me, the main elements to be found in this heightened language are the way abstract-concrete combinations challenge the distinction between 'inner' and 'outer' spaces and articulate poetic truths; the joy of surreal juxtaposition and distortion; the determination of words to combine on the basis of sound

– assonance, consonance, etc.; there's also the certainty of encountering at least one or two images of searing originality!

Finally, even the fact that the texts contain elements that can't certainly be pinned down and questions that can't easily be answered seems to me to be important, for it forces us to accept that poetry brings us up against what I can only call the mysteries. And in these days of debased mediaspeak and empty formulaic language it's no bad thing to pay a little homage to the indefinable; to 'learn to love the questions themselves', as Rilke so wisely advised . . .

Finding Out
Sara Maitland

I like to read fiction with 'stuff' in it – with content, new things I did not know before, references I can draw on and link to literary and other culture more widely. I like quotation, intertextuality – in language and structure. I like science and mythology and theology and history and *knowledge* deployed in fiction as allusion, as metaphor and quite simply as information.

If I like it as reader, it has to become one of the things I work with as writer. My interior life, although it is already stuffed with 'stuff', is not, to be honest, that interesting – not interesting enough to sustain a life's work, and to engage readers for the next two hundred or so years.

Learning new things, exploring new material, finding out, *research* is key to my fiction and something I try to infect my students with. For one thing, curiosity, wanting to learn, moving into new territory, aligns the writer with the reader. This is, after all, what we are asking the reader to do – to be curious enough about what we, the writers, are up to, where we are going and what we are saying; to stay with us, to read our texts. Where the writer's own curiosity, research exploration is engaged we will be writing in sympathy with that aspect of the reader.

This follows, I think, from the whole business of walking about with your eyes open that Alicia Stubbersfield is talking about. When your eyes are open enough to notice that different trees turn different colours in the autumn, you are probably going to want to turn to a book of information and find out which trees are the colour you need and whether they are likely to be growing in the place your fiction is proposing for them. If you have enough natural curiosity you may also learn why trees change colour, which is very interesting as it happens and will deepen your fiction, empower your imagination, expand your mind and engage your readers – even if you don't actually put it in this particular bit of writing.

Over two-thirds of my own published short stories are researched. The sources seem to vary immensely – mythological tales from a wide range of sources dominate perhaps, but there are stories based on scientific concepts, on medical, historical, mathematical, and biblical material. What seems to happen for me is that a personal or internal idea has to meet an external and very concrete image (the planet Neptune was discovered by theory not observation in 1845) before I can shape my private emotion into fiction. In the novels this is even more marked: they are *about* the history and science of infertility; about catastrophe theory in palaeontology *and* mathematics; about chaos theory and neurology; and most recently about the science, history and craft of glass working.

In *Brittle Joys* (Virago, 1999) I originally conceived the central character as a glass-blower quite casually, because I wanted a very self-conscious and self-ironizing character and I read somewhere that glass as a medium was 'hopeless at irony', which seemed a pleasing irony to me. To have a glass-blower, I had to learn something about contemporary glass and how it is made, even though her work was not at that point central to the book. I found Stephen Newell, a wonderful glass-blower, who let me sit in on his studio sessions. But gradually, talking to him and following up on suggestions he made about history and technology, the glass itself moved into the centre of the novel – and actually has turned out to be the bit that readers like most.

The personal impulse that started the book – to explore what the connection between gay men and some heterosexual women (fag hags) was about – met an extraordinary depth of congruence with the transparent fragility of glass; with its liquid heat and rigid coolness; with the way it is made – it's communal choreography made necessary by the real physical dangers of the process; and with its extraordinary history. In *Brittle Joys* glass became more than incidental image or metaphor; it became the controlling force of the novel – it shaped the characters and drove the plot. The constant effort to learn more sharpened my imaginative intelligence as well, kept me engaged and moved the novel beyond my domestic concerns into far larger metaphysical and abstract ones, while the precision of research kept (I hope) the book grounded in some social reality. For lots of reasons, the writing of *Brittle Joys* was not a happy time for me – I really do not think that I would have finished a novel on the emotional themes if I had not had a governing discipline that stirred my own curiosity and kept me in touch with something so sharp edged. And, moreover, it is still fun to know some obscure but fascinating things about glass.

I am constantly amazed by the difficulty I have luring students down this path. It is as though people who come to writing classes are escaping from, rather than moving into, *reading*. I have discussed this with other creative writing tutors, so it is not just me. Somehow students believe that reading and writing are completely different and disconnected activities, and they don't want to read, or by extension 'research', as part of the writing process. But writers need to read – not just to understand genre and form or to develop narrative strategies, but in order to enrich their language and extend their knowledge and sensibility.

So I have developed a number of writing games, designed more or less to trick writers into exploring resources they might not think of or might resist if they were just told to use them.

For weekly classes I might ask the participants to bring in a quirky story from a newspaper: they'll have to read the newspapers anyway! Then I ask them to swap stories and write a fiction based on someone else's choice. I might send them off to find out, by reading or interviewing, the arcane languages and details of particular professions (work and its processes, which consume so much of our time in the real world, and form our vocabularies, our physical presence and our mental contents are dangerously neglected in so much contemporary writing) and then use these in fiction or poetry. Learning to use what you have learned is as important as learning how to learn it. We've all read bad historical fiction that is either full of uncomfortable anachronisms or so bunged up with the author's research that you can't find the fictional woods for the research notes trees.

Or I will ask students to find an 'old' story – from mythology, fairy tales, the Bible – that engages them and retell it from a different point of view or perspective; or suggest that they find a quotation to serve as an epigraph for another student's work. (I don't tell them until afterwards that George Eliot made up all the epigraphs in *Middlemarch*.) This exercise has an interesting side effect – often the quote selector and the author will become very engaged in discussing the original intention of the piece of work – the attempt to apply a quote reveals a surprising amount about the success of the piece in communicating mood and tone as well as concept and story.

✍ But a favourite group exercise in this area – though definitely one for a group, not the solitary student – is a development of the TV game show *Call My Bluff*.

Here is a list (prepared by me and refined by a workshop I ran in HM Prison Ashwell) of eight somewhat obscure words, each with three meanings – one of these is the real meaning as defined by the dictionary, the other two are tiny works of fiction:

Knurl
1 An ancient Celtic game, still played in some Scottish islands, not dissimilar from hockey.
2 A short, stumpy person; a dwarf.
3 To hit someone from behind; to attack from the rear.

Oeps

1 Some benefit or profit earned by hard work.
2 A Victorian word for an eccentric or nutter – from the initials of the Organization for External and Psychic Studies.
3 Boys in the junior houses of Eton, called fags in other public schools (no pun intended).

Jobbernowl

1 A clerk or other lowly worker in the Stock Exchange.
2 To cheat or lie your way into a job; to fake your references.
3 An idiot; a thick stupid person.

Deipnosophist

1 A person who enjoys talking at meal times.
2 A person who believes that the gods are not interested in human beings.
3 A person who studies diseases of the mouth – gums, teeth, etc.

Haysel

1 A native officer in the Indian regiments during the Raj.
2 An East Anglian word for the hay-making season, late May and June.
3 A type of helmet, with a low visor, worn by medieval knights.

Collybist

1 Originally a money lender or banker, now any miser, skinflint or excessively ungenerous person.
2 A species of sea snail, a bit like a cockle but with a whiter shell.
3 A small explosion deliberately set off for scientific experiment.

Myrmidon

1 A wicked and seductive young mermaid, with a particularly sweet singing voice, who lures sailors to their deaths.
2 An ingredient used in expensive perfumes, extracted from the musk glands of minks.
3 A fierce warrior from a tribe in ancient northern Greece, celebrated by Homer.

Ozena

1 An unmarried woman, often a belly dancer, living in a Turkish harem and having many of the privileges of a wife, but whose children do not inherit their father's rank.

2 Putrid snot brought on by ulcerous diseases of the nasal mucous membrane.

3 A mythical beast, somewhat like a gazelle but with the legs of a bird, which the Spanish conquistadors believed to live in what are now the Peruvian and Chilean mountains.[1]

Now you have to guess which is the true meaning. It will be mainly guesswork actually, but this list is carefully compiled to reflect the major sources of English vocabulary – there are Teutonic, Romance, and classical derivations.

Next you have to write a short narrative using all seven words (which usually leads to warm admiration for the ingenious and also to merriment, since a sensible plot is perfectly possible, but weird sounding).

Finally, on the spot if you can produce enough dictionaries, or between classes if not, compile your own version of the game. With a bit of luck you will get to produce some tiny fictions within a rigidly imposed genre of dictionary entries; you will get to think about the history of words and thus of language, you will almost inevitably encounter a large number (more than the required half-dozen) of new words and above all you will spend time inside one of the best reference books available.

During feedback on these exercises it is usually possible to introduce elements of rhetoric, aspects of the way words sound and look, some history of language – a deepening of the understanding of how these basic tools of writing can be deployed in so many ways – not just for sense, but for sound and tone and mood as well.

At the very least it stimulates a kind of curiosity about language, which may be quite inspiring. The group of young male prison

1 Knurl = 2; Oeps = 1; Jobbernowl = 3; Deipnosophist = 1; Haysel = 3; Collybist = 1; Myrmidon = 3; Ozena = 2.

inmates I originally played this game with got truly excited about the muscles of language and how it worked, leading to a wonderful philosopher-poet discussion based on the question: 'What colour were carrots before oranges arrived in Britain?' Researching the answers to that (it's very complicated because of the history of horticultural names among other things) led us into Persian and Middle Eastern folk tales and thence to an extraordinary short story by one of them that used flying-carpets as a central metaphor for drug use and abuse; a new way of writing about dependence and excitement and risk.

We are used to the ideas of grounding writing in the physical senses, and of training eye (and ear, finger, nose and tongue) to observe accurately, to pick out with precision the salient detail, the appropriate image. The idea of using our intellectual senses to the same end seems less developed in writing courses and books about the creative writing process.

Poetry and Science
John Latham

In recent years there has been a significant departure from the popular assumption that science and literature (or the arts in general) had negligible common ground. It was held that the creativity and harnessing of intuition so manifest in the latter arena contrasted starkly with the clinical, cerebral, fastidiously numerical and emotionally arid qualities and processes of the former: as clear a distinction between right- and left-brain activities as could be imagined.

Increasingly, however, poets have found in science strong and vivid metaphors for the human condition; and concepts from twentieth-century physics, such as black holes and chaos, have provided fertile ground for the writing of good and imaginative poetry.

This interaction is based on the perception that science – albeit an essentially distinct discipline – can successfully be trawled by writers in order to achieve fresh insights and images. Though welcome, this view does not embrace what appears to me to be the much more fundamental and powerful reality, that the writing of a poem and the pursuit of scientific research are similar activities, in terms of their creative challenges. In both, one sets off on a journey towards a goal that can be only dimly perceived, where diversions may prove more rewarding than the main track. One is looking for links, shapes and relationships. One needs to be able to dream. Success in this first and most crucial stage of creation does not come from pushing, from imposing one's intellect and prejudices on the question being addressed – which is often, in any event, incompletely formulated – but by being open to the seemingly chaotic and irrelevant impressions and images which come to mind. The setting for this first stage is the subconscious, which is fundamental to all creative activity and owes no allegiance to a particular discipline. Isaac Newton, probably the supreme creative genius in the history of science, whose work at the age of twenty-three utterly transformed our understanding of the physical world, and whose revolutionary approach to scientific investigation still holds sway, has – because of his stature – been pilloried (so too Albert Einstein) as the archetypical narrowly focused, close-minded, unimaginative scientist. Yet if one reads Newton's *Opticks*, which presents, almost in diary form, his ruminations about light and related topics, together with the experiments he composed and executed as a consequence of his dreaming, it seems clear that he went through the same set of processes as one often does in the creation of a poem. His writing is beautiful, sheer poetry. I cannot share the view that to demonstrate and explain why sunlight is a mixture of all colours in the spectrum is to reduce a rainbow to a prism.

As mentioned earlier, science – perhaps particularly modern physics – contains many ideas and processes that have strong parallels with human life, and which can be effectively harnessed by poets. To take a few examples: Werner Heisenberg's Principle of

Uncertainty, or more accurately Indeterminacy, is based on the recognition that in order to observe something we must disturb it. At the very least, one quantum of light must bounce off the object into the eye of the observer, and this collision moves the object so that we don't know exactly where it is. Everything we see or touch we alter.

There is an echo of Heisenberg's central idea in Newton's First Law of Motion, formulated almost three hundred years earlier. Since light travels at a finite speed, what we see when we look at celestial objects is light that set out from those objects some time ago. In the case of our sun it is a few minutes, for a distant star it may be millions of years. It follows that stars we see may have expired aeons ago. Perhaps more interestingly, an observer on a star, looking now at Earth, would see our planet not as it is but as it used to be. Perhaps Shakespeare would be visible, or mammoths, or the birth of continents.

Einstein's Theory of Relativity teaches us that the length of an object, or the time interval between two events, is not an absolute, invariant quantity but depends upon the perspective of the person making the measurements: specifically, the relative motion between the person and the object or events. The concept of truth thus becomes a relative quality, requiring a more subtle definition than hitherto.

The Second Law of Thermodynamics, popularly expressed in terms of ever–increasing entropy, states that in an isolated system energy can flow only in one direction, downhill, from higher to lower forms. In our solar system the highest form of energy is gravitational: the contraction of the Sun under gravity producing temperatures so enormous that thermonuclear reactions occur, in which in the deep interior of the burning Sun matter is transformed into energy, according to Einstein's equation (hydrogen burning to form helium); this heat then being transported by turbulent convection to the Sun's surface and converted to electromagnetic energy (radiation, in the form of sunlight), which flows through space to Earth, where photosynthesis in the green leaves of plants transforms it to chemical energy, which we (humans) take in by eating either the plants or

animals that have eaten the plants. This unidirectional trans-
formational chain of energy flow continues to its inevitable terminus,
cosmic waste heat in a cold, dead universe. Human life can be
considered as an interruption, lasting typically eighty years or so, in
this inexorable degradation of energy.

Several areas of science involve the behaviour characteristics
and variability of large populations of particles, notably atoms and
molecules, which are often regarded as the building blocks of matter.
The numbers involved are immense – a gram of material contains
about a million, million, million, million atoms or molecules. The
temperature of the air can be defined as the average speed of the
molecules of oxygen and nitrogen of which it is primarily
constituted. If the air is heated the average molecular speed
increases, and thus the temperature. But not all the molecules will
have the average speed, some will be much faster, some much
slower. Science is concerned with statistical probability, which
recognizes and quantifies the distributions, variations of speed – or
any other property – around the average value. The further a value is
from the average the less likely it is, but it is not impossible, and some
degree of likelihood – however slight – can be assigned to it. For
example, somewhere within a glass of ice-cold water taken out of the
refrigerator there may be a region where the water is boiling.
Somewhere within a torrent of water rushing down a mountainside,
when snow melts in the spring, there will be some water molecules
moving uphill. Such effects are not quirks or aberrations but stable
consequences of random variability in large assemblages of particles.
More graphically, they may be regarded as a consequence of the
actions of the Maxwell Demon, a mythical creature who always
operates within the bounds of physics but only just, in the far wings,
where the almost impossible can happen. It is the Maxwell Demon
who causes boiling to occur in ice-cold water, and who causes a small
number of the randomly moving molecules in a drop of ice-cold
water to interweave into the unique configuration that is the
template for ice, thus causing freezing of the drop – a process which
has been described as no more probable than the bricks in a great pile

of rubble spontaneously interlocking to form a cathedral.

Lightning is a giant spark that releases electrical tension which has built up to an unsustainable level within a thunderstorm. Its massive surge of current along a narrow channel of air creates enormous temperatures, causing the air to expand violently as an audible shock wave we call thunder. This violent, orgasmic process may have provided the source of localized, intense energy required to initiate those chemical reactions in the Earth's primeval atmosphere that led to the formation of life on our planet.

I now provide two illustrations, from my own work, of the utilization of scientific knowledge in the writing of poetry.

In the first example, where two stanzas are presented from a long poem, an old Professor of Astronomy is giving his valedictory lecture, and the scientific ideas that he's expounding are being increasingly infiltrated, as the lecture proceeds, by images and episodes from his personal life – which he regards as a failure. The first stanza is from the prepared lecture, the second his personal response.

> I repeat, my cherished friends! There is no loss
> of information. It travels on forever, intact.
> What we can't do is retrieve it, if it's passed
> beyond our niche of space and time. Its integrity
> depends on never being found, for everything
> we see or touch, we alter. Quanta flick the moon
> to read its story – and the old man winces,
> recoils. The earth leaps up to falling apples.
> Andromeda's red shift is scarlet underneath.
> It is holy only on the dark side of the moon.
>
> Is that how I altered you, Suzanne: by spying?
> At my bedroom window throughout the afternoon
> as you picked raspberries? On your bowed head,
> a knotted handkerchief. Softening your shape,
> the smock you said would see you through. Fruit

in your basket was swelling deep. You held
each berry as if you were in church, laid it
like a wreath. At times, you'd toss one high
and swallow it. Such impertinence! Such grace!
Then you felt my gaze, bit your lip to bleeding.

In this second example, a short poem entitled 'Limitless', the
science is not providing a metaphor but simply a backcloth against
which I wished to make the point that some questions – in this case
one asked by a child – are so profound that a verbal response is
irrelevant, perhaps even diminishing.

'How much sky is there
in the whole world?'

I could answer that:
give the atmospheric mass
number of its molecules
the global area
the rate at which air thins
outwards to the sun.

But as I look into his eyes
huge, open to the sky,
galactic deep
reaching far beyond the sun
I shake my head
tell him I don't know.

✍ Some of the basic ideas outlined above form the basis of the exercises
and opportunities for writing practice that follow. In addressing
these it is important, when ranging widely with your ideas, either
to try to confine them within the limits of physical possibility or to
recognize when you are outside these limits. Courage is crucial – you
will be most creative if you are stimulated by strange concepts,
rather than intimidated by them.

1 The essential idea behind Heisenberg's Indeterminacy Principle is that the act of observing or touching an object necessarily changes it in some way. We cannot acquire information about something without disturbing it: without changing it. Embody this idea in a poem about a newly developing relationship.

2 In studying a system that contains vast numbers of particles or objects, we normally notice only the average value of its properties, such as its temperature or density. However, physics allows for the existence of small regions of the system in which the properties are enormously different from the average. Ice may exist in a glass of boiling water. The Maxwell Demon is the mythical creature who detects these highly improbable features. Describe what your senses experience as the demon takes you journeying through the unlikely regions of a pan of stew, an anthill and a densely populated galaxy.

3 Imagine a panoply of sounds and/or smells that left Earth long ago and are now wafting past you on a distant planet. Keep in mind that the speed with which these attributes travel to you is finite and variable.

Out of the Abstract
Paul Magrs

One of the old clichés about writing is that it's always best if you 'write about what you know'. Why did people ever say that? Why did the instruction gain such currency?

I think it's because we all respond to writing that makes us feel that we have 'been there'; writing in which the writer has evoked a setting, an experience, a whole lifetime that is so vivid they have transported us bodily, all our senses alert, into another time and place. Our response as readers is often to feel that such a forceful impression of authenticity is down to the writer's own experience.

They are telling us what it was like so evocatively because the experience was real and vivid to them. They were writing about what they knew. So when we read Catherine Cookson's account of growing up in 1930s Jarrow or Harriet Jacobs' memoir of a nineteenth-century slave girl, they ring true because they are grounded in immediate, sensual, recalled detail.

All the essays in this section have been about keeping your work grounded in the everyday, in immediate experience. Alison Fell talks of writing about the associations you have with the bed you sleep in, Sara Maitland about finding out what glass-blowers actually do to create their works, and John Latham explains the minutiae of molecules bouncing around in matter. Whatever they are writing about here, it's all grounded in physical objects, processes, images. But they are all also talking about those larger concepts, those things beyond the immediately observable. All the essays here are, I think, discussing how we might engage with abstract concepts and realms of knowledge, or even (as Alison Fell puts it) with 'mysteries'.

How can we smuggle these vast ideas into our writing, without resorting to generalizations or language so opaque that it alienates the reader?

Writing is how we ask questions about the world. Angela Carter said, late on in her life, that it was how she still managed to ask the 'big adolescent questions, about the nature of reality. Why are we here? What do we think we're doing here? Who do we think we are?'

Looking for the answers to these things could take you down many routes. You might become a theologian, a traveller, a quantum physicist, a mystic, a politician. Or you might just become a novelist, a poet or playwright. The novelist, poet or playwright are using language in their experiments and their explorations. Language, because it refers to things, to physical matter and everyday lives, always wants to ground these big questions, so that they make vivid sense to a reader. It wants to trigger associations for the reader and make the abstract into something that is imminent and comprehensible to them.

In her 'fantasy bed' writing workshop, Alison Fell is ruthless in not allowing us to write bland, easy generalizations. She always pushes us back to writing about the sensual and the real. It is in her cut-up process, in the random juxtaposition of discrete phrases, that she allows the unconscious to work, so that by putting these vivid snippets of language back together, we see new patterns emerging. She gets us to examine our subconscious processes, and gets us to engage with the 'mysteries'. She asks us what our real questions and preoccupations are. She wants to know what's under the surface.

Writing alerts you to what you are really interested in. Whatever you are writing about, your true preoccupations always come out.

Do this now. List five abstract nouns, five states of mind that you are interested in. Write them off the top of your head. They could be envy, hilarity, isolation.

Now go hunting through your books. Find episodes from novels or stanzas from poems or scenes from plays that you particularly like. Boil five of them down to one word each; one abstract noun that represents that scene to you. Maybe all your favourite moments in literature are to do with ecstasy or triumph, or maybe despair or revenge. Can you see a pattern emerging? Which abstract states are you fascinated by? Which do you enjoy seeing dramatically evinced in writing?

Now look in particular at how these states are evoked in the individual pieces of writing. Which phrases give the clues? Are they grounded in character, in supple, evocative language? How does the author bring the abstract notion in?

My own favourite example in this section of the book is John Latham's conjuring of that agent of chaos and randomness, the Maxwell Demon. I can see that creature immediately and see him as a kind of mythic trickster being, tampering with the laws of probability. My imagination wouldn't be half so engaged if I'd read something about the laws of probability that used only the abstract terms. To get a handle on such subjects, we need an image, a mythic trope of some kind. We need to see a demon and suddenly it all comes clear. In this, perhaps, we're not so different to the Egyptians making up sun gods to worship and explain how the universe worked. During the millennium celebrations I was heartened to see a giant metal millipede parading the streets of Manchester, being cheered by the crowds: the Millennium Bug personified. We seem to need to give a face to our abstract fears and hopes. We need to make them into something we recognize.

Sara Maitland writes in her essay about a restless need to research and find out 'stuff' from a variety of sources – horticulture, etymology, mathematics. She talks about the difficulty of using that information in fiction or poetry. Every reader likes to find out 'stuff' about the world; stuff they never knew before. It does us good. But no one likes to feel they are being clobbered over the head by it. In her example of finding out about a glass-blower, though, I think we have the key. In that research, she was learning to see the world through a glass-blower's eyes: not only about the physical processes and skills involved, but also the kind of things that a glass-blower might think about as their thoughts go off into the abstract as they work. Thoughts, perhaps, about irony, inspiration or the divine. The writer's job is to show how that grappling with the concrete and the immediate is what gives any of us access to the bigger questions and how, in writing, you only gain access to the one via the other.

✍ Think of an occupation you know nothing about. Something you are aware of but haven't really paid much attention to. Say, traffic wardens. What exactly do they have to do? How many hours do they walk up and down the streets? Do they have a set route and timetable or do they just make it up? What kind of satisfaction can they feel? Have they ever been beaten up doing their job?

Everyone sees the world in terms of their own biography, occupation, immediate preoccupations. I want to know what a traffic warden is thinking as she goes slapping tickets on cars. She might just be thinking she needs a holiday or new shoes. But she might well believe herself to be the instrument of divine retribution. How metaphysical can her thoughts be?

Ask her. Ask your chosen person about their job. Talk to a

laundrette operator, a cinema usherette, a hot-air balloonist. Let them talk about the specifics of their work. Don't go crashing in and ask after their philosophy. Listen to what they have to say about the specifics and then you'll gradually see how they engage with abstract notions. Everyone has their own metaphors. Their generalizations about the world are always interesting and at their most useful when they are grounded in the physical and immediate nature of what they do.

Why not test this out by getting out and about to talk to some people whose view of the world you have never really considered before? Talk to your friends about their work. You might think you know what they do and the kinds of things they get up to, but it's always worth asking for a bit more detail. It's always surprising.

4 Autobiography

Introduction
Paul Magrs

Everything tends to become material. When you are writing you want to use up everything around you, everything that happens to you, everything from your past.

For me, it's people that I want to get down on the page, somehow. They might be people I knew years ago and don't any more – they've died or moved away. I want them remembered in some way. As large as life again.

Sometimes I have dreams and people from the past come back in incredibly specific and lifelike ways. The way they speak and behave are precise in a way that my conscious mind has forgotten. I find it reassuring to believe that some part of me remembers the tiny, seemingly irrelevant things. In those dreams I see how aunts and grandmothers, uncles and neighbours and school friends all behaved: my stepfather's sister Jenny in stretchy nylon trousers, sitting on her kitchen doorstep and telling me about her crush on Starsky and Hutch.

I want my writing to conjure these people up in the way my dreams sometimes can. I want to introduce some of these people to others they never got a chance to meet and see how they would get on. In my dreams and fiction I want to look at the great 'What ifs?'. I want, sometimes, to change how things really did happen.

Sometimes I have very lucid dreams about the first house I lived in, in Darlington, where I stole yellow roses from the front garden next door; where I stood in the doorway behind my mam as she talked with the postman and I imitated his chronic twitch the whole time.

Some of these things have become anecdotes; the specific memory has been replaced by an actual narrative that my family and I tell each other. (Like when I was kidnapped at the age of three by a gang of rowdy teenagers and locked in a garden shed. My father found and rescued me and when he told me not to go with strangers I told him to fuck off: I'd been having fun.)

The actual memory gets occluded by the telling of it. If I want to write any part of these things as stories, I have to get past the anecdote and recover the exact feeling of that time; and also run the risk of replacing my memory with what I actually write about it.

When I was five we moved to Newton Aycliffe to live in a box-shaped house on a black-brick estate. Ours was one of the first houses finished, in fields of toffee-coloured mud. I did most of my growing up on that new town in the seventies and eighties (where the ice-cream vans ran round the maze-like streets bonging out 'Lara's Theme' from *Doctor Zhivago*). I knew the people round the doors (precocious, chatty kid that I was), I was going to the school over the Burn, and I was using the shopping precinct in town.

When I first came to write seriously I wanted to get all of that place and time written down and captured. I didn't know of any novels that were about the seventies and eighties in a new town. I didn't know of any fiction about people like our neighbours and the people you saw down town.

I couldn't start writing about it, any of it, though, until I'd moved away. Then it became a memory and was recoverable, somehow. I could see it more distinctly when I was across the country at university. Newton Aycliffe and the people I knew, my family and my past were all something I could make real by turning it into fiction. Realer, almost, than it was in the first place.

When it's happening to you, life is terribly fast.

The one big party we had at our house was for New Year's Eve in 1980. It was the one time a whole collection of people were brought together for the first and last time; the Tyneside branch of the family, the Dutch and the Australian contingent. I was ten and the night went by in a kind of glamorous haze. I remember my Big Nanna walking up the street with our neighbour Molly after midnight, both of them tipsy on Snowballs, both wearing flowing Dutch-print skirts (presents from Rini). They were off to look at Molly's religious paintings, which she'd been laboriously executing on rolls of wall-paper.

I wanted that night to replay and replay for ever. As it turned out, the eighties weren't that good a decade for most of the people there. Last year I eventually managed to write a short story about that night and those people there and most of the satisfaction was in re-creating the characters: putting them back together in a way that could never now happen in the real world. It is as if they are stuck at that party for ever. And I can go back there whenever I want to. And other people can go now as well.

     ✍ Here's something to try. Write down the names of three people you
     have vivid memories of. Three people whom you knew but who
     never met each other in real life. Put them into a scene, maybe an
     impossible scene, in which they meet for the first time. You knew
     them all well and you can imagine how they would have reacted to
     each other, what they would have said to each other.

       Write their dialogue for them.

       What would these people have found to talk about? Would they
     have got on with each other? Would they have taken against each
     other?

In daydreams we often wonder how so-and-so would have got on with so-and-so. Give yourself some time now to make that real. Engineer a possible brief encounter for these friends or relatives you remember.

You begin this kind of effort at salvaging the past by reminding yourself. What you learn, as you go on, is this: the means by which you remind yourself of the past are the very ones that any writer needs to use in order to create any kind of experience for their reader.

You need the exact colours and smells and textures.

These sensual clues are what can take you back at any moment to a point in the past. The tiniest of things can re-evoke the biggest, most elaborate scene. The classiest example of this is, of course, Marcel Proust dipping biscuits in his tea and having the whole lot flood back to him. But I'm thinking, more selfishly, of toast and marmalade and whisky in tea with a gang of new friends, wintry afternoons during my first year at college. Or I'm thinking about warm sausage rolls from the bakery after doing the shopping down the precinct with my mam; flakes of pastry down my jumper and the pop-eyed woman behind the counter who thought I was a girl.

Maybe the most effective way of recovering the past is through food. Tastes and textures can pull us back any time we're not expecting it; the smells of other people's dinner, a glimpse of wall-paper.

Childhood is a good place to start with recovering these exact sense impressions.

✍ As an exercise, think back to being a child and write down the most evocative smell, sound, sight, taste and touch that you can remember. Then think yourself further on in time. What were the most vivid impressions when you were twenty-two? Thirty-seven? Forty-four? Is it easier to remember the very earliest senses or the later ones? You really have to work hard at recovering these experiences. But they do come back. And they are the key to recreating those times in a text of any kind.

Another thing that can't help but draw me back is the way people talked. I wouldn't say my memory is that marvellous at all. I have to keep notes everywhere to remind me of the simplest things. I do, though, have a curious memory for what and how people have said things. If I stop and think now, I can hear my parents telling me things when I was a kid, in their exact voices, in all their specificity; all their quirks and vocal mannnerisms intact.

I can hear my Big Nanna wondering whether she'll have a last cup of tea before bedtime; her Norfolk accent hardly changed after thirty years in the north-east. 'I'll not have another cup, due I'll be wetting all night.' My other Nanna telling my mam she wasn't afraid of the ageing process in her broad Geordie accent: 'I'll fight the bugger tooth and nail.' My granda, seeing him again after years, after I'd published my first novel. He had it on the shelf the day I went back, just after my Nanna Magrs died. He said, 'Eeh, lad. You're a clever bugger, aren't you?'

Smells, tastes, snatches of dialogue and colours. When I think of the house in Darlington, the carpets are a swirling aqua and the curtains bright tangerine; there was a stark white unused room upstairs. Moving to the new house; helping to smear shocking pink Windowlene on the windows. We painted the kitchen the same deep jade as my stepdad's Ford Cortina. The spring of 1982 was yellow; the winter of 1989 silver and black (the stars like diamanté through the skylight in my student room). So I use the colours, too, to anchor me back.

These are all the things that make a piece of fiction real and vivid to me; the precise rendering of each of these elements. When I think of my favourite writers – Anne Tyler, Shena Mackay, Katherine Mansfield – they work exactly in this way upon me. They build an indelible atmosphere through a compressed, succinct accretion of observed, transformed detail. They make their stories seem like memories of my own: they become that immediate and pressing to me.

If you are drawing upon memory and autobiography for your writing then you have to remember this and work from the ground up; conjuring the atmosphere as fully and vividly as possible. You will always know more about these characters and circumstances than your reader will. You knew the people in real life; you know where they came from, what they did next; maybe what eventually became of them. Don't be tempted to rush in and splurge and tell all straight away in an explosion of unmediated confession.

Let your reader get to know these people and places you are salvaging and re-creating from the past. Build them up carefully in all their specificities. You might change things and transform them to make it into a better story. You are free to do this. Once they're on the page, they're not real people any more. It's impossible really to create people on the page; it's a confidence trick. You are putting together an impression of them through gesture and colour.

You have to give an impression of them as three-dimensional people; ones that you and your reader can walk all the way around and could imagine meeting. It's difficult because you have to be honest about yourself and the time and the people you knew then. You have to start seeing the things you didn't see at the time.

It's not always best to use the first person and begin 'I remember'. Best, instead, to recapture some tiny part of a scene you recall and keep yourself out of it for a while.

Learn to fall in love with these people all over again. Remind yourself why you loved them in the first place, whatever happened later. Don't let hindsight colour the picture you are putting together. You've got to return, Tardislike, to that exact point in time – and learn how to stay in that moment longer.

The characters in that moment are not flesh and blood, but neither are they ghosts. Now you've got characters and you have to make them into your own. You've got responsibilities and you've got an amazing amount of freedom in writing about them.

Let them start talking to each other, again.

Memory: The True Key to Real Imagining
Lesley Glaister

I am on a beach. I don't know where – Southwold perhaps. I am very small and wearing a blue ruched swimming costume, which scratches the tops of my legs and fills with bubbles of water when I go in the sea. But I'm not in the sea. I'm sitting on a big striped towel, shivering. My dad is sitting beside me and I'm thinking how hairy his legs are, like gorilla's legs. Then I notice something: a hollow in the soft bulge of his calf, big enough to cup an egg in, not hairy like the rest but dull pinkish, fuzzy like newborn mouse skin. I want to put my finger inside and feel but I don't. Somehow I know I can't do that and I must not mention it. Then Dad gets up and hobbles down the shingle towards the sea. He breaks into a run when he gets to the flat bit before the sea begins. He plunges in and swims out and out and out. My mum is reading and my sister shovelling pebbles into a bucket. No one but me has noticed how his head gets smaller and smaller the further out he swims, until at last I can't see him between the waves. He has gone. But I don't shout or scream. I turn over and lie on my tummy on the towel, feeling my heart thudding against the lumpy pebbles. I have seen my daddy drown but I don't say a word. I lie there with the sea or my heart roaring in my ears.

I lie paralysed by fear and guilt for what seems hours until I hear the crunch of footsteps and feel the sprinkle of cold drops on my skin. Daddy is back and is standing above me waiting for me to get off the towel. He is fine, invigorated and oblivious to my terror, rubbing himself dry, slurping tea from the thermos.

That experience encapsulates for me a key moment of growing up: the sudden realization of my dad's vulnerability and his mortality – and by extension that of everyone including myself. An apparently insignificant moment when the bottom fell out of my safe child's world.

It wasn't until my father died, about twenty years later, that the seaside moment came back to me. Only then did it occur to me that the hollow in his leg was the scar of a tropical ulcer contracted during the war. He was one of the soldiers captured by the Japanese when Singapore was taken in 1941. He worked as a slave on the construction of the Burma/Siam railway, suffering cerebral malaria, cholera, dysentery, beatings, near starvation – an unimaginably traumatic time about which he never spoke. It was a deep area of silence. Not only was it never spoken of but there seemed an embargo even on wondering. It wasn't until years after his death that it even occurred to me why, as a naturally curious child, I never even *wondered*. About ten years after his death I became fascinated by the idea of that deeply layered silence – not unique to my family, I know – and began to plan the novel which became *Easy Peasy*. The seaside memory – only a tiny moment in the book – was the seminal one from which that novel grew, the true key to real imagining.

There are very few literally true moments like this in my own fiction, although naturally writers vary enormously in the way they process and utilize memory. Much of what I write feels as if it is made up – but that really means that it is memory refracted through imagination, often unconsciously, into something new. This might mean a scrap of a childhood memory is blended with something I heard yesterday and comes out as something unrecognizable as either. That, I think, is the real stuff of fiction – memory blended, refracted, transformed. That is why something that is apparently entirely imagined can have the real force of emotional truth.

For instance, my mild dislike of confined spaces was transformed into a potholing disaster in *Limestone and Clay*. And the queasy embarrassment I felt as a child at an accidental glimpse of my father's genitals (again on the beach!) dramatized into Jennifer's mortification at the spectacle of her naked grandparents in *Digging to Australia*. This latter was quite unconscious, indeed I didn't realize where it had stemmed from until years later.

And this unconscious salvaging is another and more fundamental way in which memory is employed in the making of fiction. Every impression ever made on a person from newborn babyhood onwards will contribute to the shape and texture of the imagination. And an individual's personality is largely shaped by early experience: unconditional love, disappointed hunger, rejection, displacement by a newborn sibling, star or scapegoat status within the family. These all affect the deep patterning of expectation, the rhythm of a unique world view. This affects the deep structure, the rhythm that becomes apparent within a piece of writing. This is why with many writers similar tropes recur, similar themes are visited and revisited. Whatever the actual consciously chosen subject – from true romance to sci-fi fantasy – that pattern or rhythm is very likely to recur.

The most exciting moment in the writing of a novel comes with the onset of the wonderful trance-like state when a book seems to begin to grow itself, seems there to be discovered rather than created. Some writers describe this as the moment when the characters take over. It seems that the writer has little choice but to let them have their way. It is thrilling and feels somehow *real*. That is because it is. It is simply the deep unconscious patterning rising up and taking over the conscious critical planning mind. The unconscious rhythm that dictates the shape of most deeply felt fiction that has its germ in the structure of the writer's personality; and which also bestows on each writer a unique and precious voice.

Would-be writers often object that they have no memories to draw on, or that nothing interesting ever happened to them. This is not possible. Memory can be hard to access, but it's a skill that can be learned. And it's not so much interesting things but unique ways of seeing ordinary things that makes the most original and satisfying fiction. Catching one little tail end of a memory and patiently teasing it out can be a way to start. And it doesn't matter if the memory is not complete, nor entirely true. Remember you are writing *fiction*. A little kick start from the memory can set off your imagination – and who knows where that might lead . . .

✍ Try this: close your eyes and remember a pair of shoes or boots that you wore as a child. Maybe some pink satin ballet shoes with scuffed toes; maybe the Wellington boots inside which your socks always went to sleep; or the pinching toes of your best party shoes. It doesn't matter, just take some time to picture them, then jot down everything you remember about the look, the feel, the smell of them. Now remember an occasion on which you wore them. Where were you going? What did you feel like? Maybe you were dawdling along behind your mum cracking icy puddles with your heel; maybe you were scared or bored or excited; maybe you were running a race in your brand-new rubbery smelling plimsolls. Write the memory and if the memory runs out, start making up. That is fiction.

Writing from Experience
Nell Dunn

It is said that all fiction is an autobiography. What we write about has to be felt and therefore experienced, but it can be experienced in the imagination and needn't necessarily be lived experience, or so I believe. What we choose to write about usually has an energy that agitates us. There is a sense of adventure as we sit down to write. What remains somewhat of a mystery is how real experience hits and provokes the imagination into a work of fiction.

I was evacuated during the war without my mother. I was three. In *Steaming*, written in 1981, I created a mother–daughter relationship, Mrs Meadows and Dawn. Mrs Meadows rules the roost. Dawn, the apple of her eye, now thirty-five, behaves like a three-year-old. She can't even open the cat's tin. She can't bring in the milk from the doorstep when her mother is ill. They sleep in the same bed. We know something dreadful happened to Dawn but we never quite discover what it was. In real life I missed my mother. Dawn's mother is not allowed out of her sight. By the end of the play Dawn has the upper hand and is defying her mother outrageously. In *Steaming* I got my own back and something inside me was satisfied.

In *Babe*, another play written a few years later, Babe, the daughter, is attempting to break free of her mother. She goes to Spain and finds a rich older man to take care of her, but this time it is her mother, Cecile, who can't live without her and comes to find her to make her come home. At the end of the play Babe realizes, in order to be free, to have her life, she has to take care of herself.

Finally in *My Silver Shoes*, written in 1996, the mother, Gladys, is old and her daughter, Joy, devotes herself, with quite a few hiccups, to caring for her. Shortly before I wrote this book my own mother became ill and needed taking care of till she died. I visited every weekend and sometimes took care of her, and finally she died in my arms. A great gift from a mother to a daughter. But I needed to write about a daughter who had really 'got there' with her mother. Joy and Gladys knew everything about each other and the deep love was, in *My Silver Shoes*, lived out.

Sometime after finishing this book I dreamt my mother took me in her arms and hugged me and kissed me and told me she loved me.

✍ Start with fifteen minutes' notebook writing: odd scraps of dialogue overheard, descriptions of people and places, a dream from the night before.

The following exercises are intended to free up the memory and imagination. And to put the writer in closer touch with her or his own self.

1 Shut your eyes and put yourself back in a childhood bedroom. Spend some time there remembering the wallpaper, the furniture, the smells, the noises. When you are ready, write about it in as minutely detailed a way as you are able. Don't put any people in it. Try to use your memory and be absolutely accurate.

2 Now remember yourself at this time. Put yourself to bed in that room. Who were you? Write about yourself from the pen of the six-year-old or ten-year-old boy or girl. Tell what you liked and disliked about your bedroom.

3 Now your mother comes in to say goodnight. What happens? Write some dialogue between you and your mother. What does she look like when she comes through the door?

4 Now your father comes in to wake you up in the morning. What does he say? What does it feel like? What does he look like?

In all these exercises except the first you can mix in reality and imagination. Put a time limit on each exercise. They should all be done quite quickly. At most thirty minutes each. It is a liberating exercise to get students to read out their work to one another soon after writing it.

If you are working in a group, there may only be time for one of these exercises at each session. It is important to leave space for reading work out loud as this is often the most enjoyable part.

✍ Working in Pairs

It can be energizing and exciting to write another person's 'autobiography'. For these exercises you work in pairs. Here are some possibilities.

1 Take it in turns to tell your partner something drastic that has happened to you in the last year with as much detail as possible. Take five to ten minutes in the telling. Your partner need only listen attentively. No questions. Then write one another's stories, changing the names and locations. First or third person can be used. Write taking two steps back as if you were writing a short story. Give a time limit of thirty or forty minutes for the writing.

   Read out the story to your partner and check that any identifying evidence has been cleared. Ask permission for what you have written to become yours. Then the stories can be read to the wider group.

   After the reading leave time for the stories to be discussed and polished. This exercise encourages the thought that everywhere there are hidden stories. It also encourages trust and intimacy between students.

2 Again in pairs. Take it in turns to tell of an ongoing problem in your life around a relationship. Take five or ten minutes in the telling. Again your partner need only listen. No questions. Then, once again, swap situations and write for thirty minutes an imagined dialogue between the protagonists in your partner's story. Feel free to create a setting for your dialogue. A café, perhaps, or a garden or a room in a house. Anywhere you care to make them meet. Trust your instinct to guess or imagine or even overhear what they might say to each other. You may break the dialogue to describe the setting but stick mainly to dialogue.

   Experiment with saying things that maybe haven't been said.

This is an exercise in developing the writer's natural intuition and learning to trust it. It is also great fun writing dialogue. Leave time for the reading out and discussion of writing dialogue.

3 Spend a few minutes thinking about your own family. Include grandparents, aunts and uncles and cousins. Now consider who was the 'outsider' in the family. The one who didn't really get included. Who was nobody's favourite. Who somehow got left out and forgotten. Who often had bad luck. Describe as accurately as you can what he or she looked like. Focus in on a precise moment when you remember seeing them at a bus stop, in the kitchen, coming out of the bathroom. Write down exactly what you see with as much detail as possible.

In the second part of this exercise create a dialogue with your 'outsider'. What would you like to tell them? Listen carefully to what they might like to say to you and write it down. You can also place this dialogue somewhere you know or somewhere imagined.

Read what you have written to your partner, then write down how reading your 'outsider' piece to another person makes you feel. How did hearing your partner's piece make you feel?

Finally write a dialogue between yourself and your partner's 'outsider', telling him or her how you feel about them in relation to your own life and problems.

The Shared Past
Anna Garry

Our memories are our ways of making sense of the past. Memory can be individual and personal, a sharp flash of recollection, an intense moment where feelings are concentrated into short, everyday events. A smell in the street can take you to your childhood or anywhere in your past, bringing back words, sounds, images. Or the smell might only haunt you, refusing to be identified, but filling you with longing for elucidation, or with strong feelings of recognition. The purpose of the writing exercise that follows is to give you ways to link into this powerful process, to write about memories, and then to learn about yourselves as writers, from what you and others have produced.

One of the most powerful impacts of guided writing from memory is the element of surprise, pleasure and energy that can arise from doing this exercise. It is important to come at it spontaneously, with minimum self-judgement, and not to worry about the coherence of the writing. In what follows I first outline what you need to do to produce the writing, and then I explain what can be learned from this exercise. If you are going to do the writing exercises yourself, I recommend that you write first and then look at the analysis afterwards. One of my students, in his seventies, said at the end of a writing session, If I'd known what your purpose was, in getting me to write about memory, I would have tried to meet it. This way I found out about my writing for myself.

✍ It is important that you or your group spend little time thinking, and instead get down to writing, swiftly and without stopping. What may come to you are ideas, images, words, a narrative, even poetry. The main thing is to write whatever comes naturally. I assure my students that they may find some of the suggestions trigger more writing than others.

If you are concerned that you, or your class, may not get going easily, it is possible to preface this exercise with a warm-up session. For example, I might give my students a line of prose and then ask them to write for two to three minutes on anything that might follow from this line. I do find that the exercise works without this, and if time is limited, I do not bother. What is important is to get the students to write for about twenty minutes, without stopping, and then to give them sufficient time to read out their work to each other in groups. The session ideally ends with some guided class discussion about what this writing has produced.

I first experienced a form of this writing exercise on a weekend course run by the poet and novelist Mary Dorcey. I have developed it to suit my needs in both my evening and undergraduate creative writing courses. The aim is to get students to write for about five minutes on each of three potentially memorable moments in their lives. One of the advantages of the suggestions that follow is that they produce writing of validity and energy but, on the whole, they do not tap into memories that are hugely painful or could dissolve someone emotionally. If this is a first, or early, meeting of a group, this is important, because people may be feeling excited, anxious and vulnerable.

If you are guiding a group, you should do the timing. Ask the participants to write for about five minutes on each of the three subjects below. Reveal the topics in turn, without telling what the next piece is about. If you are doing it alone, sit with a clock and respond to each topic in sequence. It is possible for you, as group leader, to participate in this exercise, i.e. writing with the group. I imagine this decision will depend on your familiarity with the group or whether you are part of an informal writers' group, where this could also work well. If it is a larger group, it is advisable to leave your own writing and concentrate on how the participants are doing.

The Topics

1 The first day at school/kindergarten you remember
2 The first journey you remember
3 The first room you remember

I say to my students that it is not important to search for precise memories, rather to write down the first things you remember. One of my evening-class students couldn't remember her first days at school, because she had started during the Second World War. What she remembered, and wrote about, were the effects of the war around her, the bombing, the air-raid sirens. And indeed, when it came to her writing about the first journey she remembered, it was the one where she was evacuated, by steam train. My students in their late teens and early twenties have vivid memories of that transition from home to school, of the colours, the smells and the emotions.

Looking at the Writing

Once the writing is completed the students stop. Some have produced over a thousand words, and even the ease with which this amount is produced can be a surprise to new writers. At this point I break the class into small groups and remind them that everyone is in the same position. They have all produced spontaneous writing. What I want them to do now is read out the writing to each other.

Use of the Senses

At this point I introduce an extra purpose to the discussion, one that is beyond discussing memories and sharing the communality and differences in their experiences. I want students also to focus on the use of the senses that has appeared, naturally, without thought, in the writing they have produced. Here, I say, they will find out which senses they use, spontaneously, in their writing. I write on the board the five senses: sound, sight, touch, smell and taste. I also introduce the important point that good fiction is based on the effective use of the senses, and that the senses, or concrete detail, in a piece of writing gives a reader a fundamental link to a writer's work, allowing the reader to feel and experience the fictional situation (this is discussed further at the end of this piece). The groups then work on their own, reading their writing and identifying where the emphasis on the use of the senses is.

I circulate round the groups, listening to what people have discovered about themselves as writers. Some have remembered sounds and smells, like the foods they had to eat, which is the most common. The majority have written down visual memories: a room with an orange settee, a calf-skin rug, a lamp with a woman holding a torch, a holy picture whose eyes followed you wherever you moved to in a room. The intricacy and specificity of the memories are really impressive.

What also comes through strongly in the writing is a written expression of emotional experience, which underlies memories. Sometimes these emotions are so powerful that students don't want, at first, to look at the use of the senses, but rather to examine how they felt at these times: fear of the first day at school, excitement about new clothes, tears at leaving your mother, anger at a journey that was forced upon you as a child, sadness about a room where there was no space and which had to be shared, and even terror at what might be under the bed or in a chest of drawers. Many students then suggested that emotional expression should be added to the list of the senses, as a way of looking at the writing. It is the expression of these moments of intensity in vivid detail that has this impact.

The exercise usually ends with a group or class discussion of the experience of writing. As this is an exercise that I do in my first class, the way I organize this discussion depends upon the group. It is very important that students should feel confident and comfortable about participating, and not feel forced to read out work before they are ready. With my undergraduates, this is usually not a problem, and we usually hear an extract from each student's writing, though no one is obliged to read out. The writing is always strong, and it gives me the opportunity to point out the quality and richness of writing that can be produced by such a short exercise, with its focus on real experience. There are often common experiences, toys that the group remember, fashions or clothes that students may have shared, but until then have forgotten. There are often interesting choices in the perspective of writing voice. Sometimes students write as though the memory is in the present moment, others let it drift into a narrative, which explains, at a distance, what it felt like to be, for example, four or five.

In my evening class I am working with adults of all ages and backgrounds. They may have, for the first time, chosen to take what they see as an enormous step, they are allowing writing to be part of their life. I do not ask anyone to read out to the group at this point. For some people it is enough that they have got through the first meeting and have managed to write something. There is, however, always a lively discussion about what it felt like to write these pieces, about the particular senses that were focused on and why, and the surprise people felt at the differences and similarities of their memories. One great advantage of this exercise is that it shows people both their individuality and shared humanity.

I bring the discussion to a close by summarizing how memory can show us our natural use of the senses, how it reminds us of powerful emotions, how it shows us the individuality of our experience. This is where our originality of viewpoint will come from. I emphasize how memory gives us details: the faces in the playground, the toys we had, the mood behind our first journey. There is often a discussion on how memory does not have to be factual, indeed, often is not factual, and that the borders between fact and fiction are difficult to delineate.

✍ Writing from Memory and Difficult Emotions

This particular memory exercise is good to use at an early stage in teaching because it rarely taps into memories that are deeply distressing for the students. This is a vital factor to remember in teaching creative writing. For some students writing may quickly lead to an unfolding into difficult or traumatic areas of their lives.

Another memory exercise I also use is called 'The Indelible Place You Lived In', and comes from Liz Allen's chapter of *The Creative Writing Handbook* (edited by Singleton and Luckhurst). It focuses on a sequence of steps to remember a house that the students have lived in. This is an excellent, lengthy exercise, which unfolds slowly and with concentration on one particular experience. It can, however, lead people speedily into difficult memories. When I use this, I tend to warn people at the beginning that this exercise may lead them to somewhere with negative associations, and they need to decide whether they feel up to exploring them before they start. Once a group is established, however, and has some familiarity or connections between the people, this exercise can yield complex and strong writing.

Final Words on Memory and Using the Senses

One of the outcomes of this exercise is that it produces snippets of very strong writing from everyone, full of richness of detail and sensual description. They can also become the starting point for lengthier stories. For instance, one of my American students wrote about a hospital room where he visited his mother as a small boy. This led him to develop an excellent story about a seven-year-old boy. The story was focused on a room in his home and showed a little boy moving from having a strong relationship with his mother and going through the painful and funny experiences of trying to find some independence.

The short story writer Flannery O'Connor writes that, 'Fiction operates through the senses, and I think one reason that people find it so difficult to write stories is that they forget how much time and patience is required to convince through the senses.' In addition she says that, 'Fiction writers who are not concerned with these concrete details are guilty of what Henry James called "weak specification". The eye will glide over their words while the attention goes to sleep.'

This is one of the challenges of making writing fresh and interesting: to produce concrete and unusual detail as a way of showing the world. In my experience, returning to use of the senses, again and again, ought not to be underestimated. When we try to write larger pieces, and get focused on ideas and themes, this is the first thing that, disastrously, can go, leaving writing lifeless and unspecified.

What this exercise does, to all levels of writers, is produce a level of rich detail, without a great deal of effort. The freshness of remembered experience can enhance writing, and can be returned to as a way to remind people of the depths that can be achieved if you use details to make your reader feel the experiences of their characters.

Where You're Coming From
Julia Bell

Most of the inspiration for my work comes about as a part of my engagement with the world in which I live: it's the things that happen to me that make me want to write. This is not to say that all my fiction is autobiographical. It is not, it *is* fiction. I make things up, embellish, exaggerate, lie. I remake my world in a new kind of way for myself, in a way that allows me to make sense of things, imagine scenarios, draw conclusions, plot revenges. It is the safest kind of place to explore my own territory, think about the things that bother me. If the writing wasn't for *me* in the first place, I doubt very much whether I'd be writing at all.

All of us have experience. It's the pull, or the fracture, of our formative experiences that often drives us to writing in the first place. When we say that a writer has found their voice, what we mean is that they've staked out their territory, they've found their subject, as well as a style that will carry it. If you study the careers of most major writers their early novels or stories are often very autobiographical. As if the writer has to write inside out in order to start 'making things up'. Look for Martin Amis in the *Rachel Papers*, Philip Roth in *Portnoy's Complaint*, Jeanette Winterson in *Oranges Are Not the Only Fruit*. These books aren't *true* but they are based on true experience, real emotion.

Often writers will start as far away from themselves as possible. But eventually as the writing progresses, the subject circles closer and closer around their own experience, eventually settling on a narrative that carries something of real importance to the writer. To start writing extended narratives, a writer needs to have a subject, a cause, an aesthetic on which to hang their metaphorical hat, and perhaps the most successful of these (in literary fiction) are the ones drawn from a writer's real-life experience. The only problem with this is that it requires self-knowledge from the writer. It demands that they assess their own experience and look at the world in the light of it.

There are, of course, big drawbacks to this, either the writing becomes impenetrable self-therapy or it becomes didactic, the writer moralizing from their own experiences. How to avoid this? Character. This is where the real task of creating fiction rather than auto-biography lies.

The me-replacements in my stories are the most important part of the narrative to get right. They aren't me, they are fifty degrees to the left or the right of me, but they take my place in the story. I want to be able to empathize with my pro- or ant-agonists. I want them to experience things I have experienced, reflect these experiences back at me so that I can have some kind of insight into the events that happen in my life. In order to do this I have to fall in love with my characters and therefore, narcissistically, with a part of myself.

✍ *Try this exercise:*

> Write 100 words on your own name. Do you like it? Do you hate it? Who gave it to you? Have you changed it? Do you have nicknames?
>
> For example, my full name is Julia Hephzibah Bell – hours of fun to spell down the phone. Initially my father wanted Hephzibah as a first name, which my mother said would be far too cumbersome for a baby. They settled on Julia. So my name comes about as a compromise between my mother and father. My surname, being short and easily rhymed, gave me a headache at school: 'hell's bells', 'ding dong', and, most humiliating, 'Bell's smells'. My friends and family usually refer to me as 'Joolz', or 'Jules' or 'Jools' or 'Jewels'. There is certainly a distinction between who I am when I'm Joolz and who I am when I'm Julia. I'm more informal, less on show, amongst friends. In origin, Julia is Roman, Hephzibah is Jewish and Bell Anglo-Saxon. So in name at least, I have a very mongrel heritage.

✍ Do this exercise for yourself, and then consider it in the light of your characters. How do they feel about the names you have given them?

What do their names say about who they are? If you have given your characters improbable or fantastical names, reconsider them or, at least, ask your characters what they think about it. I read once about a traveller who called her two children Ambulance and Layby after where they were born. I often wondered what the children felt about this and if they would feel compelled to change their names as they grew up. What does it mean to change your own name? What does it say about how a person might try to reinvent themselves, become someone new?

You need to have empathy for your characters, so in some way they have to be like you in order for you to identify with them. This doesn't mean that you can't write about any character, but think about *why* you are writing about them. If you always write about 60-foot women or men with big muscles, what is it that you are identifying with? Be honest. No one else has to know the answers, but the added layer of self-knowledge will give your characters more impetus and bite. Knowing where you're coming from is not something that will be immediately revelatory. It takes years, a lifetime even, and there is never any certain conclusion. Like our characters, we can be capricious, elliptical, mercurial, but knowing even this much about ourselves, we are in a much better position to begin writing convincingly about others.

Shaping

5 Characterization

Introduction
Julia Bell

Without character there is no story. Characters are often the reason we read. As well as *what* the story is about, we want to know *who* the story is about. A reader needs a protagonist to empathize with, someone to identify with for the duration of the story or novel. The best characters become part of our shared cultural experience: how many of us have discussed the characters from our favourite books or TV shows as if they were real people? But where does a writer start? How can character become convincing on the page?

Conflict

A good character always has some kind of internal conflict. A character who has no problems becomes unbelievable and boring very quickly. Chances are, if your character suffers no conflict you will be finding her hard to write. Dialogue, for example, is almost impossible to write without a really clear sense of how your character views the world and her place in it. How can a character with nothing to struggle with have a perspective on the world? How can they speak? Without conflict a story will have no shape. These conflicts might be heightened, more dramatic than real life, but they are what give your character a perspective on the world. Where would Lady Macbeth be without her guilt? Hamlet without his desire for revenge?

Development of character relies on consequence, on the way in which the world creates and shapes us. Before you even start to write a word of your story, write some character sketches. Write an imagined history for your characters. Always ask, Why? Why is my character like this? Why do they feel this way? Characters, like real people, have histories: places they came from, ideas about the world, families. Ask your character thirty questions about themselves, from 'What is your favourite colour?' to 'How do you feel about your parents?' It may take a while for them to take shape, you may write plenty that is irrelevant or unnecessary, but this kind of imaginative sketching is vital to the development of a convincing character. It's your job to know your characters inside out, to have their psyche at your fingertips.

Take this opening sentence from *Portnoy's Complaint* by Philip Roth:

> She was so deeply imbedded in my consciousness that for the first year of my school I seemed to have believed that each of my teachers was my mother in disguise.

The narrator starts the story with a conflict. The novel, which is all about men escaping from women – and more specifically, a domineering Jewish mother – begins as it means to go on. It lays down a gauntlet, it starts with a character in conflict with themselves and the world around them.

What makes a character interesting is not the way that the world impacts upon the character, but the way in which the character impacts upon the world. If all you are doing is describing things that happen to your character, the likelihood is that you haven't thought them through properly. They will remain passive, have no impetus, no reason to act. To get your character doing and saying things in an active, engaging way they need to be vital, visceral. They need to have reasons, motivations, conflicts.

Surprise

Characters evolve through being tested by the events of a story. Often writers will say things such as 'the characters started to run away with me' or 'they surprised me, I didn't know they were going to do that'. Writing character sketches is only half the task. Once you start putting your character into an environment and writing her through scenes and dialogue, she will start to have life on the page, she will start to do things, say things of her own accord.

Characters don't have to jump out of cupboards and say 'boo' to be surprising, they need to reveal themselves to the reader in an interesting way. Consider this character sketch:

> *A young man in his early twenties, works in a crisp factory, shovelling heaps of potato chips out of vats of boiling fat. Makes his skin greasy; he's underconfident with girls. On Saturday nights he gets drunk with the boys but doesn't feel as if he can really talk to women. Still has a strange obsession with Airfix kits. Lives with his mum who's sick; she's got lots of animals, fourteen cats, two dogs, rabbits and a parakeet. His wages have to go towards keeping the animals, which he is beginning to really hate.*

The character already has plenty of potential conflict there. Put him in a few scenes to see how he'll react. Imagine him at work in the crisp factory: What does he think of the people he works with? What does he think of his job?

Surprise has much to do with expectation. It's only when you know how a character is expected to behave that you can make them defy their own conventions. Perhaps the young man could really enjoy his job, or find some kind of solace in being out of the house away from the animals. It would be too easy to make him hate everything; it would make him quite passive. What if his mother died, leaving him with a house full of animals? How would he cope? What if he found a girlfriend, a boyfriend? All these scenarios allow for the possibility of surprise.

Characters who are not surprising can become stereotyped. They behave in a way which is all too familiar to us already. Do drug addicts always have to be poor? Working mothers always have to feel guilty? Boys into football and cars?

A good exercise is to give your character several different settings and try to write them in each one. Iceland, Ibiza, Iowa, Indonesia, for example, or, less exotic, at work, at home, in the pub, in the supermarket. How does your character react and adapt to new environments? How do they feel about their home town? A really good character should be able to go anywhere and still have something interesting to say about it.

Voice

Voice creates character on the page. It is the way they talk and think, or the implied way in which they talk and think, that gives your characters life. We all use language differently, we all have a voice that is unique to us, even fictional characters. To have some idea of how your characters think and speak you need to think about where they come from. What figures of speech are natural to their environment? Do they have an accent? Do they have verbal tics unique to them?

To be convincing, you need to think about how your characters talk. Not just in dialogue but also in the narrative. In a first-person narrative, a story is all character, but in a third-person narrative, character is revealed through description, dialogue and implied speech. Writing from a child's perspective, for example, limits the kinds of words and ideas you can express. The child character shouldn't sound too 'adult', and yet she mustn't be so childish as to render the story incomprehensible.

Even in third-person narratives you need to have a clear sense of how a character talks; the narrative needs to be soaked in the character's voice. Consider this example from Jane Austen's *Emma*:

The hair was curled, and the maid sent away, and Emma sat down to think and be miserable. – It was a wretched business indeed! – Such an overthrow of every thing she had been wishing for! – Such a development of every thing most unwelcome! – Such a blow for Harriet! – That was the worst of all. Every part of it brought pain and humiliation, of some sort or other; but, compared with the evil to Harriet, all was light; and she would gladly have submitted to feel yet more mistaken – more in error – more disgraced by mis-judgement than she actually was, could the effects of her blunders have been confined to herself.

Though ostensibly in the third person, this passage is a reported version of Emma's real speech. Austen reveals Emma's character by reporting to the reader what she is thinking. The sentences with exclamation marks show the progression of Emma's feelings of mortification. She has just been proposed to by Mr Elton, the bumptious local vicar, whom she has been grooming as a match for her friend Harriet. Having raised Harriet's expectations, she now has to face an unwanted suitor as well as the social humiliation of explaining to Harriet what has happened. Austen is so close to her character at this point that narrator and character are almost of the same voice.

Detail

Finally, good characterization relies on detail. Well-placed details give a sense of authenticity and help the reader to build a mental picture of your character in their mind. Much of this depends on visualization, on the writer being able to see their characters as physical beings.

What kinds of clothes do they wear? How do they look? What kind of expressions do they pull?

Look at this passage from Hemingway:

> Robert Jordan looked at the man's heavy, beard-stubbled face . . . his head was round and set close on his shoulders. His eyes were small and set too wide apart and his ears were small and set close to his head. He was a heavy man about five feet ten inches tall and his hands and feet were large. His nose had been broken and his mouth was cut at one corner and the line of the scar across the upper lip and lower jaw showed through the growth of beard over his face.
>
> ERNEST HEMINGWAY, *For Whom the Bell Tolls*

Against the backdrop of the Spanish Civil War, the protagonist, Robert Jordan, has just met Pablo, the leader of the guerrilla group that he is keen to join. The description of Pablo's imposing physical presence adds weight to the muscular, masculine tone of the novel. This is a story about war, about hardened, physical characters.

Even if you don't use them verbatim, it is useful to write a couple of paragraphs of physical description for your characters. If you can't visualize them, chances are your reader won't be able to either.

Arguments over the nature of character in fiction were the topic and focus of much twentieth-century literary debate and writing. The modernist movement was obsessed with it, bent on resisting a Victorian notion of character that believed in a tightly constructed, preordained 'human nature'. Virginia Woolf's later novels, for example, are meditations on the construction of character, a question that pushes beyond the pages of her books into life, asking what it means to have identity. In these texts, character is fluid, represented through streams of consciousness; a fictional trick that attempts to mirror the minute-by-minute thought processes of a human being. In other writers, Italo Calvino, for example, in *If on a Winter's Night a Traveller*, character is acknowledged from the start as a construction, a product of the writer, whom we are kind enough to read. Or, as in

Angela Carter's *The Bloody Chamber*, character is an archetype, written in capital letters – Princess, Mother, Wolf, Witch, Queen, Beast – which traps the protagonist into a string of set responses that they must struggle to escape.

Whichever side of the critical fence you choose to sit, a writer at the beginning of their writing life has to learn the art of characterization before they can attempt to break the mould. Picasso learnt to create perfect life-drawings before he dared to fracture the human image with his cubist paintings. Many students, enthralled by theoretical ideas of character, try to write experimental or stream-of-consciousness narratives without having first tried to create character on the page in a realist way. Virginia Woolf's first novel, *The Voyage Out*, is a homage to the Victorian novel. There are hints of the stream-of-consciousness style she would later go on to adopt, but this novel is an example of a writer finding her feet by working through the confines of convention first.

The Things They Carry
Susan Perabo

People are immensely complicated. The best fiction recognizes this, creating characters so utterly convincing that we fully expect to bump into them at the bus stop. Developing characters with this depth of being and richness of spirit is difficult. Too often we have a sketch of a character in mind when beginning a story and we never allow that character to grow beyond his or her initial sketch. Why is this? It is because we have not successfully fooled ourselves into believing that our characters are real people. We *know* we're making them up, right? We're caught up in the exhilarating process of lying, of playing God. We know our characters will do what we want them to do, say what we want them to say. But – if we hope to write a successful story – we must believe in our characters as living breathing humans. If we don't, then how can we possibly expect our readers to?

Tim O'Brian's story 'The Things They Carried' (a section in the novel of the same name) is an extraordinary example of how a multitude of characters can be defined with minimal exposition. The story, about a platoon in Vietnam, develops the characters – both major and minor – by telling the reader what each carries with him through the terrain of war. Each man carries something related to his role in the platoon: the radio, the M-60 machine gun, the maps, the code book, etc. In addition, each carries a little part of the self he has left behind: a comic book, letters from a girlfriend, an illustrated Bible. Finally, each character carries a memento of the self he has become: pot, earplugs, the blackened thumb off a VC corpse. We know almost nothing of these characters except for what they carry, and yet as the story develops each man comes alive as a unique individual.

Another effective, if less literary, use of the same technique can be found in the American movie *The Breakfast Club*. In one scene, a young woman who finds it impossible to connect with her peers dumps out the contents of her purse in front of a young man in an attempt to share herself with him. With little dialogue, the young man – and the viewer – is able to gain insight into this woman simply by taking note of the contents of her purse.

Try it yourself, with those around you. Imagine you are at a family gathering and your mother asks you to retrieve something from her purse. Problem is, you don't know what her purse looks like, and there are a dozen purses to choose from. And yet, quickly, you are able to determine which purse is hers. Why is this? What items make it uniquely hers? Is it the flavour of chewing gum? The colour of lipstick? The selection of credit cards? The pencil with the end chewed off? The lucky coin?

The way to apply this technique to your fiction – obviously – is to discover what it is that each of your characters carries. The 'vehicle' for the carried items can be anything: a backpack, a suitcase, a lunch box, a handbag, a briefcase, etc.

This technique can be quite useful at two points of the writing process: in the initial creation of a character and in the task of revision.

✍ Building a Character from the Ground Up

In this method, you start with a literal and figurative blank slate. With a clean sheet of paper and a clear mind, simply start listing items off the top of your head. List the first ten things you think of, no matter how random or dissimilar they may seem. When you have finished, look over your list and create a character based on those items. Say your list looks like this:

- Used tissues
- Zippo lighter
- Dog-eared copy of poems by Robert Frost
- Three pounds
- A fork
- A whistle key chain with twelve keys
- Hand lotion
- A small china dog
- Three pens, two of which don't work
- An aged and wrinkled photo of a man in uniform

Now, what observations can we make about this character? The zippo lighter might indicate that the character smokes, yet there are no cigarettes. Perhaps the lighter is of sentimental value? Perhaps the character does not smoke himself but has friends who do? Or perhaps the character cannot afford cigarettes – after all, he/she only has three pounds. Now, what of the whistle key chain? Does that suggest that your character is anticipating danger? Does he/she have reason to suspect a threat is imminent? And what about the small china dog? Surely this has no practical value. Was it a gift? A remnant from childhood? Did it once belong to the man in the wrinkled photo?

This list – which I came up with in less than five minutes – offers me innumerable possibilities; it gives me a place to begin, a foundation to build upon. Once I have unravelled the mysteries behind these ten items, my character will come to life.

✍ Understanding Your Characters

This exercise is also extremely helpful when revising a story that has already been drafted. If you feel your characters are under-developed, lacking humanity, make a list of the things each of them carries. The things on your list may never show up in the actual story – certainly not all of them will. But the better you know your character, the better realized he will be. Making the list for a character who already exists will offer you new insights into his personality. These insights, in turn, will enrich your understanding of the character as you revise the story, helping you to create a convincingly complex human being.

Somebody Else's Shoes
Paul Magrs

If you want to write fiction it's often because you are nosy.

You want to know about people. You want to know what makes them tick. You've spent most of your life listening to the way people talk, watching how they behave. They intrigue you, they madden you, they fascinate you.

Perhaps you grew up like this: a little apart from the rest of the crowd. Hanging on to the sidelines. Feeling rather awkward and too thoughtful while everyone else was charging around. You were astonished by the way they seemed to know, without apparent effort, the way they needed to behave.

You were watching as the class got rowdy while the teacher was out of the room. Knowing she was going to come back any minute and catch the rowdiest as they were drawing filthy pictures on the blackboard. You knew that the teacher was going to walk in just then; you knew she would look flustered and annoyed in just that way.

When you got older, still watching other people, talking to them, you realized that they weren't as straightforward as that. They felt awkward, too. They were just getting on with it. They were extemporizing and feeling perhaps as alienated as you were.

But the obsession stays with you: Why does everyone else seem to feel so at home in themselves, when so much of your own time is given over to not being you? When you spend so long imagining what it must be like to be them instead?

The writer Tony Warren has said that as a child he would sit under the kitchen table, hiding there and listening as the adults talked. He would listen to the way women talked and the way men talked, and he would appreciate and catalogue the differences. He did a lot of research under that table before he even knew that it was research at all.

If you are going to write fiction, chances are that you've been collecting up just that sort of research all of your life. We all have stories we like to tell: outrageous ones about the doings of various aunts and acquaintances; sad ones about neighbours and friends. These stories always congregate around characters we already know and have observed. We have taken down their particulars in the most avid fashion; we just haven't written them down yet.

The best storyteller I know is my mother. She can spin them out for hours on end and range over a huge cast of characters; the full gamut of human emotion within the space of a single phone call. She also has amazing recall; far better than me. She says she could never write any of it down; she's not sure she has the grammar or the correct form of expression. I try to tell her there is no correct form; there's just technique.

The real business is the story in the first place; the story that is set into motion by the characters inside it – behaving in all the random, selfish, adventurous, brave, ludicrous ways that people behave.

When you write fiction you have to remind yourself that fiction doesn't have to be grandiose and stuffed to the gills with profundity.

What's the most memorable bit of *Ulysses*? Someone cooking kidneys, someone else rolling about on a bed. What's the most memorable episode in *A Room with a View*? Lucy gets her first snog in a field of wild flowers. All of these things are based in everyday behaviour; they're all things we've seen or experienced.

It doesn't have to be massive, profound or outrageous to catch our eye. To stay with us. To make us think: What's really going on in that person's head?

I was walking to catch the bus to work one day and I saw this old man bent double in the street. He was stuck still, as if his back had locked, but it turned out he always walked that way. He was in an old mac and he had a rather smug-looking cat sitting on his back. He looked at me imploringly and asked if I would scoop the creature off.

'It's a very nice pussy, but it always does this.' Up the street, high on scaffolding, builders were laughing, as I knocked the cat off and shooed it away.

Two weeks later I saw him there again, with the cat sitting on top of him again. He didn't recognize me, but he asked if I'd mind coming to the rescue.

The poor old bloke walked that way every day, bent double with rheumatism. Each time he passed that particular wall the cat would be there waiting for him, ready to stride blithely out and stop him in his tracks.

What I couldn't help thinking about afterwards was what was going on in the old fella's mind. Did he think the cat was persecuting him? Did he think this happened to everyone? He wouldn't walk for fear of hurting the cat, of dislodging him and knocking him to the ground. His behaviour was bound up with a curious kind of complicity with and tenderness towards a cat who, as far as I could see, was just having a laugh.

Then I started to wonder about the cat's motives in all of this.

This is, it has to be said, though true, a somewhat outré story. I'd think twice about writing a story about a man with a cat on his back. It's useful as an example, though, of the kinds of things you see that you aren't expecting to; the odd bits of surprising behaviour you see in people that lodge in your head and won't let you go until you do something with them. You either have to tell someone else about them or you have to write them down. You have to find some way of seeing that behaviour from the inside. 'What makes someone act like that?' you end up asking yourself all the time.

A friend of mine went to Sunday lunch with people he hardly knew. The husband was affable and nervous; a computer programmer who filled the awkward silences with talk of nothing else. His teenaged kids were subdued and his wife was strangely distracted as she gulped her way through a bottle of Chardonnay. My friend said that they'd all held it together pretty well for a while, until the tipsy woman suddenly burst out: 'I saw that Lulu on the television last night. She's sorted out her life. She's got rid of her partner and a life that wasn't working. She's got her independence back. That's what I want to be! Just like Lulu!'

'Mam, don't,' said the eldest daughter, and suddenly the whole family started talking to cover up the mother's sobs.

My friend told me he didn't know where to put himself.

So here's a scene less outrageous, more everyday than that with the man and the cat on his back. It still gets your mind going. How many Sunday lunches go on like that all over the country, all over the world, every week? We've all been sat there when someone suddenly erupts into an epiphany about what they want their life to be like. We find the revelation and the pathos endlessly fascinating. However embarrassed we are at the time, afterwards we still want to know what it was all about; how it was that tensions like that happened to come to such an abrupt and compelling head.

As a writer what I want to be doing at that point is coming at the scene from a number of different angles. I want to know what her husband is feeling, as he tries to keep the lunch party together, pretending nothing is going on. I want to know how he squirms as his wife gives the lie to their happy gathering. I want to be the children; one of them, the youngest, delighted at the spectacle of the adults behaving like kids and shouting out the first thing on their minds. I want to know about the older child, shushing her mother, trying not to let the strangers hear, being embarrassed and flinching at everything her parents say and do.

And I want to be in the mother's shoes as she looks up and down the immaculate dining table; at these children, this husband and these friends she doesn't even know. How did she end up here, eating with all of these people? Will she be here Sunday after Sunday, for ever, until the end of her life? When the kids go to college will it just be him and her and other strangers? Will they be talking about new computer systems for ever, each of them giving her odd worried looks now and then as the conversation so obviously passes her by? What exactly is it that goes through her head in the seconds before her outburst? What is it that makes her seize on Lulu as the image, the icon, the emblem of her possible escape? Does she really mean to hurt everyone's feelings? Make them feel uncomfortable? Is she completely unaware of the effect her words can have? What is the secret story that drives her to this?

That scene seems to me to be behaviour in its purest form. It's a scene we can turn over and over in the light, seeing it from all angles. It's the kind of scene you mull over for ages, even when you are not writing. It's the kind of thing you thought about even before you called yourself a writer of fiction.

One of the best responses I ever got about a piece of writing of mine was when a friend read a scene in which a woman spends a whole day obsessed with getting all her washing done, out of guilt, in order to have earned the previous night out and the hangover she now has. She makes her hangover worse by watching the suds slosh round. 'How do you know that?' my friend asked. I didn't really have an answer. It just seemed like the way people carried on.

I tend to believe in what the American writer Charles Bukowski said: that even the time we don't spend actually writing words on pages, we are writing all of the time. I really think that we spend hours drinking in, observing, miring ourselves in what's going on. I think Bukowski was saying something slightly different to me. I think he also meant something about spending time completely drunk and cogitating Profound Themes. Here I'm more concerned about the way we become intrigued by other people and their specific behaviours and details, and the way we move through sympathy, empathy, towards putting ourselves in their shoes.

In real life, of course, wearing someone else's shoes isn't a good idea at all. Once I was on an outward bound course (not willingly, and not something I would ever do again) and we were forced to wear other people's fell-walking boots. I wanted to wear my trainers but we weren't allowed; we had to be properly equipped.

My feet ballooned. After a day's walking I could barely stand up. Within a week I had blood blisters the size of saucers on both heels.

In writing, of course, trying on other shoes is far less perilous.

It is a cliché about acting that you can feel your way into a part by getting the footwear right. For writing I would say don't wear anything on your feet at all. You've got to put yourself, at a moment's notice, into somebody else's shoes and you need to feel free enough to do that.

✍ *Try this exercise in order to get your character to come to life.*

Imagine them in conversation with someone. They are describing the plot of a film they have seen on TV the night before. They can't remember the name of the film and they talk their friend through the whole plot. The point of the exercise is to discover how your character would tell a story differently to you or anyone else. What would they find interesting or important? What fascinates them or offends them? Here's your chance to find out things about your invented character that you don't know yet.

Keep this character in your head. As you read, talk with people, go shopping, eat dinner, watch TV, keep asking yourself: What would *they* think of this? How would they respond differently to me?

Room of Leaves:
Voice and Character in a Sequence of Poems
Amanda Dalton

Some years ago I came across a newspaper cutting I'd kept: 'Jilted Woman, 70, Found Dead in Nest of Leaves'. The article concerned the sad and bizarre circumstances of the 'bird woman's' life and death. Jilted at the altar some thirty-five years earlier, she had never returned to her work as a pharmacist or to living in her mother's bungalow. Instead she made a home in the garden, a giant nest-like construction of twigs, leaves and rotting cloth. The article included one or two quotes from neighbours, their descriptions of her regular appearances at the library and in the fields (her face daubed with flour), the police discovery of her body and the overgrown garden, plates of food for the birds, pink ribbons hanging from the trees.

An extraordinary story, tantalizing, too, in its details and omissions. I decided to try to write a poem in the woman's voice, and to find a vocabulary and state of mind for her, to understand her reasoning at the turning point where she decides to set up home outside. A line came to me quite immediately: 'I'm setting up home in the garden / unpacking my trousseau in a room of leaves.' I called the poem 'Nest' and it was my first attempt to create character in a poem.

Nest

I'm building a nest in the garden
and watching my breath disappear
into splintered trees.
The sky is scratched and freezing;
birds are trapped in it.

I finger veins on damaged leaves

and put my ear to the cracked soil
but there's no pulse.
My nest will be of dead and aching things,
lined with my wedding dress,
decorated with our broken flowers.

I'll sing a marriage song behind my throat
where everything is cold and trapped.
Save me from losing my breath in the hard air.
Save me from screaming like birds
and wondering how things disappear.

I'm setting up home without you,
unpacking my trousseau in a room of leaves,
singing.

(FROM *How to Disappear*)

I found the experience absorbing and challenging in quite different ways from my previous attempts at writing poems. It was also oddly freeing – perhaps not unlike a performer working with a mask. Although I'd tried writing in first, second and third person, present and past tense, and in voices where 'I' was quite certainly not 'I', this was the first time I had consciously 'constructed' a person and 'her' voice. What I liked about working in this way was how the distance allowed me, paradoxically, to write directly and personally and to explore intense emotion, without falling into the trap – as I perceived it – of writing private, hideously untransformed, 'spill your guts' stuff.

I called the woman Grace, and her circumstances gave me an almost ready-made pattern of images (leaves, nest, room, cage, shelter, wedding, birds) through which to build an evocation of her immense loss, sense of 'outsider' status and of what I wanted to portray as her oddly calm and brave state of mind.

After I'd written 'Nest' I knew I'd only just started with Grace and her story. I guessed I should be writing a novel or a play, but I wanted to write poems and I wanted to see if I could create an entire story as a narrative sequence in verse. For a few weeks I set myself writing exercises and made copious notes about the, by now, imaginary Grace and, later, Frank – the man who jilted her at the altar. I worked, as I suppose some novelists work, creating a life for Grace and Frank: What do they wear? What do they love? What do they want? What frightens them? What do they own? And why? Why does Frank jilt Grace at the altar? Why does she never return to her mother's home? I was, by now, quite unconcerned with the literal facts of the story, fascinated instead by the puzzle of creating an internal logic for Grace's apparently very odd behaviour and the challenge of understanding, if not empathizing, with Frank's betrayal.

I played a version of the Furniture Game that I'd first come across in a writing workshop, and then in a book by Peter Sansom. You write a list of categories: furniture, weather, car, drink, animal, room, flower, etc. Then you say: 'If Frank was a piece of furniture, what piece of furniture would he be?' I decided Frank was a fantasist and that I needed two replies for him. Frank would want to be a chaise longue but he would actually be an inexpensive, slightly fragile kitchen chair. And so on . . .

Grace, I decided, was a hippopotamus but, in part *because* of this, she was obsessed with birds. More than obsessed, she comes to believe she *is* one – the logic for much of her behaviour. So I read up on garden birds and collected words for the things birds do. (Take a look at Selima Hill's 'Maisie' for an interesting treatment of the usually insulting cliché of woman as cow.)

There's a Maura Dooley poem that delves into the contents of someone's bag. She transforms what is found there into a wonderful piece of writing. I didn't do this, but I did, in note form, decide what Grace might carry with her and what was in the pockets of Frank's coat.

Another idea I tried was to write the five senses down the side of a sheet of paper and some key moments from the 'story' along the top. I didn't fill it in with examples of what Grace or Frank were seeing, touching, hearing at this moment, but with examples of the senses as metaphors for their states of mind. For example, the day after jilting Grace at the altar, the taste of being Frank is cold metal on your tongue and fish in your windpipe. In the months before she dies, the sound of being Grace is of echoing in hollow bones and a flapping loud enough to fill the fields.

And I did some very simple research on the late fifties and early sixties. Once I came to know, for example, that Frank loved the movies – old movies – I needed to find out a bit more about screen goddesses and popular films of the time. If Grace was a pharmacist, I might want to name a few popular 1950s remedies, so I talked to a retired pharmacist, and a doctor gave me some medical terms for her likely condition at the time of death.

I remember gathering all of these fragments in a notebook, which I've still got, but then realizing one day that I had more than enough material and that I was in danger of using the research as a fine old excuse for not writing the actual poems. For me, poems don't come from ideas; they come, usually, from a single image or from a phrase that lodges itself in my brain. Most usually they begin visually, and from this visual moment comes a word image or metaphor and so on. What the 'research' and the writing exercises had given me was both a strong sense of Grace and Frank as people, and a series of images and metaphors, details from which to select and through which to construct their stories and their inner lives. (I could see Grace in her size 9 shoes, accidentally breaking a blown egg; Frank on the edge of a cliff, feeling like a hooked fish dangling from a rod.) However, what I felt I now had to do was forget everything, pack away the notebooks at the back of my brain, and try to return to 'real', authentic writing, trusting that the important fragments would present themselves when and if I needed them.

This worked for Grace, but I found Frank difficult. I had decided he was an immature and emotionally inarticulate man and that his speech would be cliché-ridden and often stilted. But how to find a voice for him that articulated this without being simply 'dull'?

In the end I found something, through playing around with draft after draft of Frank's proposal to Grace. I abandoned any attempt to construct something that sounded like what Frank might *actually* have said – that wasn't even interesting. But Frank's inner, imaginary world is anything but dull. So instead I saw the marriage proposal in terms of the emotion driving the moment as Frank's childlike stuttering to himself; a naive, urgently gushing plea to be rescued, not from his dream, but from the harshness of the real world. I started to find a voice that juxtaposed repetition and colloquial speech patterns with the imagery of Frank's obsessions (in this case, the movies), and combined the mundane with the heightened. Just as important, I tried to find a rhythm and a pattern of words on the page (especially line breaks) that echoed his state of mind: breathless and quick in his excitement, anxious, self-doubting and full of dreams.

Frank's Proposal

I want to start again.
I want to start again
against a New York sky.
Tyrone Power on the thirteenth floor
breathing silk. Will you do it?

I want to board a liner to the USA.
I want to go there.
An Affair to Remember on the open deck,
sky full of stars and Vic Damone.
Remember?

When I become The Man with the Golden Arm
will you save me?
Will you be Kim Novak in a haze of smoke?
Will you help me break the habit of a lifetime?
Will You?

(FROM *How to Disappear*)

I'm not sure if it entirely works or even if it's a poem! If it is, it comes from the collision of two 'languages', which is what I think any voice in creative writing, essentially, must be. There's the voice of the 'person' who's apparently speaking, then there's the voice of the writer. In overtly personal or confessional writing, I guess the two are almost one and the same thing, in that the reader can't separate the voices – that which comes out of trawling for very personal, subjective, maybe formless, raw material. And the cool, crafting, editorial voice that the writer often only allows in later. However, in a poem that's concerned with constructing a sense of character through voice, the distinction between 'character' and 'writer' is usually more clear. In a later 'Frank' poem, for example, I wanted to suggest his crass lack of awareness and inadequacy, revealed in the inappropriate tone and content of a letter he writes to Grace. So he speaks almost entirely in film titles and the letter has a strong rhythm as well as a formal rhyme scheme, used in this case to suggest Frank's unwitting trivialization of Grace's situation as well as his own need for formal politeness and constraint. I think it is a poem entirely in his voice – but, of course, he wouldn't really write like that.

Not all of the poems in the sequence that became *Room of Leaves* are written in the first person. As poem after poem began to collage into a jigsaw kind of narrative, I felt the need for a kind of balance, a move away from the intense, personal, and often rather desperate registers of Frank and Grace, towards a flatter, more objective note. I could only see this being achieved through a third-person narrative, but I didn't want to move right away from my exploration of characters and voice.

In the end, I came up with some notes from the autopsy report – almost a 'found poem' from the real notes given to me by a doctor. And in the poem that ends the sequence, with the discovery of Grace's body, I deliberately used direct and reported speech in amongst barely altered references from the original news report. This, I hoped, was in keeping with the italicized interjections from Grace's mother that appear throughout Grace's poems: *'stupid girl'*, *'clumsy ox'*, *'Breathe in, Gracie'*.

In giving the reader suggestions of 'other' voices, I wanted to evoke fragments of character that were never fully explored or developed and, in the case of PC Ainsley, the voice of a kind of Joe Public or Everyman. He has the final word:

Half a battered suitcase in the undergrowth,
a screwtop jar with nothing in it but a ring,
a tarnished ring, set with a clear blue stone.
Ainsley held it to the light. *Poor bitch.*

Character and Characterization
Malcolm Bradbury

1 Stories and Characters

The power to create and develop character is at the heart of all fictional writing. The other essential motor of narrative is plot. But plot is itself often the product of a character or characters in their processes of development, growing self-knowledge or interaction with others. So plot itself is the product of human actions or adventures. And it is frequently from the idea of a key character, the emergence of a central figure, that the whole notion of a story starts.

So Henry James, describing in one of his late-life prefaces the creative process that brought what is perhaps his finest novel *The Portrait of a Lady* (1882) into being, emphasizes that the book came out of a character, Isabel Archer – the young American girl affronting her destiny. But how, he asks, does a character become a subject? 'Millions of presumptuous girls, intelligent or not intelligent, daily affront their destiny, and what it is open to their destiny to be, at the most, that we should make an ado about it? The novel is of its very nature "ado," an ado about something . . .' So the problem of writing the book is to make an 'ado' about Isabel Archer.

James splendidly describes how he goes about the problem: how to build 'a square and spacious house around her'. He observes that a whole gallery of other characters begins to take shape around her, once you ask the questions: What does she want? And what will she do? Some of these characters will be central to the form; others will be secondary characters. Out of them all, but above all out of the wants and needs of the central character, Isabel, the story will take shape. James emphasizes that, in the case of this novel at least, he did not know, when he started to create Isabel and set her life and actions moving, what was finally going to happen to Isabel Archer.

Yet even when we do know – when we have a story worked out and seek characters to take us through it – we still depend fundamentally on the power of creating, developing, motivating and illuminating character. In some forms of writing this is obvious. We cannot write a play without characters: drama is a developing interaction of characters performed by actors and developed scene by scene.

But the novel, the short story, and many forms of poetry, as well as the modern media – film, television drama, interactive TV – are just as dependent on character. And the power to understand the potential of character, the elements that compose a significant representation, is central to writing and the human sympathy and recognition on which literature depends.

2 Character and Drama

In drama the centrality of character is always apparent. A playscript is not really a text but a set of instructions for performance. It opens with a list of characters, or dramatis personae: the impersonation of character, the power to be another is at the centre of an actor's skills. Writing for actors is one of the great tests of writing, and the ability to create a powerful part and keep it alive and in motion and development through the course of a dramatic narrative is one of the key literary skills. Drama provides us with many of our key notions of character and psychology. Some of the key terms of characters in interaction in the interests of drama and discovery come from the stage: the hero and the anti-hero, the protagonist and the antagonist, the tragic hero, the comic clown, the villain, the confidant, the pantaloon. We similarly recognize in some of the great theatrical heroes and heroines – Oedipus, Antigone, Clytemnestra, Hamlet, Faust, Don Juan – the deeper and more mythic aspects of character, and the fact that great characters generally have profound psychological and indeed mythological roots.

The essence of a dramatic character seems to lie in playability: the character is interesting and engaging, fascinating from the outside, clearly motivated within. An actor or actress playing the part finds in it a coherence of motivation, the basis of a performance; the spectator in the theatre finds developing interest in the actions and evolutions of the actor in the part. Characters illuminate themselves by tiny detail – habits of behaviour, types of speech. But the dramatic and narrative essence lies in those larger questions that Henry James raises about Isabel Archer: What does she want? And what will she do? A character is not complete until we perceive the drama that goes with it, and the relationships, antagonisms and developments that now come into play.

In classical drama, 'character' was consistent with ideas of grandeur and heroism: the figures represented centre stage were often gods, kings, queens or historical heroes. Modern drama, like modern fiction, has complicated such notions. Modern naturalism, from Ibsen on, introduced characters from ordinary life. New forms of theatricality – expressionism, surrealism – opened the stage to new fantasy, and therefore to realms of dream, desire and inward life. The absurdist theatre of Samuel Beckett challenged many of the key notions of character in dramatic action (the tramps of *Waiting for Godot* hardly move; the central figure of *Not I* is simply an illuminated mouth). The modern stage is a highly mobile and perspectivized space.

Yet the actor, and the character he or she plays, still stands at the centre: a human figure, a mobile performance, a bundle of motivations, a life in motion. Since drama does depend on actors, clearly a playscript itself is a process of interaction of characters, essentially developed through interactive dialogue, exits and entrances, time shifts and mood breaks. These are the main ways of developing characters, showing their histories, backgrounds, backstories; their social and sexual roles, their hopes, doubts, conflicts and fates.

3 Character in Film and TV

In a playscript we hear characters speak about themselves, disclose their viewpoints, develop their interaction; so we understand their roles in the drama. In film we go further. With modern filming the camera is essentially a character and a mode of characterization. It can stand in for an angle on things, a point of view. A reaction shot can turn our attention from a speaker to a listener or an observer; perspective and distance are completely transformed. The sheer mobility and fluidity of film narrative, the power of editing, means that, in ways quite different from theatre, character can be revealed as movement and action.

Modern film-making and TV scriptwriting is highly generic, as happens in highly collaborative media, and writers and audiences have grown familiar with multiple codes of perspective: the flashback or flash-forward, the substitution of visual symbols or icons for speech, the use of location for drama, and so on. But again character is at the centre of narrative.

Screenwriting handbooks emphasize the centrality of character and some of the conventional devices by which, in film terms, character is analysed. Thus, says one useful handbook, consider screen characters (essentially central characters, protagonists) as having three dimensions: action (physical and psychological; external and internal); emotion (temperamental characteristics and reactions); and personality (integrated interior attributes, life-history, purposes and life-intentions).

A character needs growth and motivation; he or she also needs obstruction and conflict. Other characters will generally provide these things in development. From these things come the essentials and primary structures of the story. Mechanical as such story analyses are, they generally touch on a good number of the truths of writing, showing us what is dynamic and vital in a story, what gives it its structure (growth, self-discovery, revelation, etc.) and what keeps it in motion as a human fable.

4 Character in Fiction

Fiction – meaning the novel and short story – is as dependent as drama or film on character, but the tasks and problems are different. The novel is a form highly dependent from its beginnings on character. This is what the titles of some of the great books tell us: *Don Quixote* and *Tom Jones, Emma* and *Jane Eyre, Nicholas Nickleby* and *Anna Karenina, Tess of the d'Urbervilles* and *Mrs Dalloway*. Yet unlike drama the character is not represented by an actor, and is imagined in the author's and the reader's mind. Character exists as text: all of it is made of words.

The many languages of fiction mean there are many ways of presenting a character, besides dialogue, the key instrument in drama and screenwriting. And though in some fiction dialogue is a central means – as in the brilliant early short stories of Ernest Hemingway, which are largely dialogue-based – in other novels character is established by other means, not least power of description.

In drama we see the actor; in fiction we are encouraged to imagine the person. In drama we are engaged by the interaction of the characters; in fiction we have another layer of interaction, between character or characters and their author or creator. New perspectives then open. In drama or film, characters mostly play face to face. Their emotions are uttered and their intentions are made reasonably explicit. In fiction we can live in the mind, the consciousness or the unconscious of a character, according to the relation established between human figure and author.

The novel has a wider variety of angles and standpoints, because it can exploit many angles and employ many different types of discourse. Thus a book can be told in the first person, as a confession, or perhaps as a diary, or a memoir, or a set of stream-of-consciousness impressions associated with one individual, like Virginia Woolf's *Mrs Dalloway*. It can be told more objectively, in the third person, either at a distance, so the characters are seen objectively, and mostly from outside, or close to the standpoint of one character, or as a mixture of several sets of close or distanced relationships. It can also be told in the second person, or in a complex mixture of persons and viewpoints.

In modern fiction there has been a strong tendency for fiction to move 'inward', to concern itself with inner sensations and psychology. Some of the great works of modernism – the novels of Proust, Joyce, Virginia Woolf, William Faulkner – emphasize the impressionistic nature of the mind, the free-flowing of consciousness, and the complexity of observation and intuition. But the novel can be a large and epic spectacle, crowded with vast numbers of characters. Marcel Proust's *Remembrance of Things Past* and James Joyce's *Ulysses*, two of the great modern works, are a fascinating mixture of the two: the panoramic epic and the novel of inner consciousness.

What the history of the novel seems to teach us is how much depends on the writer's human power of sympathy, the capacity to value and observe human beings, to reproduce them in all their texture, to imitate speech, to understand instincts and motives, to appreciate the nature of psychological reactions and mental processes, to note oddities and quirks, to bring out what is strange, fascinating, revealing, unusual and also representative in human figures to full life.

5 Creating Character

Where do writers get their characters from? Life, certainly. The innocent notion is that they meet them, on the street or at work: note their mannerisms, write them down, turn them into literary property. Observation has rightly been emphasized as one source of literary character, and many a literary character has been traced back to an original. No doubt a good many fictional characters do have real-life counterparts. After all, this is one thing that helps make a character convincing, and many novels have a large autobiographical element in them; they are a slice of the author's own life.

Yet characters, of course, are also made of writing. They are fictions, made for a purpose. It is our capacity to turn words into people, give them a life, a density, a past, a setting, a meaning, a psychology, to place them in a perspective, to sharpen their quirks and characteristics, that will make them memorable. Our characters must exist not just for the reader but for us, as authors. They must matter; they must become familiar. They must attract our interest, sympathy, attention, annoyance, even our aversion. We must know what we feel about them, how we place them in the culture. We must have a sense of what they are feeling, what they are wishing and desiring, what they might do next.

For that reason creating convincing and interesting characters has often been compared with getting married or acquiring a new family. We become engaged with the reality of the lives of others, to whom we give flesh, meaning and emotional time; in the writing of fiction, imaginary lives become as real as our own. We need to know far more about our characters than we will ever tell: their history, emotions, backgrounds, appearances, and choices. Good characters often overlap the book and outlast it. Henry James again, on his character Christine Light, the Princess Casamassima, who first appears in *Roderick Hudson*: 'I remembered at all events feeling, toward the end of Roderick, that the Princess Casamassima had been launched, that, wound-up with the right silver key, she would go on a certain time by the motion communicated,' he writes. What he means is that Christine has, unusually in James, simply become so powerful he feels the need to bring her back. And so he does, in the novel *The Princess Casamassima*, written ten years later, where she gets an even larger role.

And what is true for the author is often true for the reader. We often remember a character even when we cannot remember what their story is or what happens to them. We can see them in our friends or imagine them as part of our own lives. It is often those books where the focus is on the telling of the story of a life or an individual's adventures that last longest in memory. Which means that the realistic observation of characters – human figures in their livingness – and our fascination with their development is funda- mental to story.

Leo Tolstoy once defined the elements of 'the novelist's poetry' like this: it consisted, he said, of '(a) in the interest of the arrangement of occurrences, (b) in the presentation of manners on an historic back- ground, (c) in the beauty and gaiety of a situation, and (d) in people's characters . . .' which involves a sense of the complexity of human motives, which precipitates action and unifies the other elements. This is as good an account of the making of a novel as I know.

'Character' clearly has a central position in fiction. The novel has been very open to the idea of character as its primary subject, and its origins are associated with modern ideas of individualism, selfhood, consciousness and conscience. It has also been extremely concerned with the idea of character in society, and the sense of society as a rich and varied accumulation of characters, types and communities, as in the novels of Charles Dickens.

Characters have a variety of possible roles in fiction. They can be the central observers and interpreters of the story or simply key agents in it. We may learn of their 'adventures', their 'opinions', see their comedies or tragedies. We may be very close to the most intimate details of their lives and thoughts; or we may follow them to make our way through huge communities (Dickens, Balzac) or great journeys.

In modern times, the idea of character has altered greatly. Writing at the end of the nineteenth century, at the dawn of a new era of psychology, Henry James was very aware of this (his brother William was professor of psychology at Harvard, and inventor of the phrase 'stream of consciousness'). Modern literature has made much of the nature of consciousness. As the critic Erich Auerbach once put it, in modern fiction exterior events have lost their power, and now chiefly serve to release and interpret inner events.

But this is not inevitably so. Though the subjective and impressionistic central character (the Marcel of Proust, the Mrs Dalloway of Woolf) have become important representatives of modern fiction, so has 'exterior' characterization, characteristic, for instance, of comedy, satire and grotesque fiction. The fundamental fact remains that without characters literature would be uninteresting; and without the permutations that surround the strange and obscure notion of character many of the greatest devices of theatre and fictional storytelling would not exist.

Some Notes on Character

- One of the great tasks of writing is to represent the human world and the figures that populate it. We learn our characters from our own lives, from our observations, our sense of the motives of others, our fascination with culture and mannerisms. The deeper our sense of character, the richer our feeling for humanity, the more interesting our writing is likely to be.

- The writer is an impersonator, living through the borrowed identities of others and creating drama out of this multiplication of selves. The characters we are interested in are likely to be aspects of ourselves and our self-understanding. But literature is more than a confession or an autobiography, and our creative sense will enlarge if we can incorporate characters who are other than or highly different from ourselves.

- 'Character' – the depiction of a strong and interesting human being, or a variety of them, with their own voices and qualities, and with whose lives we grow involved – is generally at the heart of storytelling. Whatever genre we are working in (fiction, short story, play, film or television) we need the power to observe, depict, develop and extend characters.

- From character – and what he or she hopes for, wants, suffers or learns – an entire plot and action can arise, as the novelist finds the standpoint to explore a situation, an episode, an adventure, an extended experience, an entire life.

- A character does not have to be heroic or extreme in some way to be interesting. Fielding's Tom Jones is ordinariness personified. Flaubert's Emma Bovary is an average discontented suburban housewife from the provinces. Joyce's Leopold Bloom is the opposite to a hero, a demoted Ulysses, transformed into a seedy advertisement salesman. Some of Beckett's heroes are literally nameless: unnameable.

- The creation or invention of a character generally depends on the creation both of an inner and an outer life. Just as an actor needs a motivation to play a part, so a character needs an inner life or desire that shapes the needs, hopes and actions. Hence, as motors both of characters and action, the importance of Henry James's questions about Isabel Archer: What does she want? What will she do?

- Similarly, a character is usually observed alike from inside and outside: as a psychological human being, and a set of appearances, characteristics, and quirks about which the writer may make generalized observations. And while the character may live in the immediate present of a story, the narrator or novelist need not. The story can divert from the character or recount something the character need not know.

- As readers or viewers, in observing or responding to 'character', we generally seek psychological consistency, probability of behaviour, likelihood of feeling. We want a share in the subjectivity of the figure, even if we see him or her chiefly from the outside.

- The motives of a well-invented character generally generate conflict and contradiction, for motives are ambiguous to all of us and lead us in many directions. Desires are not satisfied easily; intentions are often ridden with contradictions. Scene by scene in fiction and drama, a character generally discovers more of life, difficulty, and sometimes the falsehood and futility of wishes and motives.

• Thus the nature of the character is the spring of the development, the enlargement and the discovery process of the story. From encounter, conflict, difficulty, obstruction there often comes self-discovery or the attainment of moral, social or psychological truths not apparent at the start.

• The novel may be – as Iris Murdoch once said about it – 'a fit house for free characters to live in', meaning that it is the writer's task to acknowledge and explore the complexity of human life and experience, rather than subject characters to over-disciplined and organized plot. Yet this idea of the 'free character' may be in conflict with the demands of plot. In Thomas Hardy plot is generally fate, a force beyond the self that challenges existence. In absurdist fiction, character disappears into randomness and chance. Thus the interaction of character and plot is one of the primary structural tensions of fiction.

• In much modern fiction 'character' is not a freestanding figure, sharply observed. 'Character' is consciousness, viewpoint, angle of vision, perhaps the narrator of the text. As we have come to believe in the subjective nature of life, the viewpoint of the single character (Holden Caulfield, for instance, in Salinger's *The Catcher in the Rye*) can appear the most truthful form of storytelling. One crucial relationship in modern fiction is that between character and author. Many writers have explored it as displaying the paradoxes of human freedom. Thus John Fowles in *The French Lieutenant's Woman*:

> The story that I am telling is all imagination. These characters I create have never existed outside my own mind. If I have pretended until now to know my characters' minds and innermost thoughts, it is because I am writing in . . . a convention universally

accepted at the time of my story [the Victorian age]; that the novelist stands next to God. He may not know all, yet he tries to pretend that he does. But I live in the age of Alain Robbe-Grillet and Roland Barthes; if this is a novel, it cannot be a novel in the modern sense of the word.

- 'Characters' are the products of writing. But it is our capacity to observe, invent and create them, to keep them sustained and alive, to make their lives quite as fascinating as anyone's, that justifies us as writers and thus creates the humane value of stories.

- Virginia Woolf summed it up in the essay 'Mr Bennett and Mrs Brown':

> I believe that all novels . . . deal with character, and that it is to express character – not to preach doctrines, sing songs, or celebrate the glories of the British Empire, that the form of the novel, so clumsy, verbose and undramatic, so rich, elastic and alive, has been evolved. To express character, I have said, but you will at once reflect that the very widest interpretation can be put upon those words . . . You see one thing in a character, and I another. You say it means this, and I that. And when it comes to writing, each makes a further selection on principles of his own.

Example: Anna Karenina

Here is Tolstoy introducing us to Anna, the central character of his novel *Anna Karenina*. We see her on a train at Moscow station, through the eyes of the young soldier Vronsky, who will become her lover, and who is there to meet his mother off the train:

> Vronsky followed the guard to the carriage and had to stop to let a lady pass out.
> The trained insight of a Society man enabled

Vronsky with a single glance to .decide that she belonged to the best Society. He apologized for being in her way and was about to enter the carriage, but felt compelled to have another look at her, not because she was very beautiful or because of the elegance and modest grace of her whole figure, but he saw in her sweet face as she passed him something specially tender and kind. When he looked round she too turned her head. Her bright grey eyes which seemed dark because of their black lashes rested for a moment on his face as if recognizing him, and then turned to the passing crowd evidently in search of someone. In that short look Vronsky had time to notice the subdued animation that enlivened her face and seemed to flutter between her bright eyes and a scarcely perceptible smile which curved her rosy lips. It was as if an excess of vitality so filled her whole being that it betrayed itself against her will, now in her smile, now in the light of her eyes. She deliberately tried to extinguish that light in her eyes, but it shone despite of her in her faint smile.

A meeting takes place; nothing is spoken. One character is established through the observation of another. What is chiefly observed is a face and an expression. But it is in the words chosen to define Vronsky's impressions that Tolstoy establishes the woman who is to be his central character, and much of her temperament and her function. Vronsky perceives, and we are given, a serious and dutiful woman, but one with a vital animation which is part of a vigorous sexuality. The encounter and the impression of personality that is conveyed in it, without a word spoken, is the motor of the entire story, and the basis of what will eventually prove first a profound and then a tragic relationship.

Nobody ever thought harder about the business of fiction, or wrote with more passion, analytical cunning or at times obscurity about its tricky arts than Henry James. The prefaces he added to the New York edition of his novels (1905–9), at the end of his life, when it was possible to look back over a career that had taken him on from the Victorian to the modern novel, are some of the greatest observations ever made about the art of fiction. 'I sat for a long while with the closed volume in my hand,' wrote Joseph Conrad, 'going over the preface in my mind and thinking – that is how it began, that's how it was done.'

James makes it clear his novels have not all started in the same way. Some have begun with what he called a *donnée* – an idea, an anecdote, sometimes an entire storyline, which emerged, perhaps, from a dinner-table conversation or hearing some striking story. Often James would write a complete plan of the book, not least in order to sell it as a serial to the magazines (though he wouldn't always stick precisely to it, for new inventions happen in the writing). The *Portrait of a Lady* – James wishes to emphasize in his preface – was somewhat different; it started with a free-standing character, Isabel Archer, the young American girl affronting her destiny. She was the subject, and the rest of the book would start from there.

> By what process of logical accretion was this slight 'personality,' the mere slim shade of an intelligent but presumptuous girl, to find itself endowed with the high attributes of a Subject? – and indeed by what thinness, at the best, would such a subject not be vitiated? Millions of presumptuous girls, intelligent or not intelligent, daily affront their destiny, and what it is open to their destiny to be, at the most, that we should make an ado about it? The novel is of its very nature 'ado,' an ado about something, and the larger the form it takes the greater of course the ado. Therefore, consciously, that was what one was in for – for positively organizing an ado about Isabel Archer.
>
> HENRY JAMES, Preface to the *Portrait of a Lady*

And he explains, a whole new gallery of characters begins to emerge around her once you ask the questions, What does she want? What will she do? James adds, interestingly, that some of these characters will belong to the 'form' – that is, they will come independently and vigorously alive in the way that Isabel herself does, as Pansy, Madame Merle, Ralph Touchett and Gilbert Osmond do in the book, and be fundamental friends or adversaries to the central character. Others, he says, really belong, like Henrietta Stackpole, to the 'treatment' – they belong with the wheels of the coach, to make it work, rather than the body of the vehicle. Hence some characters are crucial, some incidental or illustrative. What about the ones at the centre?

Isabel, in the novel, is left a large legacy to see what she will do and is set 'free'. James has awarded a similar freedom to her role in the novel. As other characters wait to see what she will make of her freedom, so, it seems, does the novelist, who has left open the plot. Isabel represents a modern notion of character as an independent figure, and the modern character demands a new role in fiction. In the end, though, Isabel is pushed towards conformity. Characters, in fiction, never have total freedom, since they are subject to their creators.

Which is why we, the creators, can become so fascinated by our characters. We will them to be free. As André Gide once put it: 'The poor novelist constructs his characters, he controls them and makes them speak. The true novelist listens to them and watches them function; he eavesdrops on them even before he knows them. It is only according to what he heard them say that he begins to understand who they are.'

Real Life
Paul Magrs

What I do to get into the heart of a situation and a group of characters engaged in a drama is this: I often take articles from confessional magazines. By these I mean those glossy mags that purport to tell the true and harrowing and sometimes heart-warming tales of ordinary folk's trials and tribulations. In these short articles we often get a whole family's history in just a page or two; ghostwritten immaculately in standard English and accompanied by photographs of the actual people.

There's something very rewarding about poring through someone else's photograph album: weddings, Christmases, holidays. The cliché is that other people's photos are boring; but that's only because everyone's are the same, essentially. You should be alert to the small, vital differences that give the true story away. Didn't Tolstoy say something about families being happy for the same reasons and their various unhappinesses being completely unique?

These are the small, specific differences that attract me to these trial-and-tribulation stories in trashy magazines.

So, say you have a glibly ghostwritten article that skims over a life story – one perhaps about a doomed love, a missing child, a fatal disease or a failed holiday romance. What you have is a drama with a cast of four or five characters, a set of locations and a particular story arc. The article gets you nowhere near the real drama of the events. In these magazines what we have is drama recalled at a safe distance, written by someone who wasn't there. These articles aren't meant to profoundly disturb or unsettle us; they are meant to assure us that everything turned out all right in the end. Often they are profoundly moralistic and cathartic.

In fiction it doesn't have to be all right in the end. In fiction we want to recreate the heat of the moment; pitch our readers back into the heart of the drama, the crucial moments of crisis.

✍ The first thing you need to settle on is one of the characters. Whose viewpoint appeals to you most? I have a great trust in instinct when it comes to these things. Do you sympathize most with the mother who puts on various forms of fancy dress to cheer up her invalid children and winds up becoming a local celebrity? Or do you feel for her long-suffering husband, who (judging by the photo) cringes with embarrassment when she dons her Tina Turner wig in public? Maybe you feel more at home imagining the inner life of the woman who shunned her mother for marrying a window-cleaning Lothario too soon after she was widowed?

It is important to let your instinct guide your first choice of viewpoint. Afterwards you can try the same set of exercises with another character.

In the first place I would try to put myself in my character's shoes by asking myself the following questions:

What is my favourite room?
What is my favourite object?
Where would I like to travel to?
Is there something I have never done that I would love to?

For each of these questions I would write fifty words or so. With these answers I might surprise myself. I'm trying to insinuate myself, carefully, into the way my character thinks. The way to do that, for me, is by thinking about what is familiar to them, what is comforting, but also what are their deepest dreams and desires.

When putting together a character, who I hope will convince my readers, it is important to me that I cover the extremes of their inner, private lives. I have to know what they dread and what they desire. I have to know how they behave when they are at their happiest and their most miserable; their most despairing and most hopeful. We have to see them at their best and at their worst.

For the next stage, I would take this character and make them confront another in their story. I would formulate three questions that one character will ask the other one. These would be the questions that would cut right to the core of the story, things like: How did you feel when your mother had you committed to the mental asylum?

We're back on this issue of the writer of fiction being inherently nosy again. These are the questions you endlessly think of when you are reading these articles or meeting these people for real. In a way, it seems to me, fiction is the place where we can ask the questions that you would never dare to ask in real life.

And you can get answers. I would answer the three questions in the first-person voice. But I would have my chosen character reply to these searching enquiries in two forms. I would write fifty words of public response and then fifty words of private response. The second fifty words would be ones that the character would know no one else in their story would ever have to hear.

Try that and see what you get. Read the two paragraphs together: the public response and the private response. Do they contradict each other? What does it mean, that the second one is at odds with the first? What deep-rooted tensions are coming out here? When you read the two responses back to each of the searching questions you will have this distinct unnerving sense of sinking more deeply into the psychology of your chosen character.

Next, have your character look at another character in their story and have them describe this person physically. We're moving out of the psychological and into the physical, the immediate. Write another hundred words like this.

Have you kept out the psychological dimension completely? What has your character given away about what they really think of this other person?

When we get into somebody else's shoes we are trying hard to make their attitudes, outlook, opinions clear, but we are also always trying to ground these thoughts in the physical and everyday.

You need to set these characters in motion, basing their behaviour in everyday locations, full of smells and sounds and thoughts that ring true.

When my friend told me the story of the woman who declared over Sunday lunch that she really wanted to be like Lulu, what convinced me of the story's truth was his description of what they were eating, the way the woman drank, her hair, the way she looked older than Lulu, even though she wasn't, the specific nature of the conversation she interrupted. Bringing these dramas to life and making these shoes fit comfortably is a process of aligning the specific details of psychology, inner life and attitude with the precise indicators of physicality, immediacy, atmosphere.

The final stage in the exercise is to have two of the characters in this story talk to each other.

You have to set them in an immediate scene: a kitchen, in the park, driving down the motorway. Conjure that scene in all its particulars and render your characters in the precise manner in which they would inhabit such a place. In the car she takes off her shoes while her daughter drives. In the park the divorced father makes sure he always wins the game of football with his sons, impressing his new girlfriend.

Then you've got to get them talking. Make one of them come to a decision. Today's the day they tell the other one what's really on their mind. They rove back over past history. They decide to describe how past events have impacted on them individually. Is the other person shocked, surprised, bored or exasperated? This is how you find out. You have to tease out the eventualities. You have to force the moment to its crisis and show them interacting, letting them interrupt each other, argue, contradict, apologize and flare up.

By getting ourselves in both pairs of shoes in a scene like this, seeing it all from both sides, we are putting ourselves right back into the heart of the drama. And that's how we find out – and prove – that Anna Karenina can happen here, now, down our street and anywhere.

6 Point of View

Introduction
Paul Magrs

Every piece of writing comes from a particular point of view. Choices have to be made as to who is writing and from where. One of the things to be clear about, from the very start, is that you are adopting a specific and consistent point of view and that you are doing it for a reason.

As writer you are controlling exactly what your reader gets to find out about the world you are putting them into. You get to make the decisions about what information to release and when. You can't let it all slip out in one disordered rush. You have to manoeuvre them subtly around this world of yours, limiting and expanding their point of view.

Your reader is effectively putting all of their sensory faculties and capabilities into your hands. While they are inside your story, poem or script, everything they will experience is governed by what you choose to tell them.

Your first major choice is that of person.

Who is telling this story? Whose voice is addressing us in that poem?

What can they see? What can they know?

First Person

The 'I' narrator is part of the action. Partisan and implicated in what is going on, the first-person narrator speaks from a position within the actual world of the story. Everything they tell us comes from their own experience, and everything within the text has to be something that is known to them.

Do you trust what they're telling you? When they describe other people or events, do you automatically believe that they're telling you the whole story? How are they presenting themselves?

As in life, if you only have one version of the events to go on, you have to decide whether to take their version on trust or to take it all with a pinch of salt.

For a writer there is a lot of good potential in this. Your first-person narrator can be a real, bravura act of impersonation. Everything you write in their voice can be a kind of mask for you. In this moment of choice, you can become anyone. You can imagine yourself a different age, gender, sexuality, class and you can be speaking or writing from any point in history. Often a writer's earliest work takes the form of a first-person account in a voice very similar to their own, describing a life very much like their own. It's good practice to distance yourself from your own position and imagine yourself as someone else. You become this person every time you sit down to write. A first-person point of view is a great conjuring act; a confidence trick.

My own favourite example here is Angela Carter's last novel, *Wise Children*, in which she has the septuagenarian dance-hall hoofer Nora Chance tell the tale of her family's history, and her own extraordinary life, directly to us. She begins the tale as she sits at her computer; opening the story with a joke and a rousing 'Good morning!' By the end of the book she is sitting in the snug of an East End pub, and we are led to imagine that we are being told the story face to face, and Nora is happily detaining us, over a drink, with her ribald memories.

We find that we trust Nora's telling of the great family saga. We take her word on trust. *Wise Children* is a book all about the unfairness of official or legitimate versions of history, and Nora's telling is an attempt to describe what it was like from the less privileged, more contingent point of view. It is a book very concerned with point of view and what might be lost or gained from a position that isn't always centre stage; one, instead, that ducks and weaves around the principal characters. Throughout the book Nora is afforded tantalizing glimpses, from under tables, behind bits of scenery, of what is going on in the secret lives of the other characters. We trust her slant and partial access to events.

A genre that uses first-person point of view extremely well is the thriller or the crime story. Here first person is employed to put us in the position of the investigator, picking up and responding to clues, moving further into the mystery. We, as reader, believe that we are being told exactly what the narrator knows and are being given information in a sequence that will allow us to piece the conundrum together for ourselves. Often, in detective fiction, we are shown a point of view slightly to one side of the investigator; someone slightly less intelligent, so we can still sympathize, but also join in with the chase. I'm thinking here of the first-person accounts of Dr Watson in Conan Doyle's Sherlock Holmes stories, or Dr Petrie, the right-hand man of Nayland Smith in Sax Rohmer's Fu Manchu novels.

The first-person narrator is someone we can listen to and be carried along by. They do our seeing, touching, listening, feeling and smelling for us. We overhear their thoughts and we can wonder about them. Are they telling us the truth? Have they become, perhaps, an unreliable narrator? My current, favourite example of an unreliable narrator is to be found in Robert Irwin's novel *Satan Wants Me*. In it the narrator gives us his diaries as he embarks, as a student, on a life of black magic and ritual. We are told early on that he has been asked to keep the diary so that his tutor can read it, check on his grammar, spelling and progress as an adept. What we learn at the end of the book, when the narrator has fled from the cult's influence, is that many of his diary entries were full of lies. The narrator was hoodwinking his professor and never wanted to be a magician at all. He was just doing research for a postgraduate sociology degree. Belatedly, we get a kind of apology from the narrator, because, as he realizes, we were hoodwinked too.

Time is an important factor, also. In *Satan Wants Me* we have a diary form, and we accept that, between each entry, each mini-chapter, time has elapsed in the lives of the narrator and the other characters. This gives the point of view more immediacy; we are much more embroiled and implicated than we would be in, say, a first-person novel that is told from a position of hindsight.

Daniel Defoe's *Moll Flanders*, for example, ranges over Moll's whole life, and she narrates her hair-raising adventures in chronological order. We know, though, that she is telling us all of this at an advanced age, retired in Virginia in the United States. However dangerous the scrapes she gets into, we know that, ultimately, she survives to tell the tale. With a novel like *Satan Wants Me*, we face the possibility of our narrator coming to harm and the diary entries stopping abruptly with his death. The Gothic novel made great play with this vulnerability of the narrator. H. P. Lovecraft's fiction often finished with the narrator scribbling an account of horrors by candlelight, bringing us up to date with the dangers he has faced, only to have, at the very last moment, the narrator tell us that the horror has caught up with him . . . and that something is, in fact, peering over his shoulder as he writes . . .

A decision, then, needs to be made, not only about the physical embodiment of your viewpoint, but in time, also.

Second Person

This is rarer than the other two options and a very interesting voice to adopt in writing exercises. Writing in second person buttonholes the reader. The writer puts the reader at the centre of things and it is the reader who becomes implicated.

Role-playing games or books often use this mode to encourage the reader to imagine themselves part of the action. 'In this adventure you are this kind of character, and these are the range of options you have . . .'

It is also the mode I have adopted in writing these pieces about writing. What you need to do is this; this is something you might like to try; why don't you keep a notebook?

With the use of the second person, I am addressing an implied reader, quite familiarly, as if you are someone known to me. In English, of course, we don't have the distinction between polite and familiar, as French or German does. In English, when we use the second person, it is always intimate, insinuating. With it you are telling your readers what they are like, what they are doing; you are cajoling them.

In Iain Banks' thriller *Complicity* certain chapters use the second person in quite a sinister fashion. You are conjured as the serial killer, the threat from outside, as you go about your terrible business. At first you aren't quite sure what it is 'you' are actually doing, but it soon becomes clear and there is a horrible frisson to your epiphany that you are looking at the world through the eyes of a killer.

Somehow it is a more horrible effect than if that killer's narrative was presented in the first person. Then you could still distance yourself from his words. It would be a kind of confessional you were reading. When it is addressed to 'you', however, those chapters of Banks' *Complicity* become almost accusatory: You are doing this, now you are doing that. At this point you realize that the title of the book describes your own uneasy relationship with the killer.

Third Person

This is the point of view with the most variations. This is the overarching voice; the one that is the least embodied. The third-person narrator can be anywhere within the text; it can know everything, like Charles Dickens' narrators seem to do, and visit every home and hideout of the characters. It can read people's thoughts and report them to us. It has a godlike power to go anywhere and see anything; it has omniscience.

It can also limit itself so that it is more bound up in the action. Jane Austen works differently to Dickens, in that she's not so given to looking out over the rooftops and taking in the bigger picture and then visiting different homes and scenes in turn. My A-level English teacher, Lynne Heritage, once described Austen as a gossip; she has the omniscience, but chooses to limit it and display it by sitting her reader down by the fire and letting them in on a secret or two.

She deliberately limits her third-person omniscience and keeps everything down to the interactions of her characters. Not for her the sweeping panoramas or the detailed, erudite digressions of George

Eliot. We get the feeling that Austen is more of a near-invisible earwigger, standing just to one side of her characters, taking everything in and reporting it to us a little later.

In choosing the third-person position, these are the further decisions you will need to make. Will you limit your narrator's viewpoint, so they maybe see the story mainly through one character? Or will they have unlimited access to everyone on your stage? Will your third-person narrator be able to look at things even when there are no characters there? Will they be able to visit rooms before any of your characters arrive? And will they be able to release important information to your reader in a fashion that will be as suspenseful as in the use of a first-person position?

A third-person account puts its reader very much in the position of a viewer. It is the familiar position from watching a film, TV or a play. The reader is the fourth wall in this world and the writer has to work to keep us feeling implicated and involved in the action.

A third-person viewpoint can be quite simple and neutral, exerting no kind of personality of its own. It can be kept subdued, quite plain, in order to let the characters take the main focus. Or it can be a voice that is full of its own personality; the implied author's voice that makes its own asides, digressions and thoughts quite plain.

Often it is this tone that a reader responds to and thinks of as belonging uniquely to the author. In John Irving's novels, for example, there is a quality of Irvingness to the third-person narrator, the implied author, that is consistent across many of his books. This is a voice that readers recognize and enjoy, but it is one that has to be very self-consciously constructed. It isn't enough simply to pitch in and start telling the story; you need to be clear from the start what kind of being this tale-teller is. How sympathetic to their characters is this implied author going to be? Do they want to be quite hard on them and make them suffer and then relish telling the reader how they're glad the characters all came to a sticky end? Or will they be a more reserved voice, letting the characters get on with it, not judging them, letting them show themselves up, for good or bad? And what will the third-person narrator do with time? From which point in time are they talking? The next day? Years afterwards? Will your third-person account suddenly be able to tell the reader what happened forty years hence (prolepsis) or what went on three months before the action of the current scene (analepsis)?

The reader has to understand what kind of being it is they are listening to when they read a third-person account. The reader wants to know if they are dealing with a godlike being who can range over expanses of time and space, or whether they have here a more localized voice; one that simply overhears and reports, keeping things very much in the moment.

Whether you choose to write in first, second or third person, and whatever powers you choose to grant that voice (to do with their access to knowledge that they will then pass on to the reader), the most important thing is to keep it consistent.

You might choose the apparently simplest point of view (a first-person, day-by-day confessional account by an honest character), or the most abstruse (a third-person narrator who identifies particularly with snakes and has unlimited access to future and past events in a story about a strike in a reptile house); what really matters is that you make your rules and stick with them.

The narrator's voice is one that governs the reader's experience of the whole text; it forms their focus for the entirety of the story or poem. If it is muddled or unclearly thought out it can jeopardize the whole piece. The reader is always looking to you, as writer, to lead them confidently through your world.

Eye Level
Jenny Newman

Point of view is the window that you, the fiction writer, open on to your imaginary world. This all-important choice determines not only your story's tone, but also its characterization and plot. Try retelling the first chapter of Genesis in the voice of Eve, or the snake, or the apple that was plucked from the tree of knowledge of good and evil. Each new slant delivers us a fresh story, with a voice of its own and a different point of attack.

Your basic choice of point of view is between first and third person, between 'I' and 'he' or 'she'. If you write in the first person, it will be one of your characters who speaks. Josip Novakovich calls this the mother of all points of view because every story is said to originate with an 'I' who witnesses what happens. It is the obvious choice for autobiographical fiction and for the 'honest account'. Because of its limited ground-level view, the first person is also used by young narrators in novels such as L. P. Hartley's *The Go-Between*, Jeanette Winterson's *Oranges Are Not the Only Fruit* and Roddy Doyle's *Paddy Clarke, Ha Ha Ha*.

But don't be misled: despite their air of authenticity, these outstanding first-person novels are more than the 'the voice of experience'. They derive – at least in part – from the imagination, which thrives on a shortage of facts. As always in first-person narratives, the author is propelled by the use of 'I' – the pronoun that Laurie Lee calls the little stick round which the story revolves – into finding a voice dramatically different from his own.

The difference can be one of years, as in *Huckleberry Finn*, written when Twain was in his fifties:

> The Widow Douglas, she took me for her son, and allowed she would sivilise me; but it was rough living in the house all the time, considering how dismal regular and decent the widow was in all her ways; and so when I couldn't stand it no longer, I lit out. I got into my old rags and my sugar-hogshead again, and was free and satisfied.

Or it can be one of race, outlook, class, gender or temperament. If you like creating a gap between you and your central character, try reading Kazuo Ishiguro's *The Remains of the Day*, written in the voice of a gullible, reactionary butler, or Iris Murdoch's *The Sea, The Sea*, told by a fussy old theatre director, then invent a first-person narrator with a past, passions and prejudices differing radically from your own. When you step back from your story, and let your character speak for herself, you may find the voice that will make your novel distinctive and set it apart from the rest. You are also less likely to slide without realizing it into your own vocabulary and way of putting things. If you are too close to your narrator, her language register may waver from time to time, and take on the colour of your own. Then a 'shadow author' creeps into your novel and diminishes belief in both narrator and story.

Though the voice of your first-person narrator is sharply distinct from your own, this does not mean that you have to abandon your favourite themes. Give a man a mask, says Oscar Wilde, and he will reveal himself. Your 'I' narrative can still be a route to your obsessions or a disguise that lets you bring out what Novakovich describes as your 'demons and angels'. Like Henry James's *The Turn of the Screw*, most fantasy novels and ghost stories are written in the first person, because it is the voice of outsiders, victims, visionaries and isolates, the sorts of people not easily assimilated and seldom believed. First-person narrators often have an angled vision and a partial understanding of events. Push any of them to an extreme and you will have an unreliable narrator such as Humbert Humbert in Vladimir Nabokov's *Lolita*, popular in today's relativistic, post-modern world. The tight focus can make the first person edgily claustrophobic, which is useful for depicting extreme states of mind, as in many short stories by Edgar Allan Poe or Janice Galloway's *The Trick is to Keep Breathing*.

Dialect, slang or non-standard English? The Irishness of Roddy Doyle's *Paddy Clarke, Ha Ha Ha*; Alex's use of 'Nadsat' in Anthony Burgess's *A Clockwork Orange*; the Scots slang of Roy Strong in Irvine Welsh's *Marabou Stork Nightmares*; the first Mrs Rochester's response to patois in Jean Rhys's *Wide Sargasso Sea*: most memorable first-person narrators have the lexicons to match their independent minds. Featuring the young, the colonized, the downtrodden or the marginalized, the language of the best 'I' narratives is rich, offbeat and blazingly original, which is why so many become literary landmarks.

Though popular and compelling, the first-person narrative has its drawbacks. Firstly, your character–narrator must be involved with most of the action: otherwise she will have to learn about crucial events second hand, and much of the drama will be lost. There are exceptions to this rule, such as Nick Carraway in F. Scott Fitzgerald's *The Great Gatsby*, who witnesses but does not influence Gatsby's passion for Nick's married cousin, Daisy. But this is the consummate work of a major novelist, and it is fair to add that even Nick is changed by his role as bystander.

Secondly, everything must be seen through the first-person narrator's eyes, so it is difficult to convey her appearance, unless you resort to the cliché of having her glance in the mirror or have another character comment on a change in her looks. Nor can you end with your narrator's death; unless, like Edgar Allan Poe in 'Manuscript Found in a Bottle' or Jean Rhys in *Wide Sargasso Sea*, you work out a clever and involved narrative strategy. As a rule of thumb, unless your character's voice is so distinctive that your 'I's cannot easily be swapped for 'he's or 'she's, it is wiser to turn to the most popular choice of all, the third person limited.

The third person limited closely resembles the first person, but written in standard English, though there are rare exceptions, such as James Kelman's original and inventive *How Late It Was, How Late*:

> He was fucking dying when he woke up the first time. He didnay know where the fuck he was. He looked about, he was on a floor and it smelled of pish, it was in his nostrils, and his chin was soaking wet and all round the sides of his mouth and like snotters from his nose, fucking blood maybe, fucking hell man, fucking sore.

Even in the above extract it is the author, strictly speaking, and not the character, who is telling the story. In the third person limited the authorial voice remains almost undetectable, thus keeping much of the intimacy of the first person while giving you the latitude to move outside your character when you wish, to describe her appearance and responses. Note how the italicized sentence in the passage below helps modulate between inner and outer:

> The cloud was lowering itself for a downpour. *Boris felt his forehead tighten, as though an inner machine was winching up the skin.* He raised a grubby hand and started to rub his brow. With his gaunt face framed by a hacked-off haircut, he looked like a missing person in *The Big Issue*, not a well-to-do barrister of twenty years' standing with a flat in Mecklenburgh Square and a cottage in Hurst Pierpoint.

Your chosen point of view is a contract with your reader, and, if you clumsily break it, or allow it to waver, you are likely to lose her. Even the deftest change may undermine your fictional world by its sense of contrivance. Instead of taking the risk, you can let in diverse voices through the usual routes of dialogue and conflict; or else you can briefly intimate how a non-point-of-view character is thinking or feeling by the use of adverbs such as *clearly, apparently, seemingly, evidently, plainly, presumably, ostensibly, obviously, surely* or *definitely*, all of which have different nuances:

> She watched the red-faced Gyorgy, clearly out of temper with himself and the world, limp up the drive in his mistress's shoes.

> Ostensibly concerned about my swollen ankle, Aunt Laetitia yanked off my riding boot so that Jeremy could see the dreadful hole in my sock.

Josip Novakovich calls these 'virtual shifts' of point of view. There are times, however, when you may wish to go further. Though some novels and stories – such as *Lolita*, Herman Melville's *Bartleby*, and Franz Kafka's *The Trial* – artfully lock on to one character's world and maintain for the most part an unbroken tone, most fiction is more like a pub than a pulpit, with multiple voices competing for the reader's attention. To see things from different perspectives is one of the pleasures of fiction and, though your novel may lose in intensity, your readers may enjoy a change – or several changes – of viewpoint. As E. M. Forster puts it:

> . . . it has a parallel in our perception of life. We are stupider at some times than others; we can enter into people's minds occasionally but not always, because our own minds get tired; and this intermittence lends in the long run variety and colour to the experiences we receive.

Forster also says that when changing point of view you should not be too conscious of your method, because then the temperature drops. Even so, it may be helpful to reflect on a couple of techniques. If you worry about losing spontaneity, then save checking for inconsistencies – which David Lodge identifies as one of the commonest signs of an inexperienced novelist – until a later draft.

The easiest method is to swap point of view between chapters or sections of chapters whenever it is relevant to your plot. But you do not have to wait for a break if you do not wish to. For the sake of irony or a point of detail, many writers prefer to dip in and out of several consciousnesses within chapters or even within paragraphs. A shift may be so subtle that the reader barely perceives it has happened:

> Asha watched the blond, well-muscled Jack as he flirted with her best friend, Meg. Though still badly hungover, he realized at once that Meg was the prettiest girl in town.

Other changes succeed by drawing attention to themselves:

Alice flung open the door and saw Spanny, a grubby little punk with green spiked hair and a nose ring. Spanny saw Alice, a mumsy-looking woman in her fifties who hadn't a clue about how to make the most of herself.

This is what Novakovich calls 'propel[ling] the reader into a new angle', and Forster calls 'bouncing' the reader from the mind of one character into the mind of another so that she does not mind the shiftings of viewpoint. The key is to look as though you are in control, and not to apologize or try too hard to disguise what you are doing, because that will distract your reader and clutter your narrative. This means establishing your technique near the start and following it confidently, as Forster does in his own fiction.

Though swapping between third-person viewpoints is probably easiest, it is also possible to move between first and third, as Irvine Welsh does in *Trainspotting*. Forster cites *Bleak House* as a model of authorial brio, with Dickens regularly 'bouncing' his reader between Esther Summerson and the omniscient narrator.

Dickens' two voices are easy to tell apart, partly because Esther Summerson's narrative is in the first person and the rest of the novel is written in the voice of a third-person narrator with limited omniscience. It is harder to swap between 'I' narrators, because once you have created a distinctive voice it can be difficult to find another to match it, and your reader's attention may flag when the lesser character opens her mouth. John Braine, for one, believes the attempt is doomed because it heightens the sense of artifice: 'I can't accept the different people being trotted on; somewhere I see a puppet-master.' If you are drawn to this technique, why not choose a daringly wide range of narrators, as Michèle Roberts does in *In the Red Kitchen*? If worried about confusing your reader, you can always label each section with the name of the new narrator.

Diving into another character's mind within a chapter is almost impossible in the first person, difficult in a tightly limited third, and easiest for the author who keeps her characters at a distance – as in the omniscient or limited omniscient viewpoints. Read the novels of Jane Austen, Henry James and A. S. Byatt for a wealth of ways to segue in and out of different points of view, and consider the pros and cons of the detachment it brings. Good writers are always on the look-out for fresh techniques such as Jamaica Kincaid's inventive use of the second person in *Girl*, or Jay McInerney's in *Bright Lights, Big City* .

But no matter how expert you grow, avoid changing perspective mid-sentence; you risk making your style look amateurish and wobbly. And remember that swapping viewpoints, like changing lanes on the motorway, is always a danger point when you risk losing your reader, so only consider doing it when she really has something to gain.

✍ Write about the earliest event you remember. Don't worry if the memory is wispy – feel free to fill in the details. For example, you can focus on your size as a four-year-old in relation to the people and objects around you. If there is a table in the room, is its surface above or below eye-level? If you are holding an adult's hand, how big is it? What clothes are you wearing and how do they feel? What can you hear and smell?

After writing as many details as you can invent or remember, wait for a few days, then rewrite the episode from the point of view of someone else – brother, sister, parent or teacher – who was present, then put the two accounts side by side. What salient changes have you made in vocabulary, details, tone and structure?

Punto de Vista
Maureen Freely

It was a professor of Latin American Literature who introduced me to this mysterious art. I am sure my own initial interest had a lot to do with the fact that he referred to it not as 'point of view' but as '*punto de vista*'. He could rave about it for hours. He had spent an earlier chapter of his life running a small publishing concern that catered to the Buenos Aires intelligentsia. To combat boredom, they had been in the habit of setting themselves challenges. They tried to invent a plot machine. They competed to find out who could write the most startling story containing a reference to a disembodied hand. And they argued, often until dawn, about the unexplored properties of *punto de vista*. How far could you take it before it exploded or imploded? What was a legitimate trick, and what betrayed the spirit of the exercise?

The champion in the *punto de vista* stakes was – most of them agreed – Julio Cortázar. In 'The Continuation of Parks', for example, he gave every indication of writing from the point of view of a man who is sitting in an armchair in a beautiful house in a handsome park, reading a rather conventional mystery story about an adulterous wife and her lover. But then we find out that the lover is going to break into a beautiful house in a handsome park to murder her husband. When he finds the husband, he is sitting in an armchair, immersed in a mystery story about an adulterous wife and a murderous lover. So could you really say it was from his point of view? The café society of 1950s Buenos Aires could never quite decide.

It was the same with 'Axolotl', another Cortázar story they admired. This seemed to be told from the point of view of a man who became inexplicably obsessed with a primitive sea creature displayed in his local aquarium. Every day he would go there and spend hours staring into the creature's eyes, trying without success to find out what was going on behind them. Until one day, in the middle of just such a staring match, he looked out and saw his former self staring at him from the other side of the glass. The shift of point of view from man to Axolotl is so smooth that you only figure out what's happened after it's all over. My Latin American Literature professor admired it because the moment of transition was handled in such a way as to add to the narrative tension. He did not believe the same could be said about a Horacio Quiroga story, which was told from the point of view of a man who fell on his own pitchfork by the end of the first paragraph, and who died in the penultimate paragraph, leaving the last paragraph to be told from the *punto de vista* of the fly on the corpse's nose. In my professor's opinion, this was a cheap and diminishing trick, which robbed the story of all significance.

I myself had similar doubts about the *punto de vista* trickery performed by another old friend of his, a gentleman novelist named Bioy Casares. He was a very wealthy man who wrote only for his own amusement. His most famous novel was told from the point of view of a castaway on an island full of beautiful people who refuse to acknowledge his presence. His suspicions are aroused when he discovers that they are on a loop, living the same week over and over. He goes on to discover that they are not real people, but three-dimensional film versions of their former selves. This is a tragic discovery, because by now he has fallen in love with one of the women, and he cannot abide the idea of life without her. So, having located the three-dimensional projector, he contrives to have himself superimposed on the original film version, so that he can spend eternity following a love object who can never be aware of his existence . . .

'So tell me,' I remember the professor saying. 'How carefully have you read this story? Locate the narrator for me. Where is he, and where exactly is he standing? How far can he see, into the past, into other people's minds? How far away is he from the real time of the story? And on what evidence do you base your answer?' It was essential, he said, for a writer to be able to answer these questions precisely. The more you fine-tuned a point of view, the more you could see.

The first thing that you saw if you did your homework properly was that there was more to point of view than just a view. In his view, the cardinal sin was to think that point of view was something that you could locate on a map. 'But this is hogwash!' he would tell us. 'It is not just in space but also in time. You forget the fourth dimension at your peril!'

Thanks to his wild and fiery sermons, I never have forgotten, and I never will. Nor will I ever be able to think of point of view as a mechanical device. For me, it is the window that takes you to the story. You can't see the window unless you are standing in the right place. Once you find the right place, the story can almost write itself. Hence my continuing enthusiasm.

It is, I must admit, an enthusiasm I have a hard time conveying to others. My students' eyes glaze over at the very mention of the P phrase. So what I usually do is to throw my students into the exercises that follow, without actually telling them what I am hoping they will learn from them.

✍ In my first exercise I get my students to help me invent a public space. This can be a bar, a pub, a hotel lobby, a restaurant, or a dentist's reception. It's up to the group to decide. Together we agree on the decor, the lighting, the clientele and so on. We fix a time, and we decide how crowded the room is. Then I assign a character to each member of the group. Most of these characters are stock figures in stock situations – a woman with a migraine, a man who has just found out he has only three weeks to live, a pickpocket, a social climber, a stoned teenager, a bodybuilder, a businessman who does not know his fly is open. I give the students an opening sentence: 'I opened the door and walked into the room.' I then tell them to continue writing in the first person past, and I give them ten minutes or so to get their assigned characters to the other side of the room. They are not allowed to let their characters identify themselves or their problems directly. Instead, they have to imagine what this room looks like to this type of person, in this type of situation. When the ten minutes are up, they take it in turn to read their passages out to the rest of the class. The others then try to work out who the person is. It is usually a great surprise to students to find out how different this room looks to different types of people. They are also surprised to discover how much their characters reveal about themselves and their preoccupations, simply by reporting what they see.

In the second leg of this exercise, I ask students to describe their characters from the point of view of a person standing at the opposite end of the room. Depending on the room, this person could be a bartender, a waiter, a receptionist or a hotel manager. Again, the person's job will help determine what he or she notices about the character who is walking across the room. By now, the student authors will know a certain amount about their characters, and so the characters will no longer be stereotypes. They will have started to accumulate quirks and histories. This means that they know more about their characters than the person who is interpreting the scene. They soon discover that this knowledge gives them a lot of power over both the characters and the narrative. Even so, they learn that they have to think very hard to figure out what a bartender might notice about a bodybuilder as he walks across a room. The more precisely they can answer these questions, the more interesting their story becomes, and the more possibilities are open to them.

✍ My second exercise tries to build on this insight. I begin by asking students to think of a real person who irritates them intensely. I then ask them to describe that person in the first person present. I then make them rewrite the scene in six other ways. In each instance, I give them the first sentence. So the assignment reads like this:

1 First person present. 'I am sitting here looking at X.' (X being the object of irritation.)
2 First person past. 'I was . . . years old when I first met X.'
3 Third person past, but this time the scene as seen by X. 'X could not understand why his old friend Y was acting so unfriendly.'
4 Third person past. This time, we get the story from the point of view of a third person, who is watching Y being intensely annoyed by X. The first sentence is: 'Z watched Y and X as they struggled to be civil to one another.'
5 Third person omniscient. 'Just after midnight in a small house on the outskirts of Manchester . . .'
6 Third person detached. X, Y and Z as seen by a woman who is

152

trying to read a book. 'She looked up from her book and wondered if she should tell them to be quiet.'

7 Third person detached. X and Y as seen by a man who cannot speak the language. 'They were smiling but it was clear that they hated each other.'

If you groan at the prospect of doing such a long and mechanical exercise, you are not alone. Cries of anguish I have heard include: 'Whatever happened to free expression?' and 'I took this course to learn how to use my imagination – not to turn it into an instruction manual!' But later on, most students say that there is at least one part of the exercise that turns out to be a revelation to them, and that they even learn a thing or two from the sections they found very dreary to write.

One thing they learn is that narrow points of view are rather easy to execute, while the omniscient point of view can be a real headache. There is too much choice. You have to know the story back to front before you've even written the first sentence. Another thing they learn is that each new point of view allows them certain freedoms while depriving them of others. They learn how much hinges on the question, 'How much does my character know?' They find out how fun it is to know a character well from the inside and then describe that character from someone else's point of view. But the thing that moves and surprises them the most about this exercise is the way it changes their understanding of X, their object of hatred. After stepping in and out of this person's point of view, they find themselves unable to hate him or her again in quite the same way. Seen from the other side, the story begins and ends in new places. It touches on material that they know well but are seeing in a new and unexpected light. In other words, it is while they are working their way through this mechanical exercise that many of them have their first taste of the thing that makes fiction worth reading and worth writing. This is the possibility of seeing life from points of view other than your own. Empathy is never an easy trick to perform, not even for seasoned novelists. Free expression is so much more fun, especially if you want to let off steam. But it's empathy, I'd say, that sets an imagination free.

Writing in the First Person
Elleke Boehmer

What does it mean to use the 'I', to take on the 'I' voice?

> She unzips her purse and extracts the rape alarm.
> I unzip my purse and extract the rape alarm.

The first sentence feels like part of a narrated action, the second can teeter between this and a page from a notebook.

Whether to write a work in the first person – close-up, comfortable, intimate, too intimate? Or in the third – rounded out, out there, objectified, remote? This is one of the central decisions a writer must make. It affects not only the angling, but the force, atmosphere and shape of a piece of writing, especially perhaps of fiction. In contemporary short poetry, other than the dramatic monologue, an I-perspective is often assumed.

A great deal of what a writer uses in their work is, of course, drawn from experience, including their reading and fantasy life, so the first person may seem in many cases an immediate and available channel, even a natural choice. The present-day popularity of confessional forms, autobiography, and works of witness, commemoration and testimony, also of diary-writing, the Bridget Jones format, reinforces this sense of naturalness. The 'I' is everywhere, and it seems modest and relaxed, as well as truthful, real, reliable. Moreover it betrays our reluctance to speak too much for and on behalf of others (where they, too, we feel, should rightly be telling their own story).

But it is within this seeming relaxed naturalness that the pitfalls of the first person lie. Writing is always an artefact, built up out of choices and splices, cutting and honing: it is not a direct translation from life. Yet, because it feels nearby and identifiable, the I-voice has the potential, to an extent, to distract a writer from fully forming and realizing their work as external to themselves. From 'throwing' the text – both as in a pot and as in a ventriloquist's voice.

So one of the first things that a writer needs to confront in taking on the 'I' is that this voice is as much of a projection, a character *out there* as well as in here, as any other. That it is as much of a construct as the third person.

This is clearly seen in those first-person narratives where the writer is evidently both circumspect about, yet sympathetic to, their central I-characters – think of Pip in Dickens' *Great Expectations* or Rushdie's Saleem Sinai in *Midnight's Children*. Conversely, there are third-person novels, particularly perhaps those using a high degree of stream-of-consciousness, in which a central character or characters come very close to passing as first persons, to speaking their story from the heart of the writing, like Woolf's *Mrs Dalloway* or Peter Carey's *Oscar and Lucinda*.

Then again, there is the device where the I-narrator is set up as a frame or continuity narrator interpreting or offering the story, but without being a central player, as in several of Conrad's novels or in Kate Atkinson's *Behind the Scenes at the Museum*. In such writing the distance of the first person from the writer, that is, their *artifactual* status, is very obvious. The labelled 'I' is in a way a subterfuge, pointing a way into the narrative, asking the reader to look further, at other characters, other narrative opportunities.

The I-decision, as I've said, pertains to all writing. But the question of how to pitch the 'I' becomes, perhaps, especially acute in confessional, autobiographical, and testimony work that has a strong stake in reality – that aims, for example, to set a record straight, to tell a 'true-life' tale, or to correct a reputation. In such cases it will be very important to writers to make sure that the first person has an independent existence in the story. They might think of themselves as taking the I-character by the arms, as it were, and pressing him/her away from them, to stand single and separate. The only child among siblings. The I-character, writers need to remember, must inhabit his/her own world, 'have a life' in the sense of having friends, family, habits, idiosyncratic likes and desires, also of having things they like to smell, sing, know; preferably, though not necessarily, separate from the writer's own.

There's an object lesson for what I've said so far in the following (at least initially) first-person account. In writing this, the shift to the third person halfway through created a clarifying and enabling distance, which then allowed me to switch back to the first person at the very end.

I began the short account by changing the central name. Immediately the story stepped away from me:

> Not so long ago I took a day trip to the outskirts of Amsterdam to attend my Dutch uncle Oom Jaap's funeral. A gentle, withheld man, the father of six children, Oom Jaap had long since become, in the land of my wish-fulfilment, a surrogate father. He was buried in a forested, hilly graveyard – for the Low Countries a steeply hilly graveyard. But even so his grave was reinforced with metal girders against the always treacherous Dutch water-table. The roses thrown on his coffin by his grandchildren and insistent niece [me? she?] kept snagging on these girders, and on the pine branches intended to camouflage them.
>
> On the way back from the funeral, in the melee of an airport goodbye, I lost my favourite hat. I had worn it in Oom Jaap's honour – or, to inflect now through third person – did she wear it in her uncle's honour?

I tried going on, in the third person. Notice how, with the shift in perspective, comes a change in tone and the points of visual focus. At a personal level it is now possible to say or imply more about this narrator's state of mind (displaced grief, a feeling of marginalization and defensiveness). But the observations of the first-person account are sharper, more immediate.

Heading out at three in the morning to catch the first airport bus, she pulled the hat low over her ears, a ceiling against a dark day, a cover for hair she had forgotten to wash. It was a soft-brimmed, grey-blue hat; she thought it suited her. Bets were that few others amongst her secular-minded relatives would be wearing a hat.

As it turned out the widow alone wore a hat, and one a lot like her own, pleated around the crown, taking shape from the wearer's head. The pairing of hats – her aunt's, her own – gave her satisfaction. She had made it over on the day, let no one in this busy and neglectful family make mistake. Under the cover of her hat, marked out but also subdued, excused by it, she wrested a rose from the bucket as it went round and aimed it straight through the pine branches, on to the coffin. A thud to show for it. The hat went missing at the airport, left on a seat in the restaurant during a crush of cheek-kissing. She missed it almost immediately but told herself it would somehow return – via lost property, the paging from the check-in desk. That hat was so much part of this day, part of the tribute of her visit, it wasn't possible it wouldn't find its way back.

It didn't though. It stayed drifting out there somewhere, for good, the lost badge of an intimacy that would now never change, grow closer or more distant. She imagined the hat dropped on the rose-clad coffin. And the process of distancing herself from it became for her, as she [I] began to write about the experience, an emblem of greater loss. An encoding, perhaps, of the loosening and separating involved in writing 'in person'.

I read the hat in this account as a tag, a sign, for a member of the funeral, separate from, yet connected to, me.

And the process of loosening involved in the writing helped in a sense to come to terms with the experience, to own it as my own account, with a sharper self-awareness and a more distinct sense of loss.

> She lost a hat.
> I lost my hat. An uncle also.

✍ As an exercise, based on the above, writers might think of creating and comparing parallel texts set up along similar lines: one in the third person, one in the first, and based on the same personal experience. They might then compare the first-person account closely with the third person, paying attention to the adjustment of distance and focus and to the objectification of the first-person speaker.

Alternatively, writers might select extracts from contemporary fiction in first and third person (for example Nick Hornby's *High Fidelity* for a highly personable I-voice; Tim Winton's *The Riders* for an involving third person) and translate these into the other voice, again looking out for the different degrees of objectification and character intimacy. It is helpful if such extracts include stream-of-consciousness and dialogue. Extracts from biography can also be useful for exercises transposing or refocusing third into first person.

Multiple Points of View
Victor Sage

Here I want to talk about point of view, not as a choice of pronouns, not as a technique of addressing the reader (first-, second- or third-person narrative voice), nor even as the creation of a speaking character, but as a sort of bias of ideas, a direction, that occurs in any piece of language. I want to talk about it not as a point but a 'view'.

When you begin anything as a writer, you intervene. And you intervene on things that have been written or thought beforehand. This act of intervention immediately brings more than one point of view into play. Let me give you an example which I have just found. Here's the opening sentence of an article from Hugo Williams' weekly 'Freelance' column in the *Times Literary Supplement*:

> I spent the morning at Camden Market looking for
> a kettle that didn't switch itself off automatically.
>
> 24 March, 2000, p. 18.

I am arrested by a sort of enigmatic crispness about this first sentence, which gets me thinking. At first, I just react: 'What a completely pointless thing to be doing!' But then the words of this apparently artless outburst give me a jolt, as I suddenly see that what I think is absurd in someone else's behaviour might, in this case, be pointing a mocking finger at my own habitual association between technology and usefulness. This is the moment at which the reversal of point of view shows itself: the new point of view taken up by the 'I' (the assumption that a useless or defective item might have a value) intervenes upon the cliché at work in the culture at large (the notion that technology is inevitably tied to progress), and the result is a feeling of enigma. A gap has opened up between these two points of view – the 'rational' and the 'absurd' – which are both created effortlessly, and kept in play, by this first sentence.

The narrative of an absurd quest is also connected, as the passage develops, with another lazy, habitual idea: that we also agree about what it means to waste one's time:

> Of course, if my old kettle had switched itself off
> automatically, it wouldn't have burnt itself out, but in
> that case I wouldn't have had any reason to waste my
> time looking for a new one. In vain, as it turned out.

Time, after all, is money – according to Benjamin Franklin, and contemporary British culture. So, for this 'I' to spend a whole morning looking for something so patently useless is an irrational activity. My curiosity is aroused: why does the 'I' do it? Then there's the nature of the object sought: it's clearly a rare, perhaps a forgotten, thing, a kettle you have to switch off, because even Camden Market didn't seem to have one. Surely, there's a touch of exaggeration here? To settle this question, divisions would have to open up between metropolitan and other readers' points of view. But after all, whether you live in London or Leeds, it's natural isn't it? Those sort of kettles have all gone. Gone where? But isn't it a bit strange, from another point of view, that now they all switch themselves off? You think: 'When did this happen? Wasn't there a time before they all switched themselves off?' Sudden vistas arise in my mind of a prelapsarian past in which kettles, whether gas or electric, just keep on boiling when you are not watching them. To your delight, because the water for your tea is still boiling and all you have to do is pour it in. Or to your dismay, because you've forgotten about it while you were out in the garden and it's boiled dry. Either way, it's a world that has recently disappeared, a bit of reality that's gone missing.

But what about the 'I'? We don't know why, on the level of biography, this 'I' did such a perverse and meaningless thing or had the time to do it in the first place. Is there a touch of obsession here? Or perhaps the 'I' is meant to teach us a lesson? Perhaps there's no biography at all. The 'I' is a didactic fiction? A mere pronoun. Will there be another reversal and an underlying endorsement of the capitalist notion of scarcity-value? Or is Williams just making up the inches of his column by sending his 'I' (and us with him) round in fictional circles?

I must read on to solve these questions. I'm hooked and plunged into a maelstrom of different points of view. I've begun to argue with myself. But imagine the pleasure of the writer in realizing the multiplicity of what he/she has set in motion. If I can feel these things as a reader, then these are some of the pleasures that Hugo Williams, the writer, must have got when he wrote these opening sentences.

Point of view is not just grammar, it is bias. When you write a sentence, you have two options. You can respond to all the other sentences it seems to ask for or sit back and listen to the silence it creates. Both are valuable and if you are writing poetry, you'll certainly need to be able to do the latter. But the first option is vital. Language is a place of differences, a noisy street, a city state; and your first intervention (that is, what you choose to present as your first intervention) actively generates a bias, a direction, a logic, which will conflict with other directions. It's your job as a writer to become aware of this process, and to exploit it, if necessary.

The process of articulating point of view is not frictionless. Of course, this sense of point of view – that it is a logic – overlaps with the notion of the angle from which a piece of writing is performed, but speaking isn't just 'seeing'. We tend sometimes to think it is, and that, if we have invented a point of view expressed in grammar or pronouns, we have invented a way of seeing. This is not always the case. Williams' innocent-sounding eccentric 'I' is important to the passage above, but it alone doesn't fully explain the presence of the other points of view that are simultaneously in it. Here I am using point of view in a different way, and thinking of it as occurring at a different level of writing practice from the technical (grammatical) question of address; of whether the narrative is first, second or third person; or, even, the position it is 'seen' from, which might be perfectly literal (an 'I' crouched behind the rose-red awning of the fourteenth junk stall in Camden market), but which also doesn't tell us anything in itself about the points of view (assumptions, arguments, opinions, prejudices, not just things seen) that are being set against one another.

Let me give you an example from fiction. The grammar of the passage, the choice of narrator, is only the vehicle of its point of view, and as such it may indicate the point at which one point of view ends and another one begins. Look at the bias in this passage, for example:

As a case history, *Lolita* will become, no doubt, a classic in psychiatric circles. As a work of art, it

161

transcends its expiatory aspects; and still more important to us than scientific significance and literary worth, is the ethical impact the book should have on the serious reader; for in this poignant personal study there lurks a general lesson; the wayward child, the egotistic mother, the panting maniac – these are not only vivid characters in a unique story: they warn us of dangerous trends; they point out potent evils. *Lolita* should make all of us – parents, social workers, educators – apply ourselves with still greater vigilance and vision to the task of bringing up a better generation in a safer world.

Widworth, Mass.   JOHN RAY, JR., PH.D.

If you listen carefully, you can just hear Vladimir Nabokov chuckle as he creates this fall-guy, 'John Ray Jr.', as the author of the 'Preface' to his most lovingly written book. Nabokov, that is, who makes no secret of his hatred of psychiatry and his contempt for Freud, whom he refers to as 'the Viennese quack'. The bias in American culture of the 1950s is towards this kind of hygienic moral earnestness. But Nabokov's ventriloquism creates another (decadent, 'European') point of view (the point of view of his narrator, Humbert Humbert), which works against this American grain. From this point of view, which suggests that the value of writing itself is amoral, and not necessarily 'progressive' in John Ray's municipal sense at all, there is only one sin: the vulgarity of thinking that art is justified by its usefulness.

Nabokov creates this writerly opportunity for himself by identifying a bias, and then writing against it, tongue-in-cheek. The deadpan nature of his parody shows how he has soaked himself in the point of view he is writing against. This is not just a narrative question; not just a matter of inventing a spoof editor, a character: it is a question of multiple points of view in the same piece of writing, a question of the logic of opinion, attitude, view of the world. Writing here is a kind of resistance to the insidiously deadening effect of a dominant point of view. It makes a hole in it, and inserts at least one other point of view.

But, if all writing generates multiple points of view, what about narrative? Despite the technique necessary to execute it, narrative is no exception to the axiom of multiplicity; and the most exciting narratives are, for me, the ones that go against some kind of grain.

We, as writers and readers, learn to read narrative often by having to occupy an uncomfortable or even blank position in language, by coming to realize its deep unacceptability to us, and in the process we insert the jolt, the counter bias. If you can't see the counter bias in a narrative, it's either because you've gone with the grain and excluded it, or (more likely) because you are it, but you haven't yet realized.

So, be prepared to reverse the logic of your selection when you explore narrative voices; be prepared to write against, even against the pretext of the voice that speaks. That position will be present whether you want it or not.

✍ Here's an exercise in constructing multiple points of view. Take any piece of writing with a strong rationale as your model and construct a story that reverses its direction without telling your reader. For example, instruction booklets usually work on the assumption that the step-by-step process they describe is in some way 'good' and has a positive outcome. Rewrite the instruction manual, adopting the opposite point of view (i.e. a character who expects or desires for some reason a negative outcome), but keep your tongue firmly in your cheek. For example, rewrite a barbecue cookbook from the point of view of a wife seeking to poison, blow up, or burn to death her husband; or a tennis manual, from the point of view of an infantile sadist. Survival manuals are very fruitful. Use the steps of the course of instruction as your plot, which can intensify in contradiction if you preserve the essential solemnity and earnestness (or heartiness) of the manual format.

I once saw a brilliant cartoon in a 1950s newspaper called 'Cain Builds a Shed' – gardening in the days before TV was often presented in a cartoon-like format by a person called 'Adam the

Gardener', who naturally had green fingers and could do DIY. But in this alternative cartoon, 'Cain' was murderous and couldn't knock a nail into a plank without making a mess of it. The resulting step-by-step explanations by 'Cain' were great, and the final picture of his 'shed' was a miracle of geometric misery that made me hoot. Let the model do the talking and the logic of the different points of view will emerge. This is what Swift does in his *Modest Proposal* – still the classic model for exploiting multiple points of view.

Whose Story Is It Anyway?
Three Short Essays on Points of View
Julia Bell

Narrative Choreography

One of the traps many writers can fall into when they first start to write scenes in a third-person voice is that they switch between their character's thoughts and feelings almost randomly. A third-person narrative is seen as an excuse for sowing everything about all the characters, and this kind of switching can create havoc with the way in which the action of the story is choreographed.

As with dance, good choreography is about choosing a focal point for the piece. A steady centre point, around which all the other action will gravitate. If you have chosen to narrate *all* your characters' thoughts and feelings you will find it problematic when you come to a scene in which two or more main characters interact. Who takes centre stage? Whose story is it? Where is the focal point?

If you are going to write multiple viewpoints you want to make sure you have a strong narrative voice. Annie Proulx, in *Close Range*, for example, is very deft at switching between characters, but only because her third-person omniscient viewpoint is so robust.

Developing a strong third-person voice takes practice and patience. You need to know how to write a scene before you can start switching between different characters.

Take this example:

> *Fred walked into the office, he was glad to see that Jane was already at her desk and sorting through his piles of mail. He looked over at her and smiled. Jane caught Fred's eye, how handsome he was, she thought.*
>
> *'Have you got the Adams report ready for me?' Fred asked, allowing himself to lean into Jane's shoulder a little. Jane flinched, feeling a blush rising up her cheeks. She wished he wouldn't stand so close.*

Now the writer has a problem. Who do we follow next? Does Fred go into his office or do we stay with Jane and her paperwork? Who is the story about? It would be more subtle to consider how Fred thinks about Jane and perhaps view her responses from his point of view, or think about how Jane sees Fred as he walks into the office.

> *Jane could see Fred walking towards her, only his head visible above the partitions. Oh God, he was looking at her. She looked at her desk and pretended she hadn't seen him.*
>
> *'Have you got the Adams report ready for me?' he asked.*
>
> *He was close now, leaning ever so lightly against her shoulder. She could feel the blush rising up her cheeks. Why did he always do this to her?*

The narrative becomes much more immediate if you stick closely to one character. It is better, to begin with, to restrict your point of view to one character. Choose a single protagonist and explore their world. If you find yourself slipping into other points of view, work out ways of implying, rather than showing, what the other characters might be thinking. Let the dialogue do the work for you. If you want to explore different characters, a good way to do this is to split them up, let each character narrate a different section of the story. Pagan Kennedy, in her novel *The Exes*, allows the four different band members a quarter of the book to narrate. Similarly, Jake Arnott in *The Long Firm* splits the novel up into sections, each narrated by a different character. The central character – Harry – never actually gets to narrate his own story; his life is told to us through an array of characters who, in some way or other, have all been witnesses to his gangster lifestyle.

A good omniscient narrator isn't simply one who switches from character to character but a narrator who can comment on the world that they have created in some kind of extra-textual way. The narrative voice analyses and explains the story it is telling, and takes a critical distance from the actions and the characters. The author, or implied author, becomes very present in the text. This is a difficult thing to get right. It takes confidence and a degree of certainty in your own perspective on the world. The long-winded and didactic narratives of someone like George Eliot, for example, where the text is constantly interrupted by a bossy author, isn't necessarily a particularly good, or modern, example to follow. Look at Annie Proulx, especially in *Close Range*, or Toni Morrison in *Beloved*. These narratives are masterpieces of narration. The author knows exactly when to give us information and exactly when to imply it.

✍ Try this: think of a small, single event, a fairground ride, a party, a night in the pub, a day by the sea. Take two characters who share the experience of this event and write about it, in first person, from the two different viewpoints. Now do the same thing with a different event, but this time write about it in third person, but stick rigidly to one character's point of view. Try to imply the other characters' feelings through the dialogue.

Up Close and Personal

You are a writer. You are not sure about this second-person thing. It's a bit strange isn't it? What kind of point of view is it? It's closer than first person, somehow, like having the writer whisper sweet nothings in your ear, done well, it tickles, gives you goosebumps. You have been reading lots of stories by Ali Smith, who does this kind of thing rather well, especially in *Other Stories and other stories* which you liked very much.

Ah, but I didn't read those stories, you say. I've never read that book in my life! Well, there's your problem then (this being a writing coursebook after all and there have to be problems), this second person is telling you what you have and haven't done. Marshalling you around, being bossy.

Not necessarily. 'You' is the voice of a shared experience, something so intimate that you want to convince your reader that you are of the same mind. It is not the hard, selfish 'I, I, I', always hectoring, rabbiting on about their experience, this is about you. As if the story is written for one person, no one else. *You.*

✒ Try this: think of the person you love most in world and write a story for them, addressing them in second person. No one else need know who your implied reader is, just you.

I Am the Walrus

And so you are. If you tell me that it's so.

A first-person narrative can be anyone or any*thing* it likes. It can be the bedsprings, the bookends, the cat's eyes, the ghost, the cook, the thief, the wife, the lover. The great joy of the 'I am' is that you can take almost any perspective and narrate it. Who are we to argue? We only have your words to go on.

✒ Try this: take four inanimate objects from different rooms in your house and let them describe the things that go on in your life. Because they are first-person narrators and very unreliable, they are, of course, allowed to make it all up. What glamorous things happen in the bedroom? What fabulous soirées in the lounge? What sumptuous meals prepared in the kitchen? What languorous hours in the bath?

7 Setting

Introduction
Paul Magrs

If I think about my Little Nanna Mason she's in the back parlour of her house in South Shields. It's the 1970s and the room hasn't been redecorated for forty years. She's chewing parma violets, sitting in a tiny chair by the old iron range. There's a faded portrait of her mother, Honoria, on the wall behind her. When she stands up to fetch a cake tin from the scullery, she's four feet tall. It's like being in a doll's house.

If I think about Jay Gatsby in F. Scott Fitzgerald's novel, then he's standing by a poolful of crazy reflections outside his ridiculous, ice-cream coloured mansion. He's watching the green light over the bay that to him signifies the proximity of his lost love, Daisy. Daisy who will one day visit and go through his cupboards and break down in tears at the sight of all his beautiful shirts.

If I think of anyone – from life or from a book – it's always in a context. They always come with a setting; a certain place and time; a whole set of circumstances and accoutrements clustered around them. Jay Gatsby created an opulent fantasy life for himself in order to show what a success he had made of his life. He threw weekly parties to flaunt himself in a fantastic light. My Little Nanna Mason in South Shields had a house crammed with generations' worth of family hand-me-downs; thick white linen and old silver stashed away in the dark, heavy furniture. Then she died and the whole street was pulled down, all of that was dismantled; the impedimenta of her life broken up and squirreled away by relatives.

When you present any kind of character in fiction they need some kind of backdrop. They need something to anchor them firmly and believably in their moment and their milieu.

There must be some novels, somewhere, in which no setting at all is apparent. Perhaps they are set somewhere timeless and dehistorisized and belong to no single place. In them, voices are simply heard, talking away to each other, probably about philosophical matters. If we were to read such a book, I imagine that even then we would, as readers, start to invent the setting for ourselves. As the disembodied voices rambled on, we would be wanting to know what the room looked like; what pictures were on the walls; what kind of curtains were hanging at the window.

The reader is endlessly curious about the circumstances of the characters they are engaging with. Not only do we want to know about the ins and outs of their personalities – the twists and turns of their psychology, the low-down on their love lives – we also want to know how and where they live. We want to know what it looks like and what it smells like. We want to find out what's in their kitchen cupboards and their bedroom drawers.

Fiction allows the reader to become the most discreet and the most untraceable of house-breakers. We get to look inside the homes of others without their ever finding out that we have been there.

Setting is one of the most useful means of getting your characters to give themselves away. Rather than having some ghastly self-revelation in the form of an interior monologue or in an exchange of dialogue, it's always more effective simply to slip in some telling detail about the place in which the characters find themselves. Much better to show them interacting with their environment.

Film, of course, is very good at this. Film is the medium in which so much about a character and their context can be explained with hardly a word being uttered. Think of the musty house where Norman Bates lives alone with his mother; those loving close-ups that dwell on the stuffed birds and the terrifying staircase. I'm also thinking of the overly neat, painfully chintzed-up house where the photographer and his wife live in Mike Leigh's film *Secrets and Lies*. Its very chintziness betrays the sterility of their lives.

This used to be called, in English literature, the pathetic fallacy, which was never a very good name for it. How everything that surrounded a character was a clue to, or an expression of, everything inside them. Cathy galloping pell-mell across the tempestuous moors in *Wuthering Heights*. That was always a good example; her spirit animates her setting.

It doesn't have to be as dramatic as that, of course.

In a stage play it is the stage manager who selects and places the props that will be needed. It is they who are entrusted with finding just the right accoutrements to help the characters behave convincingly in their environment. Writing fiction, you have to be your own stage manager and set designer too (not to mention actors and director . . .).

It's not like writing a play, though, and you need more than a few notes to tell the reader where we are and what it's like. As the story goes on, the reader needs to be reminded of the setting. They need to gather up more and more detail, all of it sensually and vividly recreated. The effect must be cumulative so that, by the end of the scene, the reader has a full, three-dimensional image of the place. It must be as rich and full as possible in order to convince them that they, too, have been in that place.

Whenever you create a character and a setting, make sure you have lists of objects, descriptions of furniture, seemingly irrelevant details about their setting to hand. Some of this material you will never use in your final version of the piece of work. But you will know what is in their room, what they are surrounded by, and this gives you confidence to bring that place to life. Try collecting pictures from magazines, newspapers; put them together with old photographs. Keep scrapbooks of pictures of rooms in which your characters might live.

✍ An interesting exercise in setting you might try is to take a photo of an unknown person from a newspaper and juxtapose it with a photo of a room from a magazine or brochure. Write them into that setting. How will they react? Do they feel at home?

Setting is a confidence trick, of course. You haven't transported your reader anywhere at all. They're still sitting in the same place. But as the action and dialogue of your scene has gone on, you've been skilfully dropping in precisely rendered snippets – smells and sounds and glimpses – of the world around your characters. The reader is always apt to be hoodwinked by these small, vibrant signs of a solid world around them.

We're always wanting to be transported elsewhere. It's why we read fiction.

The hardest part is dropping in these clues about setting in a subtle enough manner. Too many writers do the lazy thing and begin with an announcement in shorthand:

> *'Times Square. June 1927 . . .'*
> *'It was a drizzly November night in Manchester . . .'*

Then they forget to give us anything else. Maybe one or two reminders later on – a glimpse of skyscraper, pigeons, a hotdog vendor, a shop front quickly and sketchily described; bland, inexact images.

The whole setting needs creating from the ground up. It has to be full and economic at the same time.

I like the setting to be immediately vivid and often the best way to achieve this is to begin with very small details. Choose aspects of the setting that would seem most pressing to the characters in the scene; then build outwards as they notice more and more out of the corner of their eye. Writers often make the mistake of trying to go for the big picture first; get it all into one grand, bland gesture. Best to stick to the small idiosyncratically chosen details of a setting and let them do their cumulative work.

To bring a place to life effectively you have to draw upon all your resources. Every place has its own distinct atmosphere and this changes minutely over time. Everyone knows this, and that is why readers cannot be fobbed off with a weakly drawn setting. They can always sniff out something inexpertly drawn; it doesn't ring true. It reads as if the writer has no experience of this place. It doesn't anchor them in a precise, historical, geographical location. It's so indistinct it could be anywhere, at any time. Readers really hate that.

One of the reasons I love the fiction of Katherine Mansfield so much is that, in each of her stories, she immerses us in a particular flavour or atmosphere. The light is different in every single one of them – whether we are on a train in France or in an immaculate, festive drawing room before a dinner party. A bristling sensitivity is at work in her writing and she weaves these evocative phrases through the main action. Whatever row or epiphany her characters are having, Mansfield always grounds us back into her present scene. We are always anchored to the immediacy of the present moment and, when flashbacks come, we are always enticed into the past by the smells and sights of earlier settings.

What I have always done to work at getting this effect is to put myself in a variety of locations, all over the place – each distinct from the other, each drenched in its particular ambience. A Yorkshire tea room in late afternoon thundery gloom. Lost in a Venetian alleyway of blood-red brick, the place reeking of damp wool at night. A Perthshire glen glazed with frost, and Darlington town centre as the shops close and the pubs open on Christmas Eve. In each of these places I would take down reams of notes. I'd make each of my senses work overtime – work as hard as Katherine Mansfield's – and I'd take down every single thing that occurred to me or impressed itself upon me.

I would note them down any old how at first, not even trying to make sense or sentences. I'd want, at this stage, lopped-off and vivid phrases that, upon rereading, home again, would re-evoke the whole scene for me as richly as possible. And if characters had strayed upon that scene (the woman with shopping bags in Venice who looked curiously like an Italian Dusty Springfield), then so much the better. They can make a cameo appearance in the fiction that eventually comes from the field notes.

It's very like being a painter making on-the-spot sketches. The point is to get the details right and exact. It's like being a film-maker, shooting the footage for the cutaway shots that can later be spliced into the main shots, building up flavour and mood. But it's better than both these things; these are a writer's notes about setting. They are not just visual, like a film-maker's. We can also have smells and exaggerations and thoughts and distortions. And, unlike a painter or a photographer, we aren't static. Our observations exist in time. With a couple of lines we can describe the light glancing off the bank's windows as the sun sinks behind the precinct, or the way that a gondolier takes his stately time negotiating bridges and the old lady sprawled at his feet on blue satin cushions is entranced by the shifting reflections in the bottle-green of the canal.

We can take these details and slant them for our own purposes, as we reread them. Each of them tells us their own stories. Each detail sticks in our minds and our notebooks like burrs. When we go back to these notes on setting, each of them tries to snag us back, wanting to be used. We can hone them down, make them as precise as possible and use them, integrally, in the stories we tell about those places. At that point they become things that your characters are noticing or things that are thrown into sharp and telling relief by the presence of your characters.

Take your notebook somewhere. Find a spot where you can observe from. Start making these kinds of notes, slowly building up the bigger picture by noticing the tiny details. If you are thinking of a certain character, try to see the setting through their eyes. What would leap out at them as the most interesting point of focus? What would fascinate them? What would annoy them? Don't try to pull your observations into a coherent whole yet. Try to get as many impressions down as possible. Later, at home, you can choose what to use or discard.

Think of yourself as a Renaissance portraitist. Everything you painstakingly pop into the background – every little bauble and accoutrement – all of it is there for a reason. You want your reader to look long and hard and to be soaked in the accumulation of all this detail. You want them to come out of the scene understanding the whole, concerted picture you have put together around your principal figures.

People talk about virtual reality as if it were a new thing. Placing people into a fully rendered, re-created environment. Fictive settings were always about being virtually real.

Exploring Home
David Almond

All lives can seem ordinary to those who live them. All places can seem dull to those who inhabit them. It is easy to be tempted by the thought that the exotic or the exciting can only occur in other lives, in other far-flung places. It's easy to imagine that the material and setting for our fiction can only be discovered far from home. And perhaps we're all wary of the label 'local author'. As Flannery O'Connor said, 'The woods are full of regional writers, and it is the great horror of every serious . . . writer that he will become one of them.'

When I began, I wanted to be seen as anything but 'Northern'. I turned away from home. I wrote stories set in the garden suburbs of Surrey, on the surface of Mars, in the Australian outback, in totally imaginary worlds. I abstracted myself, perhaps wanting somehow to remake myself, to become something like the writers I loved: like Márquez, perhaps, like Borges. My settings and characters would be as strange as theirs. Then I turned and looked again, and saw that my true imaginary world, the source of my joys, fears and obsessions, was the small place in which I'd grown and which had surrounded me for most of my life. Despite myself, my writing had begun to focus more and more on that place.

I started deliberately to explore the place and to make it my fictional territory. I stuck its maps on my study wall. I pinned up photographs. I explored library archives. I sifted through our family files and photographs. I read history and geography. I made journey after journey back to the place, simply wandering through it and allowing it into myself. I smelled it and touched it. I copied down names of streets and shops and the names fading on gable walls. I brought souvenirs to my study: chestnuts from a graveyard tree, fragments of coal from beneath thin turf, a broken blue eggshell. Exploring the place as if I were a foreigner, I was flooded with memories and dreams. I filled notebooks with scribbled speculations, doodles, images, drawings, conversations, names, dates, maps, characters. I mingled factual details of the place with invented, imaginary details. I merged reality and dream, truth and lies. In the blending of the real and the imagined, possible stories started to emerge. This was a place where particular things happened, where things were in a particular place, but in the search for fictional truth things didn't need to stay that way. Some of the people I'd known need never have been born. The dead need not have died. Names could be changed, chronology could be changed. Imagined people could live in real houses, real people in imagined houses. Geography could be reassembled. The maps could change. I wrote a series of stories set in that tiny area of Tyneside. They were about the events of my childhood: insignificant events in an insignificant town. The stories were based on real events, but they were shaped as fiction, and contained sufficient inventions to be described as fiction. I wrote them for a tiny audience, my sisters and brother, who had experienced those events along with me. Once the stories had been accepted by this first audience, I sent them out into the wider world and, paradoxically, I began to reach my widest readership yet.

There is, of course, no real paradox. The local can contain the universal. The part can stand for the whole. Some of our greatest books – *Wuthering Heights*, *Ulysses*, *Sons and Lovers* – are 'local' books, whose authors and characters have a passionate and dynamic relationship with their local landscape. Márquez' characters and settings, even at their most apparently magical and exotic, would be quickly recognized by the people that Márquez had grown up with, by his relatives, his friends, his neighbours. But this isn't a simple restatement of the advice to 'write what you know', which can just lead to thin and undernourished fiction, flimsy sketches of a superficially observed world, quaint tales touched with local colour. Maybe the best way to 'know' a place properly is to move purposefully away from it, then to turn to look again. The journey away is as crucial as the coming home. We can then look at our local setting as both an intimate and a stranger, and our work can have that sense of risk, exploration and discovery that all good fiction needs. As soon as we begin to write about a place, the place starts to change. It is re-created and becomes an imaginary place, a place fit for fiction. Reality is the starting point, that's all. Think of Hardy's Wessex, Dickens's London, Kafka's Prague, Faulkner's Yoknapatawpha County. We can reshape our world to make it live up to the opportunities and demands of our stories.

All writing is a form of play. As soon as a child comes to know something he/she begins to play with it. The walk turns into a leap and a dance, the word turns into a gabble and a song. As humans, we test what we know and try to see what is possible, what our knowledge might lead us to. Writers organize those possibilities into stories. Those stories have to be set somewhere. Perhaps the best setting can be found in the author's home, where the deepest knowledge might release the most creative play.

✍ To begin this kind of play, visit the place that you think of as home. Travel through it. On foot is probably best. Make notes as if you were a stranger. Be objective: record the tiniest details, the scents and sounds and textures. Record historical and geographical fact. Write down the names that you see and hear around you. Gather little souvenirs. Be imaginative: speculate on the lives that might have been lived in this place. Redraw the maps: a new spring, perhaps, a new street of houses. Throughout your travels, allow your memories to be stirred. Write them down. Don't separate observation, speculation and memory. Record them on the same pages. Allow them to stimulate each other, to interfere with each other. Don't try to force stories into life. Allow yourself to be absorbed into your re-created world – in which even you and those who are closest to you

are becoming fictions – and watch for the glimmerings of new stories
that begin to come to life of their own accord.

Landscapes and Language
Graham Mort

'All art is a vision penetrating the illusions of reality.'

ANSELL ADAMS

'Everybody has to be somewhere!' muttered Spike Milligan in one of
the early *Goon Shows*. His existential bon mot hits a fundamental note
and is more various than it seems. Like it or not, we have to *be* as long
as we are alive and sentient and we have to be *somewhere*. Places are
where we depart from, move through, arrive in. Places are where we
sleep and dream of other places, until we can no longer differentiate
between remembering a dream and remembering what once was.
This perceptual oscillation is peculiar to human consciousness, its
meltdown of actuality and imagination – and most of the world is
imaginary because we only touch against a tiny part of it with our
physical senses. In this context, imagination has a very practical
function: it keeps the rest of the world in place whilst we get on with
being where we are.

Part of the fascination of landscapes is their flux of constancy and
change. They alter with each moment of passing light, with each day
of each season, yet they remain recognizable over centuries. Their
geological clocks tick infinitesimally slowly compared to their
biological ones – and *we* are all biology. Landscapes act as reference
points in literature, mediating between the living reader and the
dead writer. The landscapes of the Norse sagas are still recognizable
today as are the New Mexican mesas that D. H. Lawrence described

in the 1920s. Matrices of geological and biological time, landscapes – by which I mean urban, suburban and rural terrain – act as catalytic converters for human experience and memory, their concrete realities melting to release the ghosts of time.

The dictionary definition of landscape implies artifice, the laying out or deliberate construction of aesthetic space. This meaning of the word connects us to the shaping force of human activity; *land* itself emerges through seismic upheaval but *landscapes* are conceived, discovered, designed, perceived, communicated. In this sense they share their origins with literature. Our experience of landscape mediated through time – seconds, minutes, hours, years – finds a literary correlative: haiku, lyric poem, short story, heroic poem, novel. Landscapes are not mere present-tense actuality, they are a translation through the senses, through the energy of dreams and desire, through the conjugations of language and the fusions of literature into what *was*, what *is*, what *could* be. Landscapes are the past and the future, as well as the eye through which each present moment slips. And so literature becomes its own reality – witness the literary sleuths who walk the moors at Haworth each year to match a physical landscape to an imaginative one.

Landscapes have been shaped by, and shape, human imagination. This shaping brings a spiritual and political dimension – Arcadia, the Wasteland, Tir na N'Óg, No Man's Land, Narnia, the Promised Land, Homeland, Fatherland. From here it's a short, heart-stopping step to *lebensraum*. Beyond the notion of *terra firma* (with all its connotations of safety, stability, irreducibility) lies the notion of *land* and *landscape* – what is *seen* and what is *desired*. Land and language are central to the search for human identity, the extension of self and society through conquest. So, from the thought of land to the thought of empire – that idealized landscape, that vision of social, political and economic unity, with its own lingua franca.

Cities, those stony metaphors of empire, are also landscapes embodying what is constant and what is quickly changing in their quarried-out geology, their architectural conquest. Buildings succeed each other in archaeological layers, skyline succumbs to skyline, but within all cities there are natural constants. Most major cities have rivers and every river has its own songs – the Tyne, Thames, Mersey, the Severn, Tweed, Solway. Each country and each nation is a poem of rivers, a psalm of waters. Cities, too, have their tarmac rivers, their roads to elsewhere and otherness; wormholes through space and time that have accelerated unimaginably from their medieval origins. Routes out of there to imagined counterparts, other countries, cities, ways of speaking and being; and it is in terms of such otherness that our own identities consolidate and dissolve.

All literature is made up of stories, and the centrality of landscapes to storytelling is fundamental. The first dances, then the first songs, narratives and seductions must have emanated from journeys. Hunters left the tribal shelter and returned. Now there was something new to say, a place that was not *here*, a time that was not *now*, a people that was not *us*. And here is the effort of language bringing them to mind. Those first storytellers inflamed listeners with the fear and desire of elsewhere – places as imaginary as they were real took on mythical dimensions, dwarfed mundane realities, became parallel spirit worlds inhabited by the demons of the subconscious. With the effort of maintaining and extending imaginative worlds came sophistications of language, which could hold them in the mind's eye, make them resonant with meaning, significance, psychic energy.

Our human capacity for reflection – literally immersing ourselves in a world that is not here, but reflected through the prisms of thought – is maintained by our naming and energizing of the world through words. We are able to be in many places at once and in many ways. The intricate language of bees is often marvelled at, its complex interaction of pheromones and physical movement that describes the location of flowers in relation to the sun's angle over the land. But it does nothing that a half-dozen words in any human language can't achieve in seconds, through nouns that identify the world, verbs that energize it, adjectives that colour it, adverbs that say how it is, conjugations of tense that place it in the slipstream of time and thought itself.

Historically, landscapes are the earth from which generations of human beings have won or persuaded sustenance. Land is transformed in song and legend into human form, its hills and valleys representing undulations of a mother's, father's or lover's body. This resonates through the Australian Aboriginal notion that land shapes and landscapes were sung into existence by totemic ancestors who remain embedded in the Dreamtime, in a mythological land that became real. The same association of song and land is made in Christian culture where the land and its abundance are pronounced by the godhead. These places where we are or have to be are places that exist because we ask them to, because we are there to talk about them.

Despite an awesome accumulation of cultural baggage, we walk across landscapes carelessly, build shopping precincts on pagan burial grounds, plough up Saxon field boundaries, and dig out fragments of Roman tiles with our dahlias. Landscapes are ineffably extraordinary and at the same time hardly worth attention. Dorothea Lange once remarked that she used a camera so that others could see without a camera. Writers, too, reclaim experience for others to hold through words more intensely than they can in reality, where a thousand exigencies detain us. If we know a place that we love, our instinct is to share that place with others, to lead them there by the hand or with the tongue, or, since we are human, with both.

A landscape poem or descriptive prose passage is always more than pure description; even if unpeopled it projects and embodies the sensibility and spirit of the writer. Landscapes in this respect are psyche-scapes, metaphors representing the yearnings and aspirations, hope, betrayal, anger and bitterness that we see in them. Paradoxically, all art that figures a landscape is both more and less than the things it represents. Language, because of its complexity of associations, can never be transparent; it represents a complex array of choices, which are driven both by impulse and conscious selection.

Our litany of words for water flowing through the land – valley, river, canyon, sewer, gutter, stream, beck, rill, waterfall, gill, trickle – shows a vast range of association, each word bringing its own energy, coloration and atmospheric. Artistic truth is selective and is achieved through invention, artifice – and lies. Human language that can bring pin-sharp images of the real can bring about equally accurate images of the patently non-existent, creating fantastic illusions of unity by rearranging the components of reality into an imaginative whole.

Orientation is the key feature of a human being's relationship to the land. When we wish to replicate our journey for others, we resort to maps that both symbolize and name. Place names supply plentiful evidence of the concrete nature of that fixing of topographical features through language. The first maps were songs, and in this respect a landscape *is* language. Words shape landscapes into portable, memorizable journeys, and in turn landscape shapes language into tongue, dialect, idiolect. Just as each place is voiced, so it gives voice.

In the context of teaching creative writing, landscapes present rich opportunities. Each new place, whether it be a service station on the M6, with its complexities of architecture, reflective surfaces and human activity, or a mountain in Wales, with its rock, thorn trees and circling kites, offers new experience and puts pressure on language to map and express it. The ancient war between urban and rural cultures has shifted its locus many times. Now all that is contemporary seems urban, cool and hip. Yet the countryside is still there, still lived in; not the wilderness that city kids imagine, but a place subtly sculpted by human activity. It is the writer's job to see through surfaces, to approach the existential truth of a place. As we have seen, that truth is both experienced and invented, is both actual and beyond actuality.

Everywhere in a landscape we are faced with human presence or absence. A depopulated landscape is unbearably sad to us, as if human activity gives the landscape meaning and definition. To stand on the beach at Dun Chaoin in County Kerry, Western Ireland, is to be in one of the saddest, most beautiful and abandoned places in the British Isles. Ironically, you are a step away from a stone commemorating the filming of *Ryan's Daughter*, which made the place legendary; and the deserted houses on Great Blasket seem so close that you could lift them off by hand. The physical reality of the place is underlain by a mass of cultural paradoxes that complicate each moment of being there.

A writer tries to be a stranger in each place they inhabit, deliberately defamiliarizing it, imbuing it with their curiosity, shedding assumptions. Naming the world with our transferable vocabulary recognizes the recurrence of similar artefacts, flora and fauna in different places. Lacking the big picture, we might not fully grasp that crows are crow-like wherever they occur. Species and genus with their precise Latinate labelling system are great short cuts to orientation and identification. Generation by generation we put together that big picture, the world map, the tree of life. But knowledge can be lost within a generation, and with every cataclysm that has overtaken human settlement the process of naming the world and its lifeforms and places has begun afresh, just as language has been lost and begun again. We are both humbled and inspired by this gift of tongues. Some sense of the complications of how we are alive as sentient and articulate human beings is an essential starting point for trying out those gifts.

The first stages of writing may arrive in elegant sentences, quatrains or rhythmical lines of free verse. But it's almost a truism of the creative writing process that they are more likely to arrive as an inchoate mass of vocabulary, which tries to grab at experience without at first shaping it into literary form. Set out with a literary template for experience and you are likely to suffer from 'thinking on purpose', from contrivance that lacks vitality and freedom of association. The strategies used by creative writing tutors might not necessarily conform to their own, often less strategic, working practice, but the process of experience, response, shaping, finishing does correlate to the internal mental processes of the writer, the way in which personal experience is shaped and surrendered to the reader. In order to make a piece of writing we need verbal raw material, and writing workshops need to offer a way into the process – a model of development which the student writer can make their own.

So we turn our students loose with notebooks to absorb, explore and express in words and metaphors. We implore them to be alive in a landscape; to be alive above all through the liberties and constraints of language. After this initial, impulsive response comes the process of selection. How to make language ductile, to make it work for us? How to make it say what we mean and allow it to say whatever else it has to say, too? In shaping language we shape our experience retrospectively – and when a moment moves into the past it passes into its own fictional possibilities.

My own writing workshops try to grab at the ways in which we are alive. The simultaneous nature of experience apprehended by all five senses, by the imagination and the intellect firing together. To be alive is to act *and* to think, to do *and* to reflect, to remember *and* to anticipate. To be alive is to dilate and contract, to close down much of our experience in order to open up what seems essential. Otherwise the overwhelming richness of experience stuns us with sensory madness.

The impact of experience on vocabulary begins with the noun. What are these things around me? It extends to the verb. What are they doing? And how? And why? Each successive question puts pressure on the drafting process. The writer has to take a landscape and by describing it introduces the element of time. Just as language spills from our mouths, so time slips over the land. The simplest sentence demonstrates this:

The big black bird went slowly over lots of green trees

We have some specialized vocabulary here – 'birds' and 'trees' and 'green' indicate the application of generic principles to the scene the writer is confronting. We have a sense of place, and the bird moving through it introduces temporal action. With more knowledge of nature and its vocabulary the sentence can be energized to create a more detailed visual image:

The raven went slowly over the forest.

Now the sentence appeals to a more specialized reader, one who appreciates the specific noun for a particular large black bird and the collective noun for trees. Its content is more precisely visual. But the verb is weak, supported by an adverb, and the forest unspecified. So more specialization is called for in the drafting process:

> *The raven spiralled over the larch wood.*

or

> *The raven drifted over the beech copse.*

We might employ a nautical metaphor:

> *The raven sailed over scrub pines.*

Or pluralize the noun and hint at the mating display of ravens:

> *The ravens tumbled over stunted thorns.*

Now assonance and alliteration give the line a rhythm section, a poetic tendency.

We have played with a basic unit of description, but we have also worked carefully within a geographical and ornithological system of knowledge. When we select the word 'raven', a remote northerly location is suggested and a cultural referent invoked – the association of ravens with death and war. Once we have our basic unit of allegorical sense we might decide to intensify it, sacrificing the idea of flight to take account of plumage and light, suggesting a more sinister aspect to the already portentous bird:

> *The raven glittered over the copse.*

'Copse' echoes 'corpse' and we might choose it for that associative reason alone, but the isolated stand of trees also reinforces the singleness of the bird. We might go for a more deliberately compressed and Gothic effect:

> *The raven ghosted the copse.*

A blackbird or a little dipper or a ptarmigan would have led us down an entirely different developmental road and another step in this process is to alter the noun itself for an alternative. By transforming the initial noun on which sense is predicated, action and location also alter and the experience is fictionalized:

> *The condor flapped over the jungle.*

This still presents a big black bird flying slowly over green trees, but our location is shifted towards South America and the verb has to accommodate the hugeness of the bird by slowing itself in the chain reaction initiated by the new noun. To go a step further and change noun, verb and tense is to launch ourselves on a new and urgent imaginative trajectory:

> *The parrot explodes over the forest.*

Or to introduce the now exotic bird into a northern European location:

> *The parrot hovers above the tundra.*

Or with a touch of the surreal:

> *The macaw swoops on Big Ben.*

Now we have moved from location to dislocation. We have introduced an optical illusion, an imaginative space between the bird and its environment, disturbing the reader's expectations. We have invited the reader to fill that gap so that a story can spark across it. We have created, in the words of Susan Sontag, writing about photography, an 'invitation to speculation'.

This simple example shows some of the pressures and possibilities of language, some of the ways in which actors, activity and location must be brought together, but then can be made to diverge. In an urban context it might easily have begun: 'The long black vehicle went through the streets,' and opened a different range of possibilities. Our initial impulse is shaped by what is, but refinement is shaped by what *could, might* or *ought* to be. This not only changes language, but changes the imaginative landscape. As each moment of our experience passes and is assimilated, it extends our liberty as writers to use invention, lies, fabrication, half-truths and dissimulation to get at that other truth: the vision beyond the illusion of reality.

Imagining Rooms
David Craig

A guideline that usually works well for writing in workshops is: 'Describe a room so that we can gauge who lives there.' At one time apprentice writers tended to begin their prose fiction with an image of an alarm clock ringing and a sleepy arm reaching out to turn it off. (I rather think the film of Sillitoe's *Saturday Night and Sunday Morning* began with this classic item.) Presently, it became even commoner to come across the image of the ring left by a coffee mug on a table, which could represent almost anything from the atmosphere in bedsit-land to loneliness, meaninglessness, and general angst.

The beauty of the lived-in room idea is that it is both open and specific. The room can be anywhere on a gamut from the lighthouse in Fay Weldon's *Life and Loves of a She Devil* to the stark prison cell in Robert Bresson's film *Le Condamné à Mort*. It could have the eerie mixture of the sparsely symbolic and the physically specific that worked powerfully in Kubrick's *Full Metal Jacket*. It's probably no accident that my examples so far have come more from cinema than from literature. To ease writers away from the unduly self-centred, I've had the habit of using terms from film in discussing their work. 'How do you *see* this character?' I might ask, if the dramatis persona was remaining hazy (psychologically as well as physically, since people's characters inhere so much in their physique). Or again: 'Who would you cast for this character if your piece was filmed [or staged]?' Or again: 'Some passages of your piece are rather general, rather summarized. Can you conceive of them on camera? Can you write them as *scenes*?'

Like any approach whatsoever, it is no good taking this as a rule or all-purpose, guaranteed formula. What is the 'setting' for Molly Bloom's stream of thoughts at the end of *Ulysses*? How long would it take to specify the setting for *Krapp's Last Tape*? Nevertheless we do, most of us, live in a space that teems with things, as well as with smells and memories. When I go into someone's home for the first time, I have to restrain myself from treating it as a gallery and walking round the room peering in fascination at each picture and chair, each book and flower, which perhaps shows how specialized an animal a writer tends to become.

'Setting' is quite like 'set'. We live out our lives in the little theatres of our homes, a notion taken to a sickening extreme last year by the producer of the BBC programme *Changing Rooms*. He described our homes as 'the stages we design in order to present ourselves to our friends'. Only the most self-conscious of us would go that far. The literary case is different, it lies in the medium of art – an art that partakes of poetry, storytelling, theatre, cinema, radio, painting and dance. This means that what the writer must do is not so much to catalogue the contents of a room as to select from the dozens (hundreds, thousands) of physical items it is made up of and use them to suggest the time of day, the time in history, the light (or lighting), the habits of the occupants. After all, this setting (or set) is not a sealed box. It opens out into 'the world out there' or is shuttered against it (as in Ibsen's *Ghosts*). Say it is smoky-blue; a thick atmosphere is steadily pressing down from the ceiling to the floor, and the window square is stuffed with sacking: we're in a Highland crofter's house in 1853. The same interior is windowed, with panes of a glass in a fixed frame, and one of the occupants is coughing: it is the same house in 1912, and tuberculosis has become more prevalent with the introduction of glazed, immovable windows. The same interior is empty of people, the grate is empty of fire; all we can see, in the way of human traces, is a cup stuck to its saucer by dried-up tea and, on the mantelpiece, beside the stopped clock, a tinted postcard of an Empire Exhibition in Toronto before the Great War: it is the present and nobody has been back to this deserted house for seventy years. (This is an actual cottage I explored near Mulroy Bay in Donegal in the early seventies.)

Time is in the room, history is in it, and character, and grief and elation, and the grind of work. All this inheres in and flows from the visible, tangible things. Technically speaking, plot flows from them. (Is the writer making events start to happen at this point? Or have we dropped in on a sequence that may stretch away in both directions, in flashback and in ongoing narrative or even flash-forward, à la Vonnegut, as the work unfolds?) Unless the setting is sufficiently specific, not enough will be able to flow from it, and the writer may lurch into melodrama to kick-start the action. (I well remember Kazuo Ishiguro wincing when one of my students started a piece with the character snatching up the phone as soon as it rang. This struck him as altogether too coarse and hackneyed a grab at the reader's interest.)

A writer asked to 'Describe a room, etc.' will almost always come up with something quite characterful and atmospheric. It may not be quite distinct or vivid enough. 'Magazines lying about' – which ones? 'Gloomy wallpaper' – the colour? The pattern? How old or how fresh? In making some such suggestions to the writer you are able to work with something specific and also to explore the culture you share with her or him as you lead from the less to the more sharply focused. Here is where the *conversation*, of which each writers' workshop must consist, may either run into the sand or give rise to green shoots – the apprentice writers can feel bullied or respected, forced or helped, constrained to imitate some model or other or inspired to create something of their own.

The room you are imagining is really as wide as the world and as high as the sky. The room could be the gestalt of a person who had been blind and deaf from birth. It could have no foundations because it was the control cabin of a spaceship. It could lose its solid walls – the 'leaves of day' could grow over everything, the 'hard towers of apartment buildings' could loom up and dominate, as in Arthur Miller's *Death of a Salesman*. The degree of the actual or lifelike should never be prescribed in a guideline, since it is not a blueprint, it is a stimulus, a pang of smell or touch or sight sent into the imaginations of all those in the workshop (including the 'teacher'), and not a sort of inventory or timetable of what the writers are about to make.

It is true that in an age still under the influence of the realistic novel, from Jane Austen through George Eliot to early Lawrence and David Storey, apprentice writers are liable to feel that if they are to keep a grasp of their work as it unfolds and branches out in many directions, they had better anchor it in this or that suburb, or office, or holiday resort, and in a time quite near the present. (Think of the research you need as soon as you stray from your own time, all those different sorts of slang, all those different cars and jackets and brands of beer!) This is surely as much something to free ourselves from as to found ourselves on. We must be limber and fanciful as well as clear-eyed observers of what is there. We may want to make our moor as symbolic as the heath in *Lear*, where the audience can be persuaded with Gloucester that the ground ends in a chalk cliff teeming with crows and choughs, although there is nothing there but boards. We may wish to make it as knowledgeably detailed as Hardy's Egdon Heath, with its paths of quartzite sand and its turf-cutters with their heart-shaped spades (although when I looked back into *The Return of the Native* just now I was surprised that the Heath was more of an emotional atmosphere and less of a physical place than I'd remembered).

Writers will find their own level of the lifelike, according to the point they belong to on some gamut that stretches from the more 'poetic', where the focus is more on perceptions caught on the wing, to the more 'prosaic', where the focus is more on a known environment thoroughly specified. And 'the point they belong to' is anything but fixed. This month we may want to make the most of some store of material we happen to have on the rock scene in Manchester in the eighties or Napoleon's Russian campaign of 1812. Next month we may want to write a nightmare fable as little tied to a place and time as Kafka's *Metamorphosis*. One of the most pregnant discussions of writing I ever heard was between David Storey and David Mercer on television in 1970 or so. Storey was twitting Mercer ruefully about the playwright's happy freedom from the demands of the lifelike: if he wanted to put a bishop on stage, he didn't have to find out all about the internal management of the Church of England, whereas the novelist had to have, at least on tap, an exhaustive knowledge of the subject. Actually, it's not so much the form that counts as the particular aim of the writer using it. If we think of the setting for a work as the 'world' that stretches away in all directions from that bright-lit area in the foreground that we are mainly contemplating, it can be as strongly or as faintly drawn as the writer wishes. The 'vividness' of the work need not be a matter of specifying every feature of the environment supposedly surrounding this room or that house, and it does not have to be 'true to' a known, real place. The dust heaps, the dreary monstrous Mounds, in Dickens' *Our Mutual Friend* may have their 'originals' in Shoreditch or Hounds-ditch or any other ditch or none at all for all I care. They work in the novel because their gritty meanness is shaped to embody the hard-handed skinflints who own them and who behave as though they own their daughters. If Dickens had not known his 'setting' – that is, the entirety of London – with a physical intimacy and a great journalist's eye for a society, from its sewers to its law courts, he could not have selected from it with such fiery symbolism. What he did not have to do was 'put it all in'.

Suppose a couple are walking along the front in Skegness at half past three on a hot summer afternoon not long ago, picking their way between the heaps of plastic glasses which a barman is sweeping up into some kind of order, thinking of nothing but the enjoyment of each other they hope to have somewhere along the beach. The 'scene' is 'set' in 'an east coast holiday town. Summertime, early in the twenty-first century'. The writer may well not have felt that he/she was describing that place in Lincolnshire so much as evoking the unreal glare, the sweat between two hands, the expectancy ripening like a fruit between two people, their sense of being cut off by special feelings from the stickiness and the chatter and the throb that press in at the edges of their vision. A journalist might well write a piece with this same setting for the sake of its social actuality – this piece of holiday trade, this sample of the English at this time. The writer of the story (or the script, or the poem) is more likely to be focused on the emotional peak in the people's lives. The prom, the pub, the heatwave, the sand dunes and the sun-struck waves function in the passage, and have appeared on the screen of the writer's mind, as facets of the characters' experience. They are not mere backdrop or something to screen the embarrassing blank blacknesses behind the actors.

By the same token it will be best if the room described in our opening guideline is alive: the pint on the table half drunk, the music centre playing, the poster on the wall a little torn, the book on the arm of the chair open face down, the door half open. Since this room is really not a setting, it is not a small collection of typical late twentieth-century artefacts, it is a moment in an experience, and it arouses our expectations about what may come of it, so that we read on.

Outside Your Front Door
Julia Bell

We are all, in one way or another, a product of the landscape in which we live, but often the view from the window becomes so familiar that we stop noticing it any more. I find that when I have been away from my house for a while, especially if I've been abroad, things look very different, almost unfamiliar, on my return. As if the picture of my house that I've been keeping in my imagination is different from the real, visceral one I see every day. The dimensions of my space seem different, and it usually takes me a few hours to readjust to my surroundings again.

It's the idea that Barthes is referring to in *Camera Lucida* again. The topography that impacts upon the memory when the view is out of sight is an impressionistic memory of a landscape. The mind plays tricks, remembers bits and pieces, not the whole picture, and as a result the landscapes we keep in our imaginations are often only partial. I remember the big rectory that I grew up in in west Wales as moments, like snapshots. The cheap green carpet tiles that scratched our feet, the panes of frosted glass in the bathroom that made the light seem watery, vitreous, the velvety petals of the snapdragons in the front garden that I could squeeze to make look exactly like snapping dragons, the cawing of the rooks who built their messy nests high up in the chestnut trees every year, and then the big pats of twigs and feathers that would land on the lawn after a storm. On a recent visit to Wales I went back there and walked around the house, looking at it from the road. There is a new family living there now, a satellite dish on the wall, different curtains in the windows, no snapdragons in the front garden. The house seemed smaller than I remembered. The lawns weren't so expansive, the windows narrower, the exterior painting a different colour. It wasn't the same house as the one that I keep in my imagination.

I'm sure if I wrote down all the things I could remember about that house I would come up with pages and pages of description. I would be able to re-create that house on the page, but it wouldn't be an image of a real house. It would be a fictionalization of the house, because it would be drawn from my recollections. It would be based on the real world, but at the same time unreal because it is the product of a singular, magpie memory.

✍ Try this: write about somewhere you used to live. Describe the house in detail. Everything that you can remember from the colour of the bathroom to the plants in the front garden. Now use it as a setting for a story. Take some characters that you have created and let them live there.

Our landscapes are a part of our fictional voice. As has been said elsewhere in this book, a writer's imagination and imaginative associations are unique to them. A part of their fictional fingerprints. In writing it is best to use landscapes you know well. A writer writing about London when they've only been there once on holiday is likely to come up with a rehash of all the images of London they've ever seen in guidebooks, films on the TV. Write the landscapes that are close to home. The places you are familiar with. Don't be afraid to set your story in Caithness or Cumbria or Carmarthen or Cambridge. Write about where you know, where you live.

Recently I edited a book of stories from Birmingham for Tindal Street Press with the writer Jackie Gay. The idea of the book was to give the young writers who lived and worked in Birmingham some exposure, and initially we had asked for stories on the theme of 'transgression'. What came back to us in the post, however, was a picture of the city. Most of the writers seemed entranced by the details of the world around them, the roads, the towerblocks, the parks, the trees, the bikers, the estates, the nightclubs. Our idea of the book changed and we decided to present the anthology as a collection of stories that portrayed the topography of Birmingham, hence the title, *Hard Shoulder*.

The book has proved quite important because it depicted a place that previously had very little representation in the world of fiction. Birmingham is not somewhere we would immediately put alongside London or Grasmere or the Yorkshire moors in our collective fictional consciousness.

Recent trends in fiction have tended to favour writing from all over the world, almost anywhere but home, it seems. We don't want to know about the world around us, rather we would prefer to read stories sent from the fringes of a post-colonial world, as if these landscapes have more power to tell us who we are than the ones which we inhabit on a day-to-day basis.

Perhaps it's because we've become immune to our surroundings. We've stopped looking at the details around us. The flatlands of north Norfolk are just as strange and uncompromising and unfamiliar as anywhere in the Midwest of America, if a little smaller. Also, perhaps, there is a feeling that our landscape isn't as exciting as the rest of the world. As if our small, scruffy, mongrel country has nothing that could match the otherness or the size of the Indian subcontinent or the African deserts.

But I want to read about where I live; I want the returning traveller's frisson of culture shock. To look at home and find that I don't recognize it anymore. I want the world, but especially my immediate surroundings, to be defamiliarized through language and story telling.

📖 Try this: describe the view from your house. What is outside your front door? Make notes, describing everything in minute detail. It's not enough to write: trees, a park, a row of houses, a shop. What kind of trees? What type of shop? What apparatus do they have in the park?

Now try to describe your town or village, or community. What makes it what it is? To me, Norwich is defined by its topographical juxtapositions: it is a city where you can, in certain winds, smell the fertilizer being spread on the surrounding fields and there are only A roads linking us to the rest of the country. It is a landlocked, county town. Full of history – a castle, medieval buildings, meandering town streets – and yet impractical, dependent on history as much as modernity for its survival.

Writers are a product of the landscape in which they live, and as such they are to some extent social historians. Our vision of Victorian London would be poorer without Dickens; the social milieu of the 1800s uncharted without the minute description of Jane Austen; sixties England indigent without the fictions of Nell Dunn or John Braine or Alan Sillitoe. Without writers who tell us about the world in which we live, we have little chance of figuring out what it's really like to live there.

8 Plotting and Shaping

Introduction
Julia Bell

In a prose or screenplay, a plot is the things that *happen*. Once you have created your characters, something has to happen to them in some kind of order. A plot is the sequence of events that take place within the narrative.

Plot is also the sequence of questions that the reader will be asking the narrative as they read it. Who dunnit? Why? Did they do it? And what happens next? If the events of the narrative are badly paced, or inadequately foregrounded, the story will be turgid, hard to read, and will lack the tension required to keep the reader turning the pages. Good plotting is about managing events over time. These events need not be monumental – you don't need lots of action and adventure to have plot – they just need to unravel sequentially, keeping true to the logic of your story.

In teaching, it is useful to get students to look at, and think through, different types of plotting, to consider the kinds of stories they might be writing and the implications of structure on meaning.

The Moral Plot

In his notes on tragedy in *Poetics*, Aristotle talks of 'a whole as that which has a beginning, middle and end'. He wants to see the action played out in front of him, so that the protagonist does something at point A, which causes the events at point B, which causes the conclusion at point C. For Aristotle, a plot is a history of consequence.

This kind of plotting always has a sense of moral urgency at the end: a lesson has been learned, good has triumphed over evil, we have seen men and women ruined by their own mistakes, the lovers are happy ever after, thus justifying the means by which they got together. This is the most traditional way to tell a story and most narratives conform to this structure.

More challenging plots rely on the interplay between character and events and resist neat conclusions. They ask questions, rather than offer solutions. They resist the moral moment of closure, often leaving resolution to the reader. It is the *actions* of the characters that are important. How the choices they make affect the events in their lives.

Plots can only be figured out through writing, through testing your characters in action and giving them a world to come up against. Structuring the story will come later, when you have a history to look back on and knock into some kind of shape. Unless you are writing parables or fairy stories, you don't want to start your narrative with a moral in mind, you want to set your characters off on the racetrack of their lives and watch where they end up. Shaping a narrative is a process that happens later as you uncover meaning, and make links and connections between events.

Bestselling Plots

The books sold in dump bins at airports, supermarkets and newsagents, thick as bricks and smelling of ink and cheap paper, depend on plots. The 'bestseller' – black-sheep sibling to the 'literary' novel – is a bestseller because it has a strong plot and events unravel in a way that fit a standard formula.

Out of ten books in the paperback bestseller list this week there are four thrillers, two sex and fantasy lifestyle novels (Jilly Cooper and Jackie Collins), three romances and, the one exception, a novel written by a well-known journalist. These books aren't bestsellers by chance. They are generic and conformist. We know when we pick up a thriller or a romance or a detective novel what will happen. Whatever the reasons, the pleasure of the text lies in the repetition of a pattern: we like to know what to expect.

Consider the structure of a horror novel. At what point does the reader expect to feel uneasy? The plot must include something unsettling, or the hint of something unsettling, fairly near the beginning. A few gruesome events and a protagonist trapped and fearing for their life by page 100 and we won't be able to put it down until we know the outcome.

Mills and Boon will send you, on request, guidelines as to how to write one of their romances. They know, from dominating a successful market for years, what their readers want and expect their writers to adhere to that pattern.

Commercial novels reduce stories to their primary events. They depend on the reader asking 'What happens next?' They are easily consumable and digestible so their audience will become attached to and buy more of them. But under the relentless juggernaut of the plot driving towards resolution, the characters become puppets filling the space around which the action can happen. The characters don't make things happen, the world happens to them.

But these – trashy and somehow illicitly, immorally pleasurable – books do, in fact, conform to the oldest and most moral of structures: they have a beginning, middle and an end.

Courtroom Plots

A courtroom sets out a structure for you. There are only two real choices for the ending: guilty or not guilty. Suspense is built as the story of what happened prior to the trial is unravelled piece by piece, witness by witness. A trial is a story of the unravelling of a story.

The case of Louise Woodward is a good example of a real-life drama that conformed to our expectations of good plotting. Especially in the way it was reported. Louise Woodward, the central character, was the grey area, full of contradiction, caught in a system that could only negotiate in black and white: guilty or not guilty. It was Louise's struggle against the courtroom machine of the plot that made her case into a true news 'story'. It felt like we were watching a film. Did she or did she not kill a child in her care? Were Matthew

Eapen's parents telling the truth? Who should we believe?

In the harrowing denouement she broke down, seemed helpless, defenceless, a life sentence for a nineteen-year-old girl from somewhere ordinary like Elton, Cheshire. It could happen to us, to our daughters, to our sisters. We called up people we knew who were nannies and advised anyone who was thinking of becoming an au pair against such a dangerous occupation. The final, truly fictional twist, was Judge Zobel's release of his judgement reversing the sentence via the internet. Louise came home and though the shadow of doubt still lingered, the story petered out. Who dunnit? Nobody knew. Maybe no one even cared that much in the end. What captivated us was the tragedy – the character struggling against the plot, refusing the hand dealt them by fate – and the fact that, in the end, we had to choose who to believe. It was an interactive narrative. The story didn't come to a conclusive ending, we had to make one up for ourselves.

I was reading *Alias Grace* at the time – Margaret Atwood's novel about the case of Grace Marks, convicted of murder at the age of sixteen in Canada in 1843. Plenty of doubt surrounded the soundness of her conviction, and in the novel Atwood consistently resists the moment where her reader might discover the crucial truth of events. We never know whether Grace did it or not. Like Louise, she doesn't help her own defence by being shy, surly, frightened, seemingly 'cold'. As readers we are left to ponder a moral problem, to make a decision for ourselves. The story asks questions, it doesn't answer them.

Journey Plots

A journey is a popular way to plot a story, as the events of the book can then mirror the emotional journey of the characters. Take this scenario: two characters – two women? A boy and a girl? Mother and daughter? Father and son? Husband and wife? – start out on a journey from Land's End to John O'Groats in a battered American Chevvy that costs a fortune to run. They've hardly any money.

Eventually, they get there. The story is about all the things that happen to them in between. The ending of the story is then, ironically, at the moment of arrival. We have followed two characters through a series of experiences that have taken place in the limbo of travel. A place where it is easy to sit the characters outside of themselves and have them comment on their lives. This kind of story, like the courtroom drama, provides the writer with a clear structure to follow or to subvert.

Joseph Conrad's the *Heart of Darkness* is a classic example of a story that subverts the reader's expectations of a plot. We never really *go* anywhere, though this novel is ostensibly a 'journey' narrative. From the start we are only ever passively engaged in the story. We are on a ship, somewhere on the Thames, listening to Marlow's fractured, frustrating recollections about a series of non-events in the Belgian Congo at the height of Empire. But there's still a pull, something inexorable that makes us want to read on, despite the fact that the story is second hand and refuses to answer any of the questions it poses. Subtly, the book plays with our expectations of plot. Conrad introduces details that are never followed through. For example, near the start of the narrative, Marlow tells how he was stuck in the jungle, unable to move because he needed rivets to repair his boat. A long section describes how everybody, including the mysterious Mr Kurtz, is suffering from this shortage of rivets, then suddenly we are in the next chapter and Marlow is back on his boat, travelling down the Congo, and the rivets are never mentioned again. We have to assume Marlow got his rivets and repaired his boat offstage.

Our reading habits teach us to expect that details will be important. If the character is bothering to tell us that there is a terrible shortage of rivets, we anticipate that in some way this will affect the course of events, but Conrad constantly subverts this expectation. The main thrust of the book – Marlow's curiosity and search for the mysterious Mr Kurtz – which gives the book its narrative power, turns out to be a non-event. The quest for Kurtz is similar to a reader looking for conclusion in a story, to find out, like Marlow, what it all *means*.

✍ Try this exercise: write the story of a journey in a hundred words from beginning to end. With so few words you have to pick out all the most relevant information. Is it really important to know that they stop for a Big Mac at the service station? Perhaps the car breaks down? They run out of petrol? They argue? Everything counts, so include only the most revealing details. Read back what you've written, play around with it, try to re-narrate the story putting the events in a different order. How can you upset the conventions of an A to B journey?

Moments in Time

In Virgina Woolf's *Mrs Dalloway* the entire novel happens over one day in the stream of Clarissa Dalloway's consciousness. There is no plot to speak of. Nothing really *happens*. Yet the tension comes from the emotional development and revelation of character. The story is entirely internal. The plot that we follow becomes the revelation of character rather than the unravelling of event.

Short stories are especially suited to this type of plot. In Tobias Wolff's short story 'Bullet in the Brain' the narrator is shot by a bank robber. The story is plotted around a single moment, it tells of all the things the narrator thinks as the bullet is passing through his brain. A successful short story is like a pastry cutter, pressing out one shaped moment from a much longer and more complicated narrative. A short story can be about the moment of arrival or departure, an end or a beginning; it has the luxury of not needing to unravel events in the way that a novel does, and at the same time, it must compress a character's entire history into a single line or paragraph, and in this way it shares the density of poetry.

How to Plot

There is no single way to plot a story, but there are important questions to remember when attempting to give your narrative some shape. What is the internal logic of your story? What kinds of thing can happen in the world of your characters? Think quite carefully about this. Too many twists or events in the story can create more complications than they solve. But don't go for the obvious. The 'it was all a dream' story is one we've all heard before. If you've chosen a generic plot think about how you can subvert it, either through creating unusual characters or through playing with what you know a reader will expect from the story. A good detective novel, for example, thrives on being just slightly more intelligent than the reader, on masking its plot twists and the answer to the 'who dunnit' question until the last page.

Also, don't be afraid to unpick a plot if it's not working. If an event or a scenario is falling flat, or seems out of tune with the characters, cut it or rework it. If the characters are strong, the story won't fall apart. It can be easy to forget once something is written that it's not set in stone. It is your story after all.

On Narrative Structures
Patricia Duncker

I want to begin with the reader. A piece of writing, whether it be a letter, a work of prose fiction, a lyric, or an epic poem, always constructs an audience, in other words, readers. Some writers like to remind readers of their role – 'Reader, I married him.' Others like to woo, persuade and cajole their reader from a safe distance. Some writers only talk to their readers through a series of masks. Here is the narrative chain, the uneasy link between author and reader.

AUTHOR	implied author	narrator/ speaker	(level of drama- tization)	characters (events)	implied reader	READER

Readers are subtle, difficult people. They have two identities: their living selves – the one that goes shopping, has sex and dies – and their reading selves. Their reading self is infinite, multiple and immortal. This is the implied reader. This multiple identity is the one you offer to the reader for her to inhabit. Some writers/authors have an ideal reader in mind when they write, some write purely to please themselves. But for whoever you write, even if it is for yourself, it is for yourself *as a reader*. You forget your reader at your peril. Remember where you have positioned your reader in relation to your narrative. Don't abandon her. Don't forget to address her. Tell her your story.

I am writing a novel. I decide to interview two of my prospective readers. This is not as mad as it sounds, and proves to be very revealing. You could call it a form of market research. Jo is forty, a mature student, mother of two daughters, intriguingly called Fred and George. She is an original, demanding reader.

PATRICIA: What do you most desire from a work of prose fiction?

JO: (*pulls hair, looks anguished*) I want to be swallowed up. I like the action to be as simple as possible. I want a book that is challenging and evocative.

PATRICIA: What do you mean?

JO: (*desperate*) It's to do with the language. I want the language to rediscover the taste of words.

PATRICIA: You like edible words?

JO: (*very rapidly*) I want a language that carries multiple levels of meaning and which destabilizes the obvious. I like writing that calls attention to itself as writing.

PATRICIA: (*incredulous*) And that swallows you up?

JO: (*sticking to her guns*) And I want infinite meanings. I want to be astonished.

I then interview Jason. He is in his early twenties. He describes himself as a 'footballing poet' and as a bloke, not a lad. He has a girlfriend and subscribes to *Loaded*. He also has a wicked sense of humour.

PATRICIA: What do you most desire from a work of prose fiction?

JASON: I want the author to talk to me, but like Sterne, not like Fielding.
(Patricia is dumbfounded by the subtlety of this distinction. Jason seizes control of the interview.) I want to be entertained. I like characters that are engaging. I want a good story, a sense of the familiar, and I want to feel that I've achieved something by reading it. And I think it's good to see yourself represented.

PATRICIA: *(irate)* But I thought that you said you liked reading horror and sci-fi?

JASON: *(broad smile, with great charm)* Yes, I like to be captivated and provoked.

The results of my reader interrogations seemed to me to be very positive. They want to be captivated, entertained, provoked, bewitched. They want to be accompanied. They want magic. Jason wanted something that is easily recognizable, an author who was more than just an anonymous voice, in other words a narrator who may also be a character in the fiction, and he wanted a good story. But what was really fascinating was that Jo, who wanted difficult textual density, still wanted to be 'swallowed up', and in her own words, 'astonished'. In essence, she and Jason wanted the same thing.

The narrative structure of a piece of writing is the spine on which the entire body of the work depends. It is the central nervous system, nourishing the intelligence of the writing, it upholds the bones of character, the muscles of the descriptive passages, it supports the heart and the circulation of the blood that is the tension in the text. A narrative must have tension and emotion if it is to survive and stand the test of being read and reread. Must we always have a plot? No, not always. Plot is causal. It is the rational intelligence ordering the narrative and answering our petulant demands for reasons why. You do not always need a plot. But you must have a narrative. Even the smallest, briefest, most delicate lyric poem has a narrative. The narrative is what happens.

Sometimes the material you choose determines its own narrative. If someone is murdered in your tale then your reader will want to know who did it and why. You may have good reasons not to tell them or for obfuscating the entire issue. But it would be unwise to forget that your reader will want to know the answers to these questions. You must address her desire, even if you wish to puzzle her.

Virginia Woolf famously commented, 'And as usual, I am bored by narrative' (*A Writer's Diary*, Thursday, 28 March 1929). Well, how would you summarize the events of *To the Lighthouse*? Here is a large family and assorted guests on holiday, supposedly on the Isle of Skye. They decide to go to the lighthouse, but put off the expedition. One of them starts a picture. They eat dinner. Time passes, many die. Those that are left return to the house. They go to the lighthouse. The picture is finished. That's what happens. Apparently very little. So, clearly, the interest, tension and emotion, even the action of the narrative, lies elsewhere. A reader who is baffled and puzzled is not necessarily a reader who is bored. They can be curious and excited. It is not a crime to baffle your reader. It is a crime to bore her.

An American writer once commented to me: 'There are only two kinds of narrative, either the heroine/hero leaves home, or a stranger comes to town.' I brooded on this distinction and on the master narratives of our culture and came to the following conclusions.

The paradigm narratives that stand at the source of our Western traditions of writing are the Bible and the Homeric epics. The Bible is the ultimate book. It contains all things: lyric, epic, myth, history, law, song, war stories, love stories, biography, epigrams, parables, elegies, prophecies, apocalypse. It is a sacred text. And therefore better read than pillaged. Homer's epic narrative poems are secular texts. *The Iliad* and *The Odyssey* give us the two giant patterns on which to base our own tales: siege narratives or quest narratives. *The Iliad* is a war story. The siege of Troy has lasted ten years. Stalemate. Heroic and treacherous deeds form the basis of the narratives. Mortals are at the mercy of the cunning of the gods. The ruse of the Trojan Horse leads to the sack of Troy. And the bloodbath leads to other narratives. *The Odyssey* is a search for home. Odysseus becomes the wanderer, a voyager searching, moving from land to land. What awaits his return to Ithaca? Both the journey and the arrival matter.

Here are some of the key characteristics of these two types of narrative.

Siege Narratives

This kind of narrative can be thrillingly claustrophobic, and if it is well constructed will give you tension and intensity. Siege narratives in prose fiction work best with a limited cast and not too many sub-plots. Many war stories are siege narratives. All submarine dramas are. Family sagas are nearly always siege narratives. So are love stories, marriage and divorce narratives. Siege narratives can turn into escape narratives. Make sure that the source of danger, pressure, tension is believable. Even if it is quite fantastic it must be convincing. Life and death matters must be plausible if they are to be harrowing. A siege narrative can intensify your sense of place. Your description or detail can become terrifying, uncanny. Beware of bathos. The most common problem with a siege narrative is that the writing goes flat, the tension goes out of the narrative and the reader is bored. If you are anxious about losing the tension then put a clock on your narrative.

Great Siege Narratives
High Noon
Twelve Angry Men
La Peste
Hamlet

Quest Narrative

Quest narratives are usually driven by desire. The most powerful of these is the desire to go home. Everyone longs to go home. Very few people have homes to which they can return – your endings can therefore be either joyous or horrific. Quest narratives can be lost-and-found narratives. You can extend your cast of characters. It is easier to introduce new characters. It is easy to lose them. You need a strong central character to hold the quest or the multiplying narratives together. Your narrative can travel. You can introduce many changes of place, many startling adventures. Coincidences are easier to fabricate. Beware of writing that is rambling or diffuse. The danger is reader confusion. If your quest narrative contains too many characters, too many events, you may lose the focus and the tension. Beware of open endings with a quest narrative. Readers who love quests also love closure. Please them.

Great Quest Narratives
Gawain and the Green Knight
Possession
Jane Eyre
Star Trek: Voyager

Consider the following questions:

1 Can a narrative be exciting, tense, dramatic, even if nothing happens? If you think that the answer to this question is yes, think of an example.

2 What are the uses of cliché in prose fiction? What are the most common clichés that structure contemporary narratives? How can you make cliché work for you and serve your purposes?

3 What constitutes an *event* in prose fiction? How do you construct an event? How do you signal the existence and/or nature of the event to the reader?

4 What are the essential elements of prose fiction? What, therefore, are the optional extras?

5 Remember that it is a crime to bore your reader, and the writer who does this deserves all that she or he gets! What bores you as a reader? How can you avoid boring your reader?

✍ *Writing Exercises*

Construct a quest narrative around an object. It could be anything: a jewel, a coin, a bottle opener.

Write a siege narrative for either one voice (monologue) or two (dialogue or two linked monologues).

Choose an incident from Homer. Adapt the tale to suit your purposes but don't lose sight of the original story.

Plotting a Novel
Ashley Stokes

Plot is for readers more than writers. Readers ask 'What's the plot?' meaning 'What happens? Will I be interested? Is this for me?' For a writer the question can only be answered when the novel is finished. The ordering of events, the conflicts, motives, themes and resolutions may not yet be apparent in the draft stages. In this way plot is part of the process of writing. It is something we find in the activity itself. More importantly, it comes to us in the amorphous work of notebooks, long walks, versions, false turns, hard decisions, insomnia and staring out the window. Plotting is the underside of the stone that no one sees. It is the head labour that makes a novel realize itself on its own terms. If this sounds an uncomfortable business, it is worth reminding ourselves that this is what writing *is*, a triangular process of planning, composing and editing that occurs in no particular order. For plotting read planning.

In my teaching, I tackle the issue of plot between 'character' and 'the beginning'. The first *is* plot. The second, to a large extent, determines the realization of a plot by triggering it (if we think of plot as the ordering of events through narrative, rather than story). In fact, we are thinking about two types of beginning here, one of practice, the other the result of that practice.

If a novel starts conceptually with what Nabokov called a 'throb', or if we are being geeky 'a primary generator', we are saying we have an idea that compels us to write. Five people trapped in a lift plan an escape to the moon. A schoolgirl locks herself in her bedroom for twelve years. We start with these glimpses and then power ahead. This is exciting but poses problems for the beginner because it is easy to let this drive rule the roost. It is easy to keep going, stringing events together until they overload the narrative. Everything follows the plotline. In the end only text, not experience, is being made. The writing then seems artificial or unconvincing. Plot begins to govern character. The narrative becomes unwieldy and passionless. In the end it will feel staged and the effects will be deadened. Conceptually, therefore, what we need to do is shift backwards from our idea and work with character first. We work with character always. F. Scott Fitzgerald said, 'plot is character and character plot'. If we start with character, and keep this in mind, we can avoid our narrative losing focus or the plot gaining the upper hand.

I always start by notebooking my characters. I make lists about them. I make chronologies. I write at random about them. I make sure I know everything they have ever done. I determine the details that imply their entire lives, the landmark decisions, the key experiences, the moments of change or realization. I consider their basic values and loyalties.

I sometimes practise on these proto-characters by writing short stories that involve part of the cast before I start on the novel (writing chronologies often provides tasty predicaments that will not fit into the novel's schema). This also gives me an idea of whether the characters are interesting enough. Moreover, it lets me test them out and gives me ideas about tone and style. If a character seems too unsympathetic to sustain the reader's interest over the course of a novel, at least I know that I have to address this issue and find strategies for its alleviation. It also gives me a chance to ditch characters that I can't get enthusiastic about.

Once this process is over you have a cast. By brooding on this cast you will be able to see how they will interact within the framework of both the fictional situation and how you think a novel should be written theoretically. Sarah will hate Ernie. Jozef will not handle the predicament he is asked to unravel.

You should now have a mosaic of conflicts, motives, dreams, proclivities, dishonesties, vanities, insecurities, desires, cruelties, virtues and mindsets that make up part of the context of a fictional character. I always think a character has a context that they take into any situation. This determines how they will react or impose themselves. Knowing this context, and knowing it more than you know yourself, is what will allow you to write freely and convincingly. Most of this context will remain unseen. It is only implied or imagined by the reader. But it is the gear system of the novel's progression and a fail-safe to the sort of over-plotting or 'inappropriateness' that I mentioned above.

After this we need to think about the central proposition: What is at stake? What makes this important for the reader? What drives the narrative? You may already have an idea of this if you started with a situation or predicament first, or even with a setting or theme. But character matters most. How will the sequence of events allow the character(s) to change? How will it affect them? How many events do I need to address the issues I wish to explore? What relationship does this novel have with time? Remember that, as E. M. Forster tells us, plot is about issues of cause and effect, 'a sense of causality'. Plot in this sense answers questions of 'Why?' and 'How?' rather than the 'What happens?' posed by 'What's the plot?'

This requires a different type of plotting, the appropriate ordering of events. If we dwell on the characters we have created we will be able to see situations that dramatize or enliven the conflicts that lay hidden within and between them. Beware of overdoing this, by either continually plumping for the grand or the extreme. Understatement is sometimes more effective than overstatement. Beware also of creating too many situations, of protracting the novel and thereby straining the reader's attention (there is nothing wrong with short novels).

Use flow charts in your notebook to get an idea of the ordering of events. Plan as far ahead as you can so that when you are composing you have a definite feeling of progressing towards points that lead to new points. Consider each situation before you write. Are the events grounded in character context? If not, rework or scrap. Is this leading to another scene where it has a pay-off? Is it deepening character? Are we learning things that make us want to continue reading? If not, you may not be trusting your reader's understanding. Are we repeating information that the reader already knows? If so, the scene may be superfluous and slowing things down. Try to maintain a rhythm of active and meditative scenes. Try to maintain momentum in the middle, where there is a tendency to over-complicate. Don't use a scene that only acts as a precursor to a second scene. This elongates the narrative and drive suffers. Start in the second scene to create tension, then backfold the narrative. They were knocking on the door because G had told S about J. Not a scene where G tells S about J and then they go and knock on the door in a fresh scene. Do you start at the chronological beginning so it takes too long to get to the meat of the issue? An *ad ova* scheme may work in certain types of Bildungsroman but you may need to start *in medias res*, in the thick of things. Look for the first moment of confusion or change in the novel and use it as an opening gambit. Then backfeed or break up the background material. See what happens if you cut the first two pages. There's often too much explanation at the beginning. Don't be scared of time jumps and don't invent sub-plots or material just to pass the time realistically. 'Get on with it' is the best advice I have ever been given.

It is possible that once you start composing you will get new ideas that you want to incorporate. This can lead to confusions and the novel can lose focus. Always go back to the plan and see how the new material fits in. If it is more compelling than what you already have, replot and cut the earlier sections on the next draft. Don't be afraid of cutting. Even fine work may need to be sacrificed for the overall whole. Use your notebook flow charts and scene lists to try out new material beforehand. Think about the implications of your scene structure. Try to think of other combinations or outcomes that could occur. Are they more interesting than what you first intended? If so, you've avoided learning this after spending hours writing the scene. Be aware of how other writers have handled similar material so you avoid clichés. Don't steal in any case. Always be thinking about what is appropriate to fiction. Is this adding to the narrative? What combination of events are possible to progress the novel and deepen our involvement with the characters? Only focus on what we are not likely to expect. Anything that seems familiar or commonplace, cut or rework so the material is made strange. Make sure that the obvious is treated as background. Only use description that punctures expectation. Always keep in mind that in writing about people you are dealing with the unique. If you can't make a restaurant scene different, treat yourself to a meal and keep your eyes and ears open.

The first draft may be shapeless and fail to meet with your intentions. You may have determined things about your characters that change your original plans. It may not get started until page eighty. The characters' later actions may seem incongruous with how you have grounded them. They may need more layering. You may have chosen the wrong vantage point from which to tell the story. The conceit may be too protracted. It may not read like the novels you love. This is where many writers hang up their pens and give up. Don't be afraid of this feeling. It is an intrinsic part of writing and becoming a writer. It is a rite of passage. Use it. Learn from it. You are becoming your own self-editor. Go back to the plan and rework it by referring to what you now have beside you. Always go with your hunches. This will be only the first stage of a novel. It may take many drafts to realize, just like it took Joseph Heller and Günter Grass ten years each to write *Catch 22* and *The Tin Drum*.

The biggest misapprehension about writing is that it is as instant and effortless as its master practitioners would have us believe. It is not for them, and it is not for anyone. It is hard. It is a process. See plotting as a safety mechanism, a system of constant revaluation that goes hand in hand with the compositional, imaginative wordplay that occurs in front of the screen or with pen in hand. A novel never slithers out whole like some clever-eyed prodigy. It is made, not born.

✍ Exercises

1 Start with a title that implies time and place (*My Day with Grandma, An Evening at the Faulkner, Night in Cheam, The Last Year in Kingston-upon-Thames*, etc.). On a piece of paper brainstorm this scenario, thinking what it is likely to involve and what could happen. Make lists of both situations and details. Sift through these lists and think of scenarios that look promising as stories. Focus on the items you have listed and think about how they could be used imaginatively as conflict triggers. Discard ideas that seem either obvious or unconvincing. Look at what you have left. If you have nothing left, go back to the list and rework the situations. When you have something that seems appropriate begin to plot it out with flow charts. Do you have a story that involves conflicts and motives? Is it original? Does the end include a pay-off? Is it convincing? If you can't answer these questions, rework the story so you can.

2 Take this plot plan and break it up into its constituent parts: person, place, time. Replot the story using the following combinations:

Right person, right place but wrong time.
Right person, right time but wrong place.
Right time, right place but wrong person.

Plot out these combinations and see how the plot changes. Are any of these more intriguing than your original plot? Do any of them provide solutions to the difficulties that you found with the original plot? Does this give you any fresh ideas?

After these two exercises, consider if you have enough material or ideas to trigger a novel.

3 Use the following situation outline: There is a character waiting for a train. They have a suitcase with an object in it that they wish to conceal. What sort of character would find themselves in this predicament and why? Use the idea of 'appropriateness' to plot out a story that avoids cliché or hyperbole.

4 Think of a day when you came to a realization, when something definitely changed. Write this out, either as a draft or a plan, as faithfully as you can to what you think happened. Does this produce an original and convincing plotline. If not, why? What seems inappropriate and what does not? Can you use the techniques you have learnt in the first three exercises to augment this story? Can you change the setting or the characters? What can you invent yourself to fill in the gaps or replace those parts of the plot that seem commonplace?

Decisions, Decisions
Val Taylor

Close your eyes. Listen to the sounds around you: What do you hear? Don't worry what is actually making the sounds; let your mind just drift, and focus only on what they sound like. As I'm writing this, I'm hearing the hiss of my laptop running, overlaid with a low, pulsating one-note whine. Soft irregular clicks syncopate this undertow as I tap out 'soft irregular clicks syncopate this undertow'; deep in the background, at the edge of attention, the central heating pipes thunk intermittently, as the metal breathes and complains.

Eyes closed, and I'm in an old factory, steam pipes hissing, the whine of industrial turbines. Rats' paws skittering irregularly across the hard floor. *Thunk.* A door shutting behind me somewhere. *Where? Who's here?*

Close your eyes and listen. Where are you?

The first question an audience tends to ask is that one: Where are we? Where have we gone to today? It's the first imaginative leap; as the house lights go down, literally, a leap into the dark. The writer's answer is always the same, as she turns on the point of light: *Here*. And then she begins to show them where *here* is, begins to establish visually and aurally the 'world' within which the dramatic story will unfold.

In *The Writer's Journey: Mythic Structure for Storytellers and Screenwriters*, Christopher Vogler (following Joseph Campbell) separates the story world into two: the Ordinary World and the Special World. The Ordinary World is the protagonist's (the central character's) everyday environment – where she comes from – a mirror that reflects back who and what she is. The Special World is where she goes to, the locus within which the story action follows its course. In plotting your story – that is, in deciding how you are going to tell your audience the story step by step – the first crucial decision is to determine what it is which provokes the protagonist into stepping across from one world into the other. Particularly in drama, the arc of the story is an arc of movement, from and to.

You might begin your initial thinking, therefore, not by imagining a character or a story ('It's about this guy who . . .'), but instead by imagining a world. The exercise above is a child's game; you could just as easily begin, as playwright Stephen Jeffreys once suggested, by thinking of a place where something happens, perhaps something a little unusual. (Using this approach, one student writer came up with a tattoo parlour!) But what is useful about the child's game is that it invites you to conceive the world from the inside: the way it feels, its associations, its logic, its possibilities and its menaces. It is a first step into your audience's shoes, beginning to work right away, with both *affect* and *effect*.

Understanding how your story world feels to be in is vital; it can, for example, offer you the first glimmers of sympathy with your characters' psychology and motivation, and thus their subsequent behavioural choices. In my old factory, imagine 'my' response to that slamming door if I am at ease in this building, know my way around it. I know where that door is; but I'm curious who's there. Perhaps I think I know, but I'll go and look anyway. I'm confident, even proprietorial: *What are you still doing here? Go home, I'll lock up.* But if I don't belong there, don't know my way around, I'm edgy, ill at ease. The rats give me the willies. The whole place hissing and thumping, and *Where was that? Someone's here. Oh God* . . . Experiencing the story world from the inside, like this, gives you ideas about story, genre and character type: in one version I'm an investigator, I take charge; in the other, I'm on the receiving end, potentially a victim. In the first, I'm pro-active, in the second I'm re-active.

Similarly, understanding the world in this way can help you determine which is the Ordinary and which the Special World, and whether or not they are two different places at all. It may be that the protagonist does not move physically between the two worlds; instead, she is brought to perceive her own world entirely differently. The arc of movement is not external, in this case, but internal, in her mind and feelings. This is a familiar pattern in drama: in Ibsen's *A Doll's House*, for example, Nora Helmer, hitherto a housewife 'babied' by her husband, learns that what she once believed to be a place of safety – her marital home – is instead a stultifying prison from which she must escape at any cost. In such psychological dramas, little may change externally; it is the character – often, alone – who turns through 180 degrees.

Martin McDonagh in *The Beauty Queen of Leenane* effects a different level of transformation. The world is shrunk to the living room/kitchen of a rural cottage in Connemara, County Galway; apart from one short scene, a monologue from a bedsit in London, the action never leaves that tightly circumscribed world. We, as audience, understand this to be the Ordinary World of Maureen Folan, forty, going nowhere, yoked to her seventy-year-old, manipulative, despotic mother, Mag. As we watch Maureen's one chance of escape – physically, to London; emotionally and sexually, to the arms of Pato Dooley – mislaid by Mag's sleight of hand with a crucial letter, our sympathies are largely with Maureen, notwithstanding her casual little cruelties towards Mag. But in Scene Seven, McDonagh pulls a stroke on us: discovering Mag's treachery, Maureen puts on the range a chip pan full of cooking oil and, once it is boiling, holds down Mag's arm and pours the oil over it. She goes on, one scene later, to beat Mag to death with the fire poker, and ends by taking her place in her rocking chair. McDonagh's stroke has, however, been laid from the outset: the opening stage direction says of Mag Folan that 'her left hand is somewhat more shrivelled and red than her right'. Maureen has, in fact, been a habitual torturer of her mother; the violence in Scene Seven is not new, but part of a long, unbearable routine, and we realize that what we had thought to be the Ordinary World has been, all along, a Special World of nightmarish cruelty and mutual torment. It is not Maureen's perception of her world that changes, it is ours.

Once you have understood the relationship between the two worlds, Ordinary and Special, in your story, and know whether the arc of movement is external – Dorothy goes from Kansas to Oz! – or internal; or whether the movement is ours rather than the characters', you need to identify what it is that provokes the protagonist into motion. In screenwriting, and in theories of narrative, this provocation is frequently termed the initiating event. It may be small, in itself quite innocuous, even a matter of chance: in Hitchcock's *North by Northwest*, it is a collision of unrelated circumstances misinterpreted by someone. Roger Thornhill stands up to go to telephone his mother at the exact moment a hotel bellboy is paging a completely different man to answer a phone call; but the call has been set up by the villains, who are trying to identify this 'mysterious man'. By this quirk of timing, they assume Thornhill to be their target, and pursue him.

The initiating event can be anything, but it needs to happen within the plot. We really need to see it happen in front of us, rather than be told that it has already occurred earlier in the story before your plot begins. There is a nice example of this distinction in Anthony Minghella's screen adaptation of Patricia Highsmith's *The Talented Mr Ripley*. The film opens on Tom Ripley, sitting in his cabin on board a ferry from Venice to Athens; he has just strangled his lover,

Peter Smith-Kingsley – 'his own chance of happiness'. In voice-over, Tom explains, 'If I could just go back. If I could rub everything out. Starting with myself. *Starting with borrowing a jacket* [my italics].' We then flashback to the earlier time, where Tom, in his borrowed Princeton blazer, is playing piano at a private concert and encounters Herbert Greenleaf Sr.

It is easy to see that borrowing the blazer could be taken to be the initiating event; indeed, the protagonist tells us it is so. But we don't see it happen; it has already happened, it is part of the 'backstory', and we don't flashback quite that far. What we do see is Tom's response, when Herbert Greenleaf alludes to the jacket: 'I see you were at Princeton . . . Then you'll most likely know our son, Dick. Dickie Greenleaf . . .' Tom hesitates, then lies: 'How is Dickie?' – when in fact he was never a student at Princeton, and consequently has never before heard Dickie's name. From that moment on, Tom's arc through the story is set: he will reflexively lie himself into situation after situation, with murderous consequences for Dickie, Freddie Miles and Peter.

What we see is a moment of choice occurring on screen before us, a determining moment for the protagonist. Borrowing the jacket could be seen as a practical matter, which need not have led to any such consequences as occur. Tom could, after all, simply have explained that it was borrowed, and the whole course of events would stop there! It is certainly a crucial event, a catalyst, but it doesn't make the unfolding of the story inevitable; Tom's decision to lie does. It is an act of will.

The initiating event needs to be the one thing that makes everything else occur. But why does it need to be dramatized for us, ideally, rather than us simply being told about it? We need to see it, onstage or on screen, rather than off, because the event itself is only part of the equation. The other part of the equation is what someone chooses to do as an immediate result of it, that is, a human choice of action. It may be a conscious decision, or it may be a subconscious reflex: both are forms of choice. Here, in *Ripley*, Tom's decision to lie is not the immediate result of borrowing the jacket, but of Herbert Greenleaf's mistake in assuming it means he's a Princeton alumnus. It is the human choice that makes the subsequent dramatic action inevitable. In *North by Northwest*, though the collision of timing is chance, the villains' decision to act on the (mis)identification is not. In this case, the protagonist (Thornhill) is subject to someone else's choice.

In both films, choice is completely embedded in the psychology of character will and desire, a psychology that is, as I've suggested, both constructed by and reflected in the world the character inhabits. The two interact throughout, mutually shaping each other. In my factory scenarios, the door shutting (which we don't necessarily see, but do hear occurring) is the initiating event. My response is the same in both – I go and investigate: in the first version, with confidence, in the second, with trepidation. It is *my* action that makes whatever happens next, happen. If the door slams and I ignore it, no story!

Rooting your plot in a series of human choices, which are then acted upon, gives you a spine that carries your story. It allows the arc of your story to develop from character. It encourages you towards a more original series of twists and turns in your story, because you can ratchet up the degree of challenge your character confronts – the rising arc – with each new set of choices. It is easier to avoid stereotypical decisions if you remain rooted in choices and their acting out; it only requires one slightly unusual decision – the character choosing to do B instead of A – to create an element of surprise and freshness. So, if the factory door slams and I do ignore it, the story is poised; sooner or later, in order to move the story on, I'm going to have to go up there and check it out. But there are a whole raft of different ways of plotting me into the decision: *It's the wind, what the heck.* I start to leave the building. I stop. *There's a window open, then. Blast. I'll have to go and shut it.* Or I leave the building, lock up, get in the car. *Long day.* I reach for my cigarettes before I turn on the engine. Empty pack. *Fresh pack in my desk drawer. Uuuhhh. Can I be bothered? Yes, I can.* I go back, unlock the place, stomp up the stairs to the back office and *wham!* You could try to work out how many different strategies you can create to get me up to that door.

Creating a causal chain of events, choices, actions and consequences forms the basis of mainstream approaches to plotting your script. There needs to be some form of resistance or opposition for your protagonist to push against. It is resistance that provokes characters into making choices, planning strategies and acting them out. Creating resistance in the form of blocks or obstacles encourages your characters to formulate objectives, which will gradually crystallize into goals. The goal sets the stakes for the character: what he wants, and how badly.

Resistance can be constructed in many forms: it can be another character – an opponent or antagonist, who need not necessarily be a negative character. In *The Talented Mr Ripley*, Tom, the protagonist, is a psychopath described by his first victim, Dickie, as 'a leech' and 'some third-class mooch'. His ongoing opponent-character is Marge Sherwood, Dickie's fiancée, who first welcomes Tom but then gradually realizes what he is and what he has done. But she is a weak opponent incapable of defeating Tom; his real opponent – his nemesis – is his own nature, as we gradually discover. In finally killing Peter Smith-Kingsley, whom he loves, Minghella's Tom defeats himself.

The situation itself can create the resistance. In *The Beauty Queen of Leenane*, though Mag and Maureen are clearly opponents, it could be argued that it is Maureen's situation which provokes her. Stuck in a small rural cottage, in a claustrophobic relationship, forty years old – young enough to have prospects, hopes and yearnings, but old enough to understand that they are fast running out – deprived of love and sexual fulfilment: Mag's treachery is only the final straw. The tremendous pressure imposed by her intolerable situation has Maureen wound up to the point where it will only take one more thing for the lid to blow. In my scenario, the resistance comes from my own curiosity – *I don't know what that door banging means but I'm going to find out.* (Or from my nicotine indulgence!)

The best form of resistance is created by constructing mutually exclusive goals for your protagonist and antagonist. That is, if your protagonist gets what she wants, your antagonist cannot get what he wants, and vice versa. Think of both sets of goals and objectives in positive rather than negative terms; make both characters actively want something, rather than simply having your opponent want to prevent the protagonist achieving her goal. It is immensely helpful to your plotting if both characters are simultaneously moving forward: collision therefore becomes inevitable.

Working through character, provoked by desires into making willed choices, which she then acts out, points you inevitably towards the shape of your plot resolution: she gets what she wants or she doesn't. Or the antagonist does. Or she gets what she wants and finds it isn't, after all, worth what it's cost to get it. Or neither is rewarded by achievement, and both are left standing in the wreckage.

The majority of mainstream drama on stage, in cinema and television tends to work through these kinds of patterns, though they are by no means the only ones available. A number of playwrights, in particular, have found the idea of causal structures of action very restrictive: Martin Crimp (*Attempts on Her Life*) or Sarah Kane, for example. Women writers have raised pertinent objections to the idea of goal-driven character, finding it to be more reflective of male than female behaviour. Frankly, I have problems with all of these areas myself; but they are still dominant patterns, and still powerfully effective. If you find yourself reacting against them, use them to help you clarify the patterns you do want.

In my factory scenario, the door slamming might have no direct bearing at all on what happens next. It might just be a door slamming. Or I might decide I can't be faffed to go and retrieve my cigarettes after all, turn on the car engine and drive home. However I plot my story, I will have to find some way of 'hooking' the audience and drawing them in, some way of making them stay with me for the next couple of hours.

Close your eyes. Where are you? Who's there?

What happens to you?

Peaceful Symmetries
an account of teaching an undergraduate poetry module at Queen's University Belfast
Carol Rumens

Students often enrol for the creative writing course with the perception that writing poetry is all about 'self-expression'. Without crushing their optimism, I try to refocus this expectation. Yes, the creative writing workshop *is* an arena for the play of individuality and imagination. There will be verbal opportunities unlikely to have been offered elsewhere on the curriculum, perhaps. And, yes, any piece of imaginative work will, ipso facto, express the self. At the same time, self-expression is not poetry. it is a by-product, a side effect. Poets learn, and often have to re-learn, that to concentrate on the self and those emotions for which lyric poetry apparently has a boundless appetite, is counterproductive as technique. This is not to banish the I but to emphasize that it is an 'I'. It is a construction, and its fables and reports must be re-made, reissued, fashioned in the image of language. Many of the students will come to the class with a sense of urgent things to say: this, after all, is Northern Ireland. They will have tried to get their emotions and ideas across, and they may have seen the emotions and ideas evaporate – or revolt. Fewer will be oppressed by a want of subjects to write about – those who are will probably have been mistaught that poetry has a specialized subject matter. But the issue we will most frequently address is shape. (The subject-matter question invariably looks after itself.) During the course of the poetry module we examine various set forms that have stood the test of ever-evolving linguistic and social contexts (often, in fact, migration and translation) and still retain their appeal for modem poets. These forms include the villanelle, triolet, sestina, sonnet, and haiku. In choosing which forms to present it was necessary to take into account their popularity: the better loved the form, the wider the range of interesting twentieth-century reworkings. We look at these texts in some detail. Reference works such as J. A. Cuddon's *Book of Literary Terms and Literary Theory* and Peter Sansom's *Writing Poems* will be consulted. Cuddon provides signposts to the historical origins of some of the forms, well worth following up in a longer course. With ten weeks only at our disposal, any deeper exploration a student may wish to make has to be undertaken independently.

Because the art of poetry is the art of speaking metaphorically, and of making linguistic objects that are themselves metaphors as well as metaphor-laden, the first 'shape' we look at is that of the riddle. A good metaphorical riddle is like a cross section: it is a single-celled, relatively primitive kind of poem opened up, the organs and connective tissue laid bare. This connective tissue, in its inner and outer reaches, is all important. As the editors, Laurence Sail and Kevin Crossley-Holland, of *The New Exeter Book of Riddles* declare in their foreword, 'To say that an apple is not only round and red or green but that it weeps when you bite it; that it is speckled and freckled; that it is a sphere and contains dark secrets: all this suggests and establishes relationships between the apple and a number of other subjects.' By foregrounding metaphor, the riddle exposes inner form, the interplay of imagery and allusion at poetry's heart. The best riddles will also involve other subtleties of interplay – between sound, syntax, line, etc. I think it important to have this reminder, early in the course, that poetic form is not simply poetic 'forms'. Neither are such forms ends in themselves. They are fascinating ways in (not inevitably short cuts!) to the true form of the interior, the linguistic nerves and musculature, of the poem. Within the strictest form is embedded a multiplicity of possible connections and sub-symmetries: here is the core of art, the point where the self submerges in the energy and delight of original creation – or its nearest thing.

The exercise in riddle composition is best done in class. It is informal in every sense. Methods of organizing the work, derived from the (contemporary and Anglo-Saxon) examples handed out, may be suggested, but most writers will be happier letting the content shape the form. It is ideal for the new class: impersonal, stimulating and sociable. Students anxious about reading out their work (most are) suddenly find it's more fun and more fruitful than they ever imagined. Interesting discussions have centred on what makes a certain riddle stand out as a 'real' poem. (There is often a surprising degree of consensus on the quality of the published texts.) It is particularly instructive to try to tease out the ways in which a curiously strong sense of personality and individuality imbues a piece of word spinning done by Anon hundreds of years ago! With luck, the students will leave the class having discovered in themselves perceptions both unique and communicable, and sensing that their endeavour, as poets and critics, will involve huge pleasure as well as hard work.

As early as possible in the course we will also look at the use of refrain, one of the most attractive and accessible formal devices available. Those students who have confided truculently that they 'really write rock lyrics' will usually have played with this device and may have work well worth looking at in connection with the songs and ballads of tradition. (An opportunity to bring the alienated into the fold should never be sneezed at!) But the main focus in the handouts will be on literary writers. Louis MacNeice, Edwin Morgan and, of course, Charles Causley yield up fine twentieth-century examples of refrain poems. At this point in the course I make the first of many pleas to the students to read as much as possible – by these authors, specifically, as well as any and every poet that takes their fancy. It is not only for the students' benefit: I feel I owe it to the poets whose work I've cherry-picked for forms. God forbid that I should send anyone away with the impression that, for example, Elizabeth Bishop wrote nothing but villanelles! And, of course, the more widely read the students are in the work of the poet concerned, the better they will see into the translation-like process of the formal piece of writing, the more they will understand of the unique conversation they are overhearing.

It is a short step from the single-refrain poem to the double: i.e. the villanelle. I fell in love with this form at the age of seventeen, while reading Auden's 'If I Could Tell You'. I have practised it ever since, with numerous abject failures and the occasional totally unpredicted success, and I pounce on every contemporary example I can find. My current handout consists of Bishop, Muldoon, Mahon, Roethke, Elizabeth Garrett, Dylan Thomas and, of course, Auden. I have had some thrilling villanelles composed by students – and also some very odd ones, which nevertheless contained a pulse of real poetic life. There is an innate sparkle and bounce to the form, rarely completely suppressed by poor technique.

In the dance of the villanelle, the repeated lines may mean something different each time they reappear – like an actor who has rushed offstage and executed a quick change between scenes, or, a better analogy, like a chameleon adapting to a different background. It may be that an image is taking on new colouring from the preceding stanza but it is more likely that syntactical repositioning is effecting the change, as when Thomas turns a simple predicate ('Do not go gentle into that good night') into a ringing imperative. The inter-weaving of the refrain lines can be as complicated as your skills allow: you can twitch out a comma, tweak in a colon, run on across the stanza or cut mid-line; you can even do some minor cheating as to word order and grammatical case. (I have to say I encourage cheating, though usually as a separate formal enterprise: there are discoveries to be made in breaking as well as obeying formal rules.) Yet the best villanelles are usually those in which the author, more or less, leaves the refrains to dance by themselves. The real trick of villanelle composition is to make the form look as if it were organizing the content. Refrain lines of both wonderful independence and wonderful compatibility are the first requirement, and the more throwaway they look, the better. The moment at the end of the poem, when they meet and mate and hint at miraculous progeny, is of course the whole explanation for writing the villanelle in the first place!

Towards the end of the course we turn to the light-verse forms such as the clerihew and limerick. Students usually have a sense of humour and I don't see why they should leave it at the door. (After all, the troubadours were also court satirists.) Of the 'serious' forms, the sonnet is usually found to be the most demanding, and initial results may be disappointing. I am sure this is because echoes of Shakespeare and Milton inextricably cling to A-level or first-year memories of the forms: pastiche is often the result. This is not, of course, to say students shouldn't read Shakespeare and Milton! But they need to hear examples in which contemporary diction and idiom are acclimatized. I give out samples of work by Berryman, Muldoon, Marilyn Hacker, Tony Harrison, Carol Ann Duffy. Conversely, young writers take to the sestina and haiku often with extraordinary facility – something to do with the flatness of the modern vernacular? It is strange that the longest form as well as the shortest should demand most rigorously that frilliness and fakery be put on hold. The haiku is sheer economy – especially as I urge the writers to aim for a lower syllable count than the traditional (but inauthentic) 5-7-5. But the sestina is tall, of course, and wobbles if it lacks a strong, plain narrative skeleton.

It might be thought that the more organic or free-form writing is squeezed out by the set-form regimen. In fact, half of all workshop sessions will be occupied with the presentation of students' own work, and most of these pieces will be 'nonce' poems (i.e. poems in one-off, original forms of the writer's own devising). However irregular or improvisatory, these pieces too have 'shapes', which are discussed in detail, raising issues of lineation, stanza construction, etc. In particular we discuss the rationale of the line break. It can be more difficult to get a student to listen to his or her own line breaks than to construct a sestina – but the writing of the sestina should teach something about lineation that will benefit all the writing (prose, too, I suspect). The advice to any poet is: know the rhythm of your voice and the rhythm of your language. Know them at every moment. The formal aspect of the course may be said to teach the rhythm of the language. The nonce poems tell the poets about their own pitch, tone and rhythm.

Students submit a minimum of two examples of formal poetry in their final script – many offer more. A new benefit becomes apparent during the finals flurry. Producing creative work to a deadline is tough on the most experienced professional: the very least the formal requirement achieves is a strategy for writing that minimizes the paralysing general anxiety by focusing on a limited number of soluble problems. It maps the points at which you can effectively be self-critical and frontal-lobed, but otherwise leaves the subconscious mind free to play. This is not, of course, true only at exam time, but the benefit is more appreciated then. Formal writing is, in fact, a beautiful device for liberating the essential powerlessness of the artist, Keats's negative capability. Outsiders may see formal composition as rule-fixated grind: practitioners know it as rule-forgetting delight.

I have heard it said that the least talented writers benefit the most from practising form. This is only partly true. Those students most likely to lose the thread in a nonce poem (usually in agonies of attempted 'self-expression'), or whose ear for rhythm and cadence lets them down, may discover unsuspected abilities and fluencies when writing formally. The more talented, though, will exploit the forms richly and inventively. Sometimes the less artful writer will get a better result, producing something that looks effortless, whereas the sophisticated writer conjures effects a little too obviously brilliant. In general, though, form urges all degrees of ability to optimum performance.

There is a contemporary stereotype of the well-written 'literary' poem, a work that may display a clever but somewhat imitative facility in pulling off certain fashionable tricks of style and diction. The fixed-form poem insists on a more fundamental, candid and perhaps dangerous engagement with language. Year after year I have been impressed, charmed, moved to tears and occasionally to envy as I witness a fresh young risk-taking imagination with a set of newly acquired technical skills, renegotiating its rights to the ancient properties, dispelling in a bold flourish or two every last whiff of dust and mothball. Suddenly, the student becomes a poet (if, so far, only momentarily) and the old heartbeat of the English language is heard as if newborn. How did he or she do it? Wonders, like the forms themselves, will never cease.

Shapes of Things
Paul Magrs

We write things in order to make sense of the world. It cheers me up to put something together, some written object that didn't exist in the world before. All too often events in the world seem frighteningly random and arbitrary, and I think I use writing to put some kind of order on things. I know it's an artificial order, of course.

The shape of a poem, a playscript scene, a short story – they're all my attempt to make sense of the chaotic relations of people, events and objects, and sometimes the illusion of cause, effect and reason can be quite consolingly seductive.

It is why I've always been obsessed with novels and have spent much of my time living inside of them. They are a structured space giving an illusion of the world; we feel safe within their programmed chaos. We know that we're going to come out of the other end intact, even if the characters who have engaged our sympathies don't.

In writing, we are attempting – in a fairly modest way or perhaps in a sweeping, grandiose way – to impose a pattern on life.

I grew up on a council estate in Newton Aycliffe, a new town in the north-east of England. Living there I heard hundreds of thousands of narratives over the years; lives spilled over and interconnected, becoming ever more complex as time went on. My first three novels, which together form *The Phoenix Court Trilogy*, were, in a way, an attempt to corral certain of these kinds of narrative that multiply and overlap when many vivid characters live in close proximity. It is extremely difficult to give a shape to the messiness of life and interrelated lives. In my case, I did it through plotting and mapping and drawing diagrams that the writing could follow. I chose social comedy as the model for bringing these characters together.

Narrative is present everywhere, the French critic Roland Barthes tells us. We can never have narrative without language. We seek it out, by our very nature, everywhere we look.

✑ Try this: assemble five inanimate objects – say, an empty wine bottle, a dress, an aerosol can, a scarf, a potted plant. For each of them, write its narrative in any form – dramatic monologue, lyric poem, short story. It is bound to have one. Think about the life that the object will have led. What was its moment of crisis? What was its moment of triumph or bliss? Let these turning points in the object's biography shape the tale you tell about it.

In any kind of writing we want to stay true to the complexity of real life, but we also want to impose a shape, an artificial structure. You know the world or the experience you hope to relate to the reader; you know it inside out. But you have to take the reader by the hand and lead them through it. You have to coax and seduce and persuade them, as Patricia Duncker says in her essays, and as Ashley Stokes says in his: plot, shape, structure; these are devices for the benefit of the reader. Plot in a novel is the guide rail down into the dark cavern, as the readers inch down the steps cut into slippery rock. They haul themselves along with your guidance, and they're wanting to see the subterranean grotto where the slumbering dragon guards a treasure trove. They're waiting for that kind of pay-off.

As writer you have to promise them two things. That you will guide them carefully: you'll put the guide rail and the steps so they lead in the right direction, with no dangerous gaps. But you also have to promise that you are taking the reader somewhere worthwhile. You have to keep hinting that this is a journey worth going on. That, eventually, they will get to see that dragon and the glittering wealth it protects. You've invented a structure that is a safe, negotiable space through which your readers can be led. You keep them moving through it by a dual process of building up their expectations and paying them off, bit by bit.

Shaping in this way is also about what Oscar Wilde called 'elegant circumlocution'. You can't deliver everything at once. The reader wants to be teased along. Any piece of writing toys with us and prevaricates before delivering us to the exit. If it didn't do this, then any poem or short story could be accomplished in just one line and we wouldn't need any more than that. Coleridge's 'Rime of the Ancient Mariner' could be reduced to 'This awful man kept following me about,' or Lolita might become 'He ran off with a girl young enough to be his daughter.' Naturally, readers want more than that.

The shape we impose on writing is an elaborate machine; something that drives the reader on, through all the variations and peregrinations. They want to get to the ending, they want to feel they've been through the whole experience – but they want to get caught up in it, too. They want to feel as if the delays and detours have been important to the whole experience. They need to feel enriched by them en route.

The Wizard of Oz would be nothing if Dorothy had simply called a cab in Munchkin Land and zoomed straight off to the Emerald City and demanded to be sent back to Kansas at once.

The reader needs to be treated to exciting detours, delays, encounters and pay-offs. Through chapters of a novel, scenes in a play, stanzas of a poem, they learn a little more through each variation the writer teases out. The reader feels like they've lived through something.

✍ To explore the way in which the writer imposes a narrative framework, try this out. Write down two distinct locations and make them quite different: a ski slope, a tropical island. Write down two names plucked from a newspaper and give both these characters random occupations. List four household objects. Write down three abstract nouns, and these will be the moods you hope to convey. Write down in two or three words, at most, a particular kind of accident. This last event will be the motor that will set the whole thing running. Without this trigger, all you have is a list. The event will set these items moving. It puts the whole lot into time.

Now is when you coax your characters into life. You start asking questions. Who has the accident? What caused it? Was the other person involved? Were they responsible? What is the relationship between the two characters? How has the accident forced them to move from one location to the other? How do your abstract nouns come in? Are these the emotions at play? Why is this one person in this particular state (terror, torpor, jealousy) while the other is quite different (ecstatic, betrayed, guilty)?

By taking a whole list of random items and introducing a trigger (a plane crash, a body washed up on a beach, a giraffe in a zoo suddenly savaging its keeper), you are forced to start linking all the items up. We can't help doing it. Try it now and write it out as a causal list, making sure that all the elements in your original list are used up. There are endless permutations, far more than there are in Cluedo, a game that operates by the same principle (who killed who with what object and where).

This narrative game, of linking up random, juxtaposed items, is our habitual response to the world. We want to make a pattern, a scheme and we seek closure to narratives. This exercise is useful, in that it makes us aware of how we individually set about that. Sometimes, in writing, the possibilities seem limitless and dizzying. We could write about anything – so how do we choose? It's good to close down your options a little sometimes and to become aware of your own processes of shaping and making sense.

So how does your structured narrative based on the random list work out? Does it conform to either of Patricia Duncker's models of stories – is it a quest or siege narrative? Is it a revenge tale or a romance? Take a long look at the thumbnail narrative you've constructed. What does it need adding in order to make it work? Another character? Further intrigue? More twists and turns in the plot? At this stage you can afford to be wildly inventive. It's all an experiment in shaping a piece of work. To get a character in your piece of writing from A to Z you can think up the most outrageously improbable means.

The challenge, then, is to take that grid, that map of events, and to make it convincing and real. Using all the other skills at your disposal, you take the abstract shape, that plot machine, and you make your characters and your readers live through it.

Finishing

9 Stepping Back

Introduction
Paul Magrs

In his most successful and prolific period, Joe Orton wrote in his diary that he had just finished a draft of a new play, and now he was putting it under his bed for six months in order to let it 'mature'. When I first read that I wondered if he thought that the thing would somehow improve of its own accord, fermenting and gathering dust in the dark like a bottle of wine. I realized that he must have known that his market value was on the up and up and the improvement he was actually expecting was in financial returns for a new piece of work.

Now, though, I think he also meant that, given six months, he himself would have changed. He would be able to come back to that manuscript with fresh eyes and ears. He would be coming to it almost as another person; as a reader again.

Is it true that after seven years none of our skin cells are actually the same? That we've regenerated completely, but the old pattern still holds, so that we look the same, only older?

I think that process must be even faster with writers. The dead cells flake and drop off and a newer, sensitive skin comes up with far more regularity than every seven years. We are the continually changing product of everything we see, read, experience. We can't help but be different when we sit down to start work on something already started.

In his essay, David Lodge talks about starting the writing day with reading back what you wrote yesterday. You have to anchor yourself back into the world of your story, poem, play. You have to get the feeling back of that world and strive after consistency. You have to hold the whole atmosphere of it in your head and push on, staying true to the parameters of that vision. This is something you can only do by reading yourself over and over.

You have to ration yourself, however. You can't read back from page one every day, especially if it's a novel you are working on. As the piece of writing becomes longer, more and more of your day would be spent reading and less would be spent writing new stuff. You have to write new stuff: it's good for your self-esteem.

If you read everything from page one every day before starting again, reaching the end would be as impossible for you as it is for the frog who takes half jumps from his lily pad to the other side of the pond. As his jumps get fractionally smaller, he is doomed never to reach dry land.

So you have to push away from the beginning. It's just like going to sea. It's dangerous and you might drown. A good idea is to set yourself a fixed amount of rereading for yourself – a certain number of pages, say – and they will alter every day, progressing along with you. You need to use the fresh rereading of these pages as a barge pole to shove yourself off from your home shore, and to punt yourself into clear water.

Rereading yourself as you go along is vital, but don't let yourself get bogged down in it. Sometimes you have to leave sections of your work a little rougher, a bit more untamed, in order to move on and get on with the rest of it. You can't give it all a final polish as you go on – the end isn't in sight yet. You don't know what you might have to do to those pieces yet. When the whole thing is substantially there – when the whole shape and arc and structure of the piece is complete and you've made the journey to the end – that's the time to go back and read it, all in one piece. That's when you can think about the process of final polishings.

Who'd make the parts for a car and polish each of them to a gleam before putting them all together?

It's a two-way process – reading back and pushing ahead. But you have to do both. If all you do is read back and minutely revise, you'll end up with less and less every day. If you push forward remorse-lessly, without ever reading anything, you will have something that is disastrously inconsistent in tone and vision. It would be a great patchwork of yourself in different states of mind, with no clarity or continuity between individual parts. Without a certain amount of rereading it's a mess and quickly falls apart.

My heroine in this respect is Colette who, working in her special room, writing on pale blue sheets of foolscap, would each day produce her six pages – rigorously, energetically – and, at the end of the day, upon reading back, robustly tear up page six. She knew that the energy would have fizzled by page six – and that the first five were vintage, authentic Colette.

Set yourself suitable limits like this. You can't write the whole thing in one unbroken day. No one has the stamina for that. You have to leave off in order to do the rest of life – eat, sleep, see other people. But you don't have to carry the whole thing in your head between times, either, so that sitting down to write again involves the Herculean task of lifting up the great big rock of your work and weighing it all up again, looking at it from every angle. Read back only a certain amount of it; get the flavour again, get the mood. Prepare to launch off again across the wild water.

To me, reading back isn't just about reading words already on the page. It is also about constructing diagrams on the walls for the shape of the piece of work. It is about consulting notebooks, scribbled pages, file cards and journals. All of this extra material ought to be arranged around you, like a painter has their messy paraphernalia strewn in their studio: sketches, photos, brushes, palettes, knives. These are all tools to get you back into the textual world you are creating.

A diagram constructed on the wall can show you the whole shape of a story or novel or play. It can illustrate the arcs of development and progress your characters make, or it could record the projection of tangled lines where they meet, cross over, sleep together or exchange vital information. You might have a graph charting the downfalls and triumphs of your central protagonist, or a Chinese-box diagram – boxes within boxes – to enable you to keep a hold on narrative points of view or time frames in your story. Just about all of Alice Munro's stories involving flashbacks within flashbacks could be drawn as Chinese boxes.

Another good thing to do is to lay out your pages on the floor. It's like looking down on the thing from a helicopter. Take a look at the lie of your land; the whole artificial landscape. Sometimes it's good to go to work with scissors and Sellotape, which is always more satisfying than the rather bloodless cutting and pasting commands on a word processor. Let your hands get dirty with paper and ink.

All of these practical tasks are another way of reading yourself, in immersing yourself in your work, as seeing each day's work as another negotiable step on the way to a much bigger picture.

Getting into a complicated piece of writing is just like walking into a maze. You don't know what's waiting in the middle, you've no idea where the exit is and you are not quite sure which way you came in . . . You need some practical means of getting through it. Theseus had a handy ball of wool to twine out behind him, Virginia Woolf had a writer's diary in which she kept a commentary on her progress from day's work to day's work.

You could draw a map or diagram (no two texts' maps would ever look exactly the same), or you could just rely on the most obvious and essential method: reading back to yourself a certain amount of what you've already written.

You have to clear your mind somewhat to do this. You must regard the writer as someone who isn't you. Let them seduce you and surprise you. You are looking for the subtexts that you weren't actively aware of at the time, or that you've forgotten. You are looking for the gaps you left, the potential interesting tangents, the 'roads not taken'. You'll find elements you want to tease out and develop later. Their intrigue fills you with the kind of hunger and energy so necessary for you to continue writing . . .

✍ Try this out as an exercise. Draw a map of your story and how you want it to develop. It's up to you, the form you create for your diagram. You could use different colours for your different characters, to show how they meet up, entangle and move apart again. Or you could show them as a Venn diagram, with over-lapping circles to show who knows who, who influences who in the story. You might, as fantasy writers often do, draw an actual map of the imaginary landscape your people inhabit.

When we're writing words on pages we sometimes forget about drawing pictures. We keep the plan of something in our head. It helps sometimes to deprive yourself of words and draw the shape of your story or play or poem on a large sheet of paper. You can often surprise yourself this way. The diagram might not mean anything to anyone else, but other people don't have to see it. It will mean something to you.

Try mapping out what you want your text to be. Draw arrows between characters' names or images. Try showing yourself, at a visual level, how one thing links to another.

There must be a piece of work you'd like to finish and can't quite work out how. The first stanza of a poem, the first couple of pages of a story. Hide it away somewhere and put it out of your mind, then come back to it two weeks later. Leave a note to yourself to do this (and remember where you've hidden it!). See what it looks like now.

Sometimes these beginnings of things are only waiting for one more element in order to progress. This may be something you have learned or observed in the intervening time. When you come back as a reader to this unfinished thing, the right element might just slip into place and then you can go on.

Keep a file for these beginnings of things that you can put away and come back to. Some of them will never be of use. Others might well just contain the germ of something that you want to pick up again and develop.

✍ You could do this now. Look back to something, some idea from earlier in your notebooks that didn't go anywhere at the time. You might have forgotten what you wrote back then or what was in your mind. You will read this lost piece as any reader would, trying to puzzle it out: What was the writer getting at? Use it as the trigger for your imagination now, the person you are now. See what you can make it into . . .

But you must be careful not to let reading yourself become staring into the looking glass and falling in love with yourself. Think of the wicked queen in Snow White, who adored herself and flew into a rage when she was told Snow White was, in fact, fairer. That's like the reader who reads their own pages and decides, 'What's the point when Nabokov was so brilliant? When Anne Sexton said it so much better than I've ever done?'

It's not a looking glass you are looking into. Don't fall in love with all your best moments and all your bad habits. Don't rationalize all your weaknesses and mistakes (as we do with anyone we love. . .). Don't use that mirror to envy other writers and give up in dismay.

It isn't a mirror. It's raw, still unfinished work of your own.

Look at it carefully and hard and learn the techniques for moving off from it into new, further writing.

Reading Yourself
David Lodge

In my experience, 90 per cent of the time nominally spent 'writing' is actually spent reading – reading yourself. You write a sentence – or, more likely, half a sentence. You pause to read what you have written. You cross out a word and substitute another. Perhaps you cross out all the words and start again. You complete the sentence and read it back to yourself. Probably you make some more adjustments to it. You begin the next sentence and go through the whole process again. When you come to the end of the paragraph you go back and read it from the beginning and make further changes, additions, deletions.

You begin another paragraph, another sentence. And so on.

I am well aware that not everyone writes in such a slow and laborious manner as this. And probably most of us write more quickly, with less hesitation and revision, when we are young. As we grow old the neurones in our brains, whose interaction generates ideas, plots, images, tropes, seem to fire more sluggishly. Also, one would like to think, we grow more self-critical and perfectionist in the exercise of our craft. But whatever the tempo of composition, reading yourself is built into the process from the level of the smallest unit of sense to the largest. It is essentially what distinguishes writing from speaking. In speech, you cannot delete or edit what you have uttered. You can only rephrase it, qualify it, contradict it, repudiate it, apologize for it. In both speech and writing, you discover what it is you have to say by trying out various ways of saying it (which means, of course, that the last 'it' is never the same as the first), but writing allows you the luxury of suppressing your false starts.

When you read yourself you should be trying to assess the effect your writing will have on your readers. The ability to do this is almost as important as the ability to invent or imagine what your writing is 'about'. It marks the difference between the professional and the amateur writer, the publishable and the unpublishable. The trick is to read yourself as if the work is not your work but the work of another; or, to put it another way, to read yourself as if you are another reader. When we make our first attempts at writing, we are so entranced and impressed by our own creativity – our ability to describe actions, persons, places which had no existence before we evoked them in language – that we assume everybody else will be equally entranced and impressed. But mere creativity is not enough. The simulated world you create must also be interesting, interesting enough to lure a reader from the actual world he or she inhabits. And by reader I do not mean your mother or your lover or anyone else who is apt to be as readily impressed by your creativity as you are. I mean an imagined, anonymous, ideal reader: intelligent, alert, open-minded but demanding, equipped with what Hemingway called a built-in shit detector.

Reading yourself is not just a matter of assessing and polishing your verbal style, the diction and syntax of the individual sentence. It also covers deeper and larger structures, what we may call the cohesion of the text as a whole. In narrative literature (which is what I am mainly concerned with) cohesion is determined by the intertwined codes of causality, temporality, psychology, morality, etc., which constitute a story and affect the reader's response to it. Although in literature all this information is communicated through language, it is not inseparable from specific verbal formulations. Narrative is itself a kind of language, more universal than natural languages (demonstrated by the fact that literary stories can be translated into different media which are only partly verbal or not verbal at all, e.g. film, opera, mime). In reading and rereading yourself, therefore, you are not only assessing the expressive function of every word group and sentence, but also monitoring the contribution of each of these tiny units of sense to the development of larger narrative strategies such as enigma, suspense, dramatic irony and so on.

Reading yourself is not just reactive, but also proactive. It is not merely a way of reviewing and improving what you have written, but also a way of generating what is yet to be written. Each sentence is a springboard from which to launch your next. When you are stuck, uncertain how to continue, it can help to take a longer 'run-up' – to go back to the start of the paragraph, or chapter, or even the entire work. Reading yourself is part of the *ritual* of writing. Such ritual of course varies from one writer to another; but probably most novelists begin the day's work by rereading what they wrote the day before (and, inevitably, tinkering with *that*). Some will go back further in the work-in-progress. This kind of reading is an equivalent to the athlete's 'warming up'. Its function is partly to induce in yourself the state you aim to produce in your reader's consciousness; that is, to make your imagined world, for the duration of the reading experience, displace the real world he inhabits, with all its practical demands and contingencies. It also serves the purpose of attuning yourself to the 'voice' you have adopted or created for the work, which may be that of a characterized 'I' narrator or may be the voice of the 'implied author', but in either case differs from your own ordinary, everyday, instrumental voice.

Sometimes you may have to put aside a work-in-progress for some considerable period of time – weeks or months – in order to do something else more urgently pressing. Or you may choose to put it aside for reasons that have to do with the work itself. Having to suspend work in this way can be frustrating or discouraging, but it also affords a unique opportunity. When you read what you have just written in the ongoing process of composition, you cannot actually experience your own discourse as your first-time reader will experience it, because you know what is coming in the next sentence or paragraph. But when you reread a piece of work after a long interval, it is possible to surprise yourself with things you had forgotten you wrote, and thus to get some inkling of how the work is going to affect a reader to whom it will reveal itself in a continuous movement from the known to the unknown. This is perhaps the closest a writer comes to 'enjoying' his or her own work in the way a reader enjoys it; or, conversely, to recognizing that it is deeply and perhaps irredeemably flawed.

That kind of reading oneself was very well described by Kingsley Amis in *The Old Devils* (1986). Alun Weaver is a professional media Welshman, who in late middle age returns to his native south Wales. In Chapter Seven he arrives at a borrowed seaside cottage, with his wife, a great deal of food and drink, and forty-six pages of a novel he began some months earlier and hasn't looked at since.

> As they stood, or with some minor surgery, they were supposed to be, he had striven to make them, his devout hope was that they were, the opening section of the only serious piece of prose he had written since his schooldays.

Note how the hesitant beginning of this sentence mimics in its deviant syntax the process of revision and emendation that writing normally suppresses, and thus conveys to us the character's uneasiness about the quality of his work and his tension at the prospect of rereading it. Alun is adept at deceiving others, but he is well aware that there is no point in trying to deceive himself about the viability of his projected novel. 'A great deal . . . hung on whatever he would make of those forty-six [pages] in two or three hours' time.' Amis extracts a good deal of humour from Alun's nervous preparations for the reading he both desires and dreads, but most writers will find the comedy cuts close to the bone.

> Almost eagerly he picked up the envelope. Before he had got as far as pulling out the contents his demeanour changed to a frenzied casualness. Head on one side, eyebrows raised and eyes almost shut, mouth turned down at the corners, he condescendingly turned back the flap, exposed the top half of the first sheet and allowed himself to let his glance wander over the typewritten lines . . . he slumped and stared out at the bay and tried to reason with himself.
>
> *Of course* the first couple of sentences had reminded him of the opening passages of dozens of stories and novels by Welshmen, especially those written in the first half of the century. That was the whole point, to stress continuity, to set one's face against anything that could be called modernism . . . he laid the typescript down on the table just like that and began at the beginning.
>
> After five minutes or so he began to relax his rigid bomb-disposal posture. From time to time as he went on he winced sharply and made a correction, screwed up his mouth in pain or goggled in disbelief, but several times gave a provisional nod and even laughed once or twice without mirth.

The last paragraph *seems* to be qualifying the negative impression made on Alun by the opening lines of his novel. It seems to be saying, or to be about to say, that as he went on reading he found some merit in it. But his body language is a giveaway. Even his nods are 'provisional', his laughter sparse and 'without mirth'. We are not surprised that Alun is unable to add much to his forty-six pages, and that the friend to whom he shows them for a second opinion candidly advises him to abandon the project.

For better or worse, Alun's is the best way to read yourself for the purpose of self-assessment: to leave the work aside for a period of time, to try to forget what you have written before you reread it. But for obvious reasons you cannot do this with any frequency. There are other, less radical ways of 'defamiliarizing' your own discourse. Reading it aloud, for instance, will often reveal all kinds of flaws and imperfections – awkward repetitions, over-emphatic rhythms, unproductive ambiguities – which act as irritants and distractions at an almost subliminal level and may be overlooked in silent reading. According to Leopoldo Duran, Graham Greene always used to read his work-in-progress aloud, because 'he attached great importance to the cadence of a sentence'. This habit no doubt accounts in part for the novelist's famous 'readability'.

When I started writing fiction, and for some time afterwards, I used to write out the whole novel in longhand and then type it up. The transition from manuscript to typescript was a vital part of the compositional process: it gave the work an encouraging new appearance, more like a real book, and also made it easier to reread and revise. I still find it useful to write the first draft of almost any kind of writing except screenplay adaptations in longhand, a few pages at a time, before putting them on to the computer. The strengths and weaknesses of the handwritten draft stand out more clearly when you remove the inky traces of scribbled cancellations and insertions, and the editing facilities of word-processing programs make it easy and effortless to make new corrections and additions. Even if you are wedded to composing on a keyboard, printing out the text can have something of the same defamiliarizing effect. I cannot read a page on a screen as I read a page printed on a sheet of paper, and I think I am not unusual in this respect. I print out endless versions of work in progress, read them, emend them by hand, make the emendations on the computer, print the text out again, read it again . . .

In his essay 'The Function of Criticism', T. S. Eliot wrote:

> Probably . . . the larger part of the labour of an author in composing his work is critical labour; the labour of sifting, combining, constructing, expunging, correcting, testing: this frightful toil is as much critical as creative. I maintain even that the criticism employed by a trained and skilled writer on his own work is the most vital, the highest kind of criticism; and . . . that some creative writers are superior to others solely because their critical faculty is superior.

What Eliot is describing here is essentially the same as what I have called 'reading yourself', and he is right to describe it as a critical activity. Certainly, one can only learn how to do it by reading the work of other writers – seriously, attentively, critically. However, it is not quite the same as 'literary criticism' in the institutional sense. A critic who finds fault with a novel or a poem is not expected to explain how it could have been improved, still less to offer to rewrite it. That, however, is precisely the purpose of a writer's critical reading of his own work. He uses himself as reader as a kind of wall from which to bounce back hints and suggestions for himself as writer. The professional critic is, consciously or unconsciously, ultimately concerned to exert his mastery over the text of another, imposing his own metalanguage (rhetoric, literary history, structuralism, Marxism, psychoanalysis) on the language of the text – 'covering it', Roland Barthes observed, in his essay 'Criticism as Language', as completely as possible. With the exception of rhetoric (interpreted in the widest sense) the writer will find these metalanguages of little direct use to him in the task of assessing the effectiveness of his work, and they may be actual hindrances. The writer's interest in criticism is practical and pragmatic. He is concerned only that his novel, poem or play should, as we say, 'work'. It is for others to judge whether and why it is or is not valuable and important.

Standards in Creative Writing Teaching
Russell Celyn Jones

It occurs to me when reviewing fiction for newspapers that literary judgement is an act of faith; you know something to be 'true' but can't prove it absolutely. Literary criticism is necessarily a subjective search for truth in text (and I don't mean realism), based on many years of reading and writing. When it comes to making judgements in students' fiction the criteria are different, but related to the above.

For the past year I have been teaching at Warwick University at both undergraduate and postgraduate levels. The way students are selected for the BA in creative writing is by manuscript and personal statement – ratified at interview. The manuscript has to show some aptitude for fictional language, instead of what is most common among eighteen-year-olds – an arduous slog to the sting-in-the-tail ending, the ending being the only justification of the story existing. Yet only exceptional eighteen-year-olds know how to write in a mature style and they are often protégés. With the majority of applications you have to work on a hunch, making a predication for the future based on what exists in a manuscript.

In the UCAS personal statement a student who can demonstrate an interest in contemporary authors is important, and not just their A-level set texts. Good writing is also about good reading. So at the interview you are looking for an edge, an openness, even a little eccentricity. Does the applicant have a life? Not the kind of life suggested by two years as school prefect, gymkhanas, charity work, sword fencing, but evidence of a struggle. Better still, a struggle overcome. Writers talking about books make a different sound to academics talking about books. The way they talk about modern literature is a good litmus test of how they will perform in a workshop. The creative writing workshop, particularly at undergraduate level, is principally another way of teaching literature, designed to get students looking at literature from the *inside*. To that end I often set imitation exercises: read for style, imitate; read for character, imitate; read for dialogue, imitate. How do you show the interior life of a character? How is landscape and setting employed to reveal character? How do you build a non-autobiographical character? Students are encouraged to write about what they don't know.

At a postgraduate level the manuscript is the single most important criterion to look out for. You do not set so many exercises but edit students' manuscripts instead. The MA workshop has taken quite a lot of flak from people in the industry, principally publishers who claim that writers are born, not taught. While there is some truth in that, creative writing courses grow increasingly more popular. In my view the writer's workshop has grown in inverse proportion to a decline in editing skills among publishers and agents. Would-be writers now regard a creative writing course as a prerequisite step to getting published. The workshop is where the inexperienced writer can get into shape by honing his or her writing through close editing by a writer-teacher, who nurtures an atmosphere of experiment – and failure. Failure in writing is just another term for the creative process. The aim is to understand through practice the mechanisms of fiction. At the same time you enable students to develop a sibling critical language, so they may understand that these mechanisms are inventions too, paradigms which constantly change.

Standards at both undergraduate and graduate levels can generally be reduced to a feel for language. Fiction is about language and students should be discouraged from abusing sentences as a means to an end. Sentences are the brush strokes in the canvas. Sentences are what makes up a voice. I encourage students to practise writing through the voice of a character. Authorial voice is something else and much more difficult to teach, maybe impossible. Authorial voice is the holy grail of fiction.

As a rule students do improve their performance as the year progresses, the best improvements shown by those who have attended all the workshops, attempted all the assignments. At the year's end I have to give grades and it is my experience that first, second and third markers reach a consensus. These markers are all writers themselves, which points to an inalienable truth that only writers can teach writing. Because writers live inside the novel, the short story, the poem. Even writers of different preoccupations and genres tend to agree when putting a value on a student's work. At Warwick a third marker casts the deciding grade in the event of a dispute, but on the whole there is not a lot of discrepancy between markers' decisions.

On this subject of assessment, writer-teachers should try to make judgements that are free from taste. It is the nature of immature students to make strident attempts to be different. Their pre-occupations are often limited by youth. You often have to try to assess their work without necessarily liking it. As a guiding principle I regard fiction as operating in terms of its own procedures, rather than in terms of the procedures of, say, history or academia (and since universities are often our hosts this sometimes creates ructions). Another dilemma that seems to occur frequently is whether a less able student who imitates very well should earn a better grade than a gifted student who tries something original and fails. Can you mark up for promise? Is it fair to encourage with a high grade a foreshadowing of greater things to come? In the end, each case has to be taken on its own merits. But what makes a first-class degree or a distinction at MA is precisely some evidence of invention – about character, language, form. At the same time a sense of structure is necessary, even in the most experimental of work. Students are often inclined to remove traditional foundations from literature without replacement architecture and their enterprise falls down. Fraud is a close cousin to invention and should not be mistaken for brilliance. Some sign of a controlling hand should be apparent in the work.

There is no such thing as the perfect work of art, as there is no such thing as the perfect student or the perfect teacher. Nonetheless we strive for perfection knowing that it cannot be achieved.

Anxiety of Influence
Julia Bell

Some writers claim never to read while they are writing. As if reading will infect their style and make them write too much like the writers they are reading. Anxiety of influence is one of the problems most writers wrestle with from time to time. Chances are you will have a bookshelf full of heroines and heroes, of writers you admire and want to emulate. At one time or another we all might try to do a Martin Amis story or a Bret Easton Ellis story or an Angela Carter story. This is not a bad thing. This is part of the process of finding your fictional voice.

Reading widely and working through the things you like about your heroines or heroes will help you to assess where you are different from other writers. Where your fictional voice is yours and where it is copied or stolen from another writer.

The best way to learn how to write is to read. But you need to read widely, beyond your usual frame of reference, in order for this to be a truly effective exercise. If you spend hours deconstructing Angela Carter or Martin Amis, and read very little else, it *will* cramp your style. You will find your head full of the syntax and rhythms of their writing, which will rob you of your voice because your head will be cluttered with theirs.

Now you have been writing for a while, step back from your work and do some concentrated reading. Stop reading your influences, just for a while at least, and read books you wouldn't usually read. Go through your bookshelf and pile up all the books you've bought and have never got round to reading and read them. Learn to read as a writer, looking for the consistency of voice, the way the writer makes characters vivid on the page, their metaphors and turns of phrase, the way they reveal information and so on.

✍ Write a few pastiches. Deliberately copy someone else's style, just for the duration of a paragraph or a page or a story to try to figure out how it's done. Do these pastiches quickly, without rewriting, just to get you limbered up. Develop an ear for the patterns and rhythms of other writers' voices. Identifying the voices of others will help you to distinguish your own.

Literature degrees can often ruin reading for a writer. I know that my English course didn't leave me as hungry or enthusiastic for books as I had been when I started. The minute deconstructions required by literature essays can render a text dry and lifeless. It's a bit like putting a book on the dissecting table, opening it up, and draining out all the blood. It's a very easy way to kill the thing you love.

I had to learn how to read again, I had to learn to read as a writer rather than as a student of literature. I wasn't going to the text with an ideology or a theory, rather I was reading because, basically, I have always liked being told stories. I had to find my credulity again, allow a book to seduce me. I had to recover for myself the pleasure of the text.

The problem with overtly self-conscious writing, writing that is too much steeped in notions of 'literature', is that it puts a limit on subject matter. Always looking over your shoulder to the texts that have gone before and placing yourself within that context will stop you from being original, playful, true to your own voice. Because canonical notions of writing are linear, the writer is always at the sharp end of the process. The 'canon' compels the writer to be new and original and to be aware of all that's gone before, and this can be not only frustrating but potentially damaging to the budding writer's prospects of success.

I teach many students who, excited by theories of writing, try to emulate 'the greats' and tackle grandiloquent themes and subjects. They usually end up frustrated by their own inadequacies rather than freed up to write about whatever tickles their fancy. And, worst of all, their work is often pretentious and undisciplined. Post-modernism is a poor excuse for bad practice. Flashy tricks and structural play are all very well, but does it make sense? Is it coherent? Is it telling us anything new? There is nothing worse than solipsistic writing. It smacks of egotism, arrogance towards the reader, and it dresses up its lack of insight in the clothes of modernity, excusing itself from censure because it is experimental. Sometimes it seems there is a fundamental misunderstanding about the nature of 'originality' implicit in such writing, as if originality only exists when the writing is fracturing ideas of structure or character. I try to steer students away from these rocks before they even get in the boat. Better to encourage them to create convincing characters, to develop their love of, and feel for, language, so that they become supple and articulate writers. The originality they are looking for will come of its own accord through practice. Forcing it will simply create forced writing.

10 Revising

Introduction
Paul Magrs

Getting to the end of something is really hard. You plough on and on in the same furrow and it's difficult to lift your head out and see how far you've come and where the end of the line might be. You've got the whole shape of this piece of work in your head; you want to do justice to it all.

I think it's counterproductive to stay in that same furrow. Whenever I'm working on something, I like to have other things on the go. I always have my journals and notebook, of course. But I also like to set myself exercises as I go along, to distract me, to re-energize me. If I'm writing something long and involved I need to step away from it sometimes in order to remind myself what it is I'm doing.

For instance, something I find very useful is a warm-up writing exercise in which I give myself twenty random words and then have to write a short piece in about half an hour or so that contains each of those random words. I circle twenty words in a piece I've already written, take them down as a list and then set to work.

I make myself write some kind of precis about the bigger piece of work I'm doing. If it's a novel I have to write about its characters, its plot, its themes. There's a fair amount of squeezing and lateral thinking has to go on in order to get all of my random words in there. They could include 'Kiev', 'thighs', 'astrological'. It means I'm re-approaching my story from a completely different view. I shouldn't be too tied down to essential facts. This being just an exercise, I can change those facts and the results can be quite surprising. A little bit of lateral thought can do wonders for your writing. Also, what happens when you do a spot check like this, on what you really think your writing is about, is that you find all sorts of interesting preoccupations coming to the fore. It's like taking a biopsy of your writing mind. You can read the piece back and think: So that's what I think it's all about. It might be very different to what you initially thought.

This kind of thumbnail sketch of the piece allows you to see the shape of your work. You are looking at the work down the wrong end of a telescope and you can suddenly see it from a different angle.

To me, the process of revising any piece of writing is about looking at the work from as many different angles as possible. It's like holding up an object you've made – a pot you've thrown, a jumper you've knitted – to the light and looking for flaws and other points of view. You turn it round and examine it. You wonder how it might be different or better.

In the process of revising, it's important to scrutinize every single element of the writing to make sure they're all as good as they can be, but it's important to look away for a while, too; to regather your resources so you can come to it fresh. Otherwise you can get snowblind, still pushing away at the same furrow.

I've always thought it's better to have too much than too little. One way of looking at the process of revising is in terms of pruning away the excess. I've used the metaphor of film-making before and I will do here as well. Now you are in the editing suite, after your months out on location and in the studio. You've shot take after take from multiple angles. Sometimes your characters fluffed their lines, other times the set fell down and people wandered haplessly into shot.

Here in the cutting room you've got masses of material, stored in cans, in notebooks and on separate pages and you can piece the whole thing together in the solitary hush. Here you can get back to what your original conception for the piece was going to be. You can craft it and watch it come to life as an organic whole.

Watch how much drops away on to the cutting-room floor: ribbons of sharp, shiny film, tangles of lopped-off lines of text.

You've got to be quite brutal with yourself at times. If something isn't working take it as far as you can, and if it still doesn't work get rid of it. Get rid of it also if it's too opaque, too obscure. But also if it's too explicit and expository. Often we find lines in our work that are not so much meant for the reader, but are simply notes for ourselves. Chapters that begin, 'That day she learned something about the true nature of desire . . .' don't have to begin like that. Lines like, '"You bastard," I said, crossly,' can be trimmed and made to imply more than they already do.

Readers like to be told just enough so that what they're reading is comprehensible. But they don't like to be told too much. They like to infer things from the text. They don't need you to explain absolutely everything; that way they feel patronized and oddly redundant.

You should be complicit with your reader. Leave them telling, juicily implicit gaps. Let them do a little work in putting together the whole picture. If you are alluding to classical, Biblical, Shakespearean, Miltonian sources, don't footnote it. This isn't academic writing.

Virginia Woolf used to refer to the common reader: one whom she could assume was bright enough and wanted to be challenged enough by her writing. She could assume this person would follow her wherever she wanted to take the text; they would work to keep up with her. We have to assume this, too. Don't talk down to your reader. They'll hate you for it.

Don't over-egg the pudding. If you put too much in in the way of explanations and sudden revelations, the reader will hate you, too. There's nothing I hate more than suddenly becoming aware that the author is Trying To Tell Me Something. When suddenly the props and masks drop away and we've got what Alan Bennett calls the Author in Disguise, lecturing us. The Author suddenly dispenses with all their conjuring effects and they've started to hector us like an evangelical. Beware of telling your readers What Life Is All About. They won't thank you for it.

We all want to do it, however. We wouldn't be writing if we didn't think we couldn't, at some point or other, have a stab at telling everyone What It's All About or What's Wrong With The World. Have a look through your work at the revising stage and remove all those bits. We're in the business of writing fiction and poetry. We're not writing aphorisms. The hours are longer.

Revision could go on for ever. I've known people reduce their work to almost nothing, to doilies. Part of the skill is knowing exactly when to stop. You've got to learn to say: This is as succinct and as honed as it will ever be. It says what I want it to say. It's something I've made that has gone through a certain journey and contains details that surprise me, that I didn't know would be there when I embarked on it. It's a piece of work that only I could write.

This is what you want to have: something only you could write.

During the revising process you want to take out all the material that just anyone could have written. That's why writing tutors always bang on about getting rid of clichés. Clichés are just shorthand for other people's experience; we use them to communicate with each other in life, but we don't need to use them in fiction or poetry, where more circuitous, idiosyncratic means can be employed. We're not necessarily looking for the shortest route between A and Z. In your work it needn't rain cats and dogs on dark, stormy nights. Clichés are always dead language; a slipshod rendition of second-hand experience. Everything should come out fresh, as first-hand experience. Clichés always come about when writers haven't looked at the real world long enough and hard enough.

It's often necessary and important to have other people look at your work during the revising stage. You can look at your own writing from all sorts of points of view, but the things that other members of a writing group can tell you will always surprise you.

There will always be some criticism that takes you completely by surprise; something you would never have thought of. Sometimes it is valid and useful, other times spurious and partisan. But you need to hear as much of it as you can and utilize or jettison it at will.

You are intending your work to go before as big an audience as possible. If criticism is given with care, consideration, accuracy and sympathy, then it can't hurt you. You are talking about an object in the world, something you have created, and you are invested in; but it is still an object that can be criticized and improved. You have to let people have their views on it. You can't let yourself become precious about your work and attempt to hide it away or retrospectively defend its weaknesses.

Is it communicating everything you wanted it to? Your other readers can let you know what they get from it. Listen to them. You should be fascinated by what they have to say.

Is this character working? What do you make of them? Is this dialogue really the way this character would speak? What meaning do you get from this stanza? How does this connect to this broader theme? What do you understand by this image? Is it a concrete image, one you could almost pick up and hold in your hand? Is this plot twist really necessary or does it seem very contrived? Is this setting solid and three dimensional? Are we being dragged through this part of the story too quickly?

Has the full potential of the material been realized?

It is important to realize that writing isn't like sport or playing a musical instrument in a concert. You aren't doing this live. If your attention slipped and you played a bum note or dropped the ball, or if you were waving at someone in the audience during a boring moment, or if you were overcome with tiredness and had to have a rest and run on automatic pilot for a while, it doesn't matter.

You are not playing football and that isn't a cello wedged between your knees. What you are doing is something they would never televize live. Something that on the outside looks incredibly dull: you, sitting there with your paper and pencil, frowning and doodling away. You'll never be under any pressure to do this live in front of an audience and have one chance only to make it absolutely perfect. We don't write under examination conditions, thank God.

You have the chance to take the criticisms that you and your colleagues make and return to the text. You can always draft it again.

Going the Last Inch:
Some Thoughts on Showing and Telling
Lindsay Clarke

A novel is a game for two players. The book may get written in solitude but it kicks into life only when a reader's imagination collaborates with that of the writer, so in working out how best to secure and sustain that collaboration, writers might usefully recall what most engrosses them as readers. In the early drafts of a piece, you are still working out what you are trying to say to yourself, and too much mental trafficking with an audience at that stage can inhibit the flow of your imagination. But if you mean to go public, then sooner or later you have to consider the legitimate needs of your readers, and a large part of the process of revision will be about making sure that you have given their imagination all the room it needs to work.

In this respect Henry James offered the novelist three key words of advice: 'Dramatize, dramatize, dramatize.' His disciple Percy Lubbock turned the recommendation into a rule by insisting that 'the art of fiction does not begin until the novelist thinks of his story as a matter to be shown, to be so exhibited that it will tell itself', and the cry of 'show, don't tell' still rings across writing workshops. To understand why, you need only ask which is more immediately engaging – to witness an event for yourself or to be told about it afterwards by someone else?

A brief example will *show* what the distinction between showing and telling can mean for fiction. If, in a first novel, an author had written, 'The boy broke down and began to cry so wretchedly that the other small children started howling too,' he would, rather dully, have told us something. When, in *The Lord of the Flies*, William Golding wrote that 'his face puckered, the tears leapt from his eyes, his mouth opened till they could see a square black hole . . . The crying went on, breath after breath, and seemed to sustain him upright as if he were nailed to it,' he has unforgettably *shown* us something. By which I mean that he has brought us so closely into the presence of the weeping child that we can see him and hear him and feel our own inconsolable portion in the sense of universal grief he disturbs in the other 'littluns'. Who could prefer the told version to the shown?

Yet forty years after Lubbock's book on *The Craft of Fiction*, Wayne C. Booth pointed out in *The Rhetoric of Fiction* that showing is itself only one among the diverse strategies of telling, and that direct telling can work potent magic, too. Consider, for instance, the opening of Paul Auster's *Moon Palace*, with its recklessly overt resume of the story we are about to read – all telling, every word of it, but told to magnetic effect.

What's more, if we insist on showing everything, especially things that might more effectively be told, then it won't be long before we start to bore the reader. The error shows itself in the common tendency of young writers to begin in the wrong place, so that we must watch the leading character get out of bed, stare in the mirror, eat breakfast and so on, to the point where we begin to lose interest long before some intriguing encounter seizes our attention. In those dull circumstances, the collaboration with the reader will end before it's properly got started. So what seems to be in question is the right choice of narrative strategy *at any given moment*. Do I tell the readers this or should I show it? Which approach will most effectively draw them into the dream of the novel, and keep them there till the dream is done?

Reading and dreaming have much in common. In both we generate images out of a limited visual field. These images move and disturb us because we feel that we are immediately involved with them, at times more intensely than with our everyday experience, yet they arrive without overt explanations and require us to work for meaning. Also, unlike those of film, the images we find in books and dreams are unique to each of us, the work of our own imagination. So my Heathcliff does not look like yours, and when either of us tries to tell someone else about a dream we've had, or a book we've read, we know just how much gets lost.

Now dreams remain a great mystery, but their vocabulary of images seems to allow the oldest, pre-verbal parts of the brain to speak to the neocortex, thus opening a channel of communication between the conscious and unconscious minds. By flexing all the inward senses of the imagination, fiction can tap us into that hotline, too, and when that happens, good writing literally works like a dream. And what may most deeply excite us about it is the fact that we have been set free to dream the story for ourselves.

This freedom of the imagination is of profound, countervailing importance in a time when we are so often the passive recipients of information and reportage. So there may be more than just literary reasons for the emphasis on showing over telling in most fiction workshops. But what matters here is the recognition that, if we are to create and sustain a lively dream in the imagination of the reader, then much of our revision will be about questioning our choices of narrative strategy, altering them where necessary, then fine-tuning their effects.

In practice this means hunting down those moments that unintentionally tip the reader out of the dream. They can be considered under two broad headings: problems that arise from underwriting, when the author hasn't done enough imaginative work to secure the collaboration of the reader, and those of over-writing, when the reader is crowded out by the author trying to do too much.

Merely telling the reader something that's crying out to be dramatized is a form of underwriting. William Blake once wrote that 'he who does not imagine in minute particulars does not imagine at all', and it seems clear that if we don't bring the focused energy of the imagination to bear on the scene we're writing, then we're unlikely to activate its full potential for exciting the reader's interest. The result is inert wordage that leaves the reader cold, so it's as well to keep an eye out for the symptoms.

Prominent among them is the retreat into abstraction. Watch out for a reliance on abstract nouns in your writing, particularly those to do with states of feeling. Simply to announce that a character is 'filled with fury' or 'rotten with jealousy' is the weakest way to make your reader feel the impact of their emotions. We have your word for it but little else. However, if you show us the children wincing as Harriet throws the curry she's just cooked across the kitchen, or we see Ken straining to overhear a telephone call through a closed door, then we draw our own conclusions. It's a useful exercise to forbid yourself the use of keynote words such as 'fury' or 'jealous' when dramatizing an emotional condition. Similarly, when you find yourself writing *about* an important conversation, ask whether your readers might not prefer to hear the exchanges for themselves, particularly as characters are revealed through the different ways they use the language, and dialogue can subtly move the narrative along.

Of course, this kind of dramatized showing is much harder than straight telling, and in good writing there's no distinction between language and content, so the success of a piece will depend on how skilfully your words perform the show. When you come to revise a draft, ask yourself, for instance, how many details have been blurred by the broad-brush adjectives you've used to depict a scene. Is there a more limber way of conjuring the characters into the reader's presence than merely attaching descriptive tags? Does your use of adverbs short-circuit energy out of your sentences by labelling actions that a sharper movement of the syntax might quicken into life? And when you come across a cliché, take it for what it is – a sign that you've nodded off and it's time to recharge your imagination. Somewhere behind that prefabricated block of language lies a living moment. Close your eyes, activate your inward senses, then write and rewrite till you've hit a pitch of high fidelity. After all, if you don't care enough about the characters and events of your story to do them imaginative justice, why should the reader stay inside the dream?

Overwriting indicates a failure to trust the imagination of the reader. Consider how much of the pleasure of reading comes from inferring that which has nowhere been explicitly stated. A writer who pre-empts such moments of realization by obtrusive winks and nudges soon becomes a bore. The same is true of any lack of economy and concision in your prose. By making a careful selection of details from a scene that you've imagined for yourself 'in minute particulars', you free your readers to visualize it, too. But if you pile on the adjectives, or double the contents of your sentences through the loose use of similes, you are more likely to crowd them out.

Often enough you'll find that less can do more. A marvellous letter written by Conrad in 1899 demonstrates what this principle means in practice. A friend had asked his opinion on some stories he had written, one of which contained these sentences: 'When the whole horror of his position forced itself with an agony of apprehension upon his frightened mind, Pa'Tua for a space lost his reason. He screamed aloud, and the hollow of the rocks took up his cries and hurled them back mockingly.' Conrad sharpened the passage, to powerful effect, simply by cutting out a quarter of the words. Bearing in mind his general admonition that the author hadn't left enough to the reader's imagination, you might like to work out which words he cut.

Sometimes we overwrite out of the desire not so much to show as to show off; and sometimes, less exuberantly, out of anxiety to make sure that our meaning gets across. Either way we have to learn to 'murder our darlings' for the greater good of the book, and this can come hard. I was so infatuated with a sentence in one of my own novels that it passed unscathed through every draft, right through to the galley proofs, when my wife declared that she had always hated it. I woke up and saw that either the whole story dramatized what the sentence had to say – in which case it was redundant – or it didn't, in which case that sentence alone wasn't going to save the book from failure. It was an edgy moment, but I knew that in the end the finished work had to speak clearly on its own terms, uncluttered by the author's attachments. That sentence might have helped to keep me on track throughout the writing of the book, continuously reminding me what it was supposed to be about, but the reader had no use for it. So I struck it out, and have long since forgotten it except as a happy reminder of the satisfactions of revision.

Alexander Solzenhitsyn celebrates the importance of such moments in his novel *The First Circle*, where one of the characters, a prisoner in the Gulag, speaks movingly of 'the rule of the last inch'. It's a rule that applies near the end of a project when you sense that, despite all your efforts, the quality you were after is not yet quite attained, and there's still more to be done before the long journey of the work is over. The rule of the last inch is simply not to neglect it. It's a rule that all writers who care for their craft will strive to take to heart.

Redrafting Your Novel
James Friel

Be Kind

Don't judge your first draft too harshly – or yourself. The first draft of a novel is allowed to fail. It is allowed to do so at a second, a third and a twentieth. The idea that your prose should immediately stand to shiny attention is unreasonable and self-defeating. Its very imperfections are actually invitations to know it more deeply, to engage with it. It doesn't have to be perfect until it is finished – and, sometimes, not even then.

Be Patient

Put it aside for a while. Let it brew. D. H. Lawrence would often keep his first draft of a piece in a desk drawer and refer it to it only occasionally while he rewrote from memory. William Carlos Williams's advice was to put the draft away until 'the conditions under which it was written' were forgotten. In the meantime you become a different person, you become other than the person who wrote it and can judge it more objectively.

You might consider this relaxed attitude unwise, but where is the rush? Time spent on a book, Anthony Burgess observed, is of no real concern to a reader. If a first draft was written in white heat, let it cool down before you handle it.

Be Calm

When you are ready to face it, take out the first draft and read it. Just read it. Read the first draft without comment or addition – no matter how your hands itch to correct it and your head aches at the experience. Don't charge in. See what's there.

If you use a word processor, print off a hard copy and read that. The screen with its neat fonts and straight rows can be very deceptive. Besides, this is closer to how your reader will experience your work. You need to know this experience, too.

Be Colourful

Once you have read it, read it again.

This time attack it with red pen, pencil, scissors, glue, cut it, cross things out, tick the good bits or, taking a tip from novelist Tony Warren, invest in a set of markers. Reread the draft using one marker to make a line in the margin for plot, another for any sub-plots, one for each character's development, one for dialogue, one for style policing. This will give you a testing overview of your work and how it flows. The marks will suggest where to cut, where to amplify, where a character is being neglected or the plot stalls.

Be Versatile

You have to remain at heart that ambitious enthusiast who wrote the first draft but also become objective enough to become another person, one who can look at that work fairly and constructively. John Steinbeck's practice when redrafting was to 'become' three people. 'One speculates and one criticizes and the third tries to correlate. It usually turns out to be a fight but out of it comes the whole week's work.'

Be Curious

Ask questions. All the time. Is this what I want? What is it I want? Does this work? Am I trying too hard? Remember this is not an exam. There are no right answers, and take refuge in retaining a certain amount of ignorance. It is important to know what your intentions are in a work but too much knowledge can be prohibitive. If you can summarize your intentions too succinctly, why bother with the elaborate disguise of a novel?

Be Heard

Read your work aloud. Tape it and go for a walk with it playing on a personal stereo. It's a good way of making it other, of becoming your own reader, of taking words off the page and into that private place inside a reader's head where all the best novels come alive. Or listen to the tape with the draft in front of you. You will find that, often inadvertently, you change words as you read them, elide others, become aware of where sentences are too long and breathless and others are insufficient. It's also a useful way of testing your dialogue. Note where you stumble over your own prose. Smooth it out.

Be Flexible

There may be great changes to be made. Salman Rushdie's first draft of *Midnight's Children* was 900 pages long and written in the third person. Just one of his decisions on redrafting – to adopt a first-person narrator – meant every sentence had to be changed.

Be prepared – and brave enough – to make such enormous changes as well as small ones, but, also, if a scene bogs you down move on to another. Let the unconscious mind solve problems, too. The novel is always at work in your mind even when, physically, you are far away from it. The answer might come to you three days later on top of a bus or in the bath. It may be that the scene troubling you doesn't belong in the novel at all and its intractability is its only way of letting you know this.

Be Cautious

Sometimes it is not your work that is tired and inadequate, it's you. You are human. This happens. The text is all potential. It wants to be realized, perfected. Leave it a while and return to it in a more belligerent mood. That said, it is often when one is most dis-enchanted that one makes the most merciless cuts.

Be Meticulous

Remember, your first drafts are allowed to be messy, sketchy and inadequate. Try simply copying it out afresh. It may seem laborious but this is what redrafting is: quiet, long, patient work.

Every now and then, when drafting, try writing each sentence separately, leaving a line on each side of it. This allows you to look at each sentence, see how long, how rhythmic or, even, how necessary it is – and the space around it allows you to fiddle and rewrite it. This practice will also alert you to the sentence as a thing in itself. Prose has rhythms, metre, variety, just as poetry does, and a novelist must not be deaf to them. As John Gardner puts it:

> Prose, like poetry, is built of rhythms and rhythmic variations.
> Like poetry, prose has rhythms and rhythmic variations.
> Rhythm and variation are as basic to prose as to poetry.
> All prose must force rhythms, just like verse.

Play with each sentence. See what sounds it contains. This may lead you into some fine lapidary writing but remember that prose can work by being seemingly careless. In prose, Thomas Hardy noted, inexact rhymes and rhythms now and then can be more pleasing and effective.

Be Dependent

Is your work correctly punctuated? Punctuation is the breath of language, vital to a writer if you are to make sense, vital to readers if they are to understand exactly what you intend. To spend weeks, months, years on a novel and not endeavour to make it as accurate as possible is madness, laziness, simply ungenerous.

Use technology. Most word processors have a grammar check – you might find them hateful and you can dismiss what it throws up but, at the very least, it is a neutral – if insensitive – judge of what you have written.

Or have a friend read your work for grammar, spelling and punctuation. Friends will be much more helpful and willing to comment on such things than on its literary worth.

Be Independent

If there is someone you can rely on to read your work wisely and well, cherish them but don't abuse them. Only have recourse to them when you absolutely must. Far better, in the end, to be your own critic, be your own cheerleader, and there are days when you will need to be both. You cannot rely on others to tell you when your work is going well. Of course, everyone relishes praise and feels the need for feedback but, ultimately, you are blunting your own perceptions by replacing them with the opinion of others who may be too biased or too fond to give you the response your work needs.

Far better to use your journal and record your doubts, anxieties, victories as your work evolves. By honest appraisal of your own efforts – by the very act of putting down your thoughts – you may come to solve the problem that is currently occupying you.

Be Stealthy

Most drafts are either underwritten, overwritten or, more often, a mixture of the two. That's allowed and to be expected. Redrafting is a correcting of these tendencies. If a draft feels sketchy, in whole or in part, ask yourself if you have kept the reader sufficiently in mind. If it is overwritten maybe you are trying too hard. Lawrence Durrell said overwriting occurs when one is uncertain of one's target; underwriting may occur when you are too blithe or indifferent to it. Ask yourself, have you sufficiently kept your reader in mind? If you know a landscape really well, you may not have bothered to describe it to a newcomer. You may not have *communicated* it.

Be Intent

Identify your intention in a novel as a whole and in a scene in particular. You may have more than *one* – you will have – so what is the most important thing you want to communicate? Carol Clewlow says you should ask yourself what is the one thing you want to do in a scene and then concentrate on just doing that – the rest will follow if you let it.

Be Subtle

Perversely, having identified your intention – love is a lie or love is the only answer – try to illustrate it with maximum restraint, disguise it, imply it. A novel is not a lecture. Stendhal said, 'Find out what you most want to say and then try very hard not to say it.' This will give your writing a secret agenda. Writing with a secret agenda gives prose a pulse, a hidden but very real sense of animation. John Gardner in *The Art of Fiction* describes an exercise in which you are asked to describe a barn as seen by a man whose son has just been killed in a war. Do not, he says, mention the son or the war or death. 'If worked on hard enough, a wonderful image will be evoked, a real barn would stand before us but one filled with mysterious meaning.'

This approximates to the great mantra in creative writing circles: show, don't tell. Gardner's exercise forces you to do this. It dissuades you from explaining everything. This patronizes the reader. Let the reader also work. Readers are often intelligent and get by with hints and clues. They like this kind of thing, even prefer it.

Be Consistent

Point of view or POV is about who is telling your story. It is one of the most crucial decisions you will make when writing a novel.

When redrafting, experiment with these points of view. Negotiate with your material as to which is the best one to adopt. Whichever point of view you choose, whether you keep to one POV for the length of a novel or change it from scene to scene, be consistent. To sit in, say, Snow White's head for the majority of the story and have the action filtered through her is one thing, but dipping into the Prince's POV for a paragraph here and there just looks clumsy and diminishes tension.

Be Heard (Again)

Dialogue is not best done with absolute fidelity to true speech. We may hum and ah in real life, digress and stutter, but a novel is not real life: it is representation of it and your dialogue must *re-present* the spoken word. We may artlessly chatter but characters who do so bore and tire the reader. If you have a garrulous character, suggest garrulity, don't reproduce it.

Be Vigorous

Graham Greene learned from John Buchan and R. L. Stevenson never to interrupt an action with exposition, analysis or long description. Dialogue is also a form of action. It must propel the story. Try not to clutter it. Avoid 'he averred', 'he exclaimed', 'he riposted'. Use 'he said', 'she said' – it becomes invisible after a while – and then use this construction only to avoid confusion, say, if there are more than two characters involved and, even then, as unobtrusively as possible.

Don't stop to admire the scenery. A room is best described by the character who inhabits or visits it. To stop the action to describe landscape and then resume the narrative is just not wise.

Be Mean

Look at *all* your adverbs and adjectives. Think of them as valuable coins. Spend them wisely. Don't waste them. A table that is 'old, wooden, scratched and pine' is no longer a table, it is a list. The table is lost from view. A man who 'runs quickly' is a weak verb and a weak adverb. Have him 'pelt', 'dash', 'race' or 'rush'.

Look at anything that ends in 'ly' and consider saying goodbye to it.

Be Restrained

Do you have too many italics, words that you *strongly* feel you *must* emphasize? Perhaps with exclamation marks? Lots of them! Loads!! Cool it. This is typing, not writing. Rephrase them to convey a character's excess, not your desperate insistence that they are excessive.

Be Meticulous

Spellchecks are useful but they do not pick up the differences between 'their', 'there', 'they're', 'it's', 'its', 'whose', 'who's', 'you're', 'your', 'road', 'rode', 'where', 'wear' and so on. Such errors in a manuscript imply that while a word processors spellcheck has scanned it as methodically as it is able, the writer has not. And if the writer can't give close attention to the text, why should a reader?

Be Watchful

Watch out for any confusion of singular and plurals and, also, tenses. Such errors need the most careful of checking and you must be prepared to groom your drafts with absolute care and discrimination. In dialogue, tense changes occur naturally. In exposition, they look clumsy and can confuse.

Be Precise

Outside dialogue, you almost, nearly, never, seem to, like, just, sort of need the words 'almost', 'nearly', 'never', 'seem to', 'like', 'just', 'sort of'. Rather than suggest or describe something genuinely ambiguous, they more often signal a writer's refusal to search for the precise word. I would also add 'so' and 'then'. Most sentences can do without them and can be reshaped to sound both more active and concise.

Be Concise

Beware repetitions and redundancies. They slip in if you are not vigilant, if you are not looking at every sentence, holding every word up to the light. 'She hugged her close to him.' 'He looked up and saw that round orb of day, the sun.'

Be Active

Avoid using the passive voice in exposition. (Passive voice is best avoided.) It can give prose a dead, inert quality, not what is needed when writing a strong action scene.

Be Decisive

If in doubt, leave it out. If a word, a phrase, a paragraph, a chapter really belongs, it will find its way back. You might find it easier to slaughter a particularly admired phrase if, instead of abandoning it altogether, you record it in your journal for later use, building up a private thesaurus of good lines that have yet to find their true home.

Be Done

Writing a novel entails a great deal of working back and forth between the small detail of the novel that makes it real and the general shape that holds all these details in place. You must think of everything all the time, attend to plot and to character, make sure dialogue is convincing, that the prose is expressing what you wish it to do. Your novel will be finished when you and it agree it is. Someone asked me yesterday, Okay, when do I stop redrafting. Trust me. You will know. The text will shrivel away from you, tired of your attentions and say, 'Enough. I'll do as I am.'

And then you have to leave it be.

Judith: The Making of a Poem
Vicki Feaver

Wondering how a good woman can murder
I enter the tent of Holofernes,
holding in one hand his long oiled hair
and in the other, raised above
his sleeping, wine-flushed face
his falchion with its unsheathed
curved blade. And I feel a rush
of tenderness, a longing
to put down my weapon, to lie
sheltered and safe in a warrior's
fumy sweat, under the emerald stars
of his purple and gold canopy,
to melt like a sweet on his tongue
to nothing. And I remember the glare
of the barley field; my husband
pushing away the sponge I pressed
to his burning head; the stubble
puncturing my feet as I ran,
flinging myself on a body
that was already cooling

and stiffening; and the nights
when I lay on the roof – my emptiness
like the emptiness of a temple
with the doors kicked in; and the mornings
when I rolled in the ash of the fire
just to be touched and dirtied
by something. And I bring my blade
down on his neck – and it's easy
like slicing through fish.
And I bring it down again,
cleaving the bone.

'JUDITH', *The Handless Maiden*

M writes poems out quite often in one draft. That's
amazing to me. But I don't think it matters that it's
different for me. The way I work is like a painter, or
sculptor, slowly building up an image, or images –
and that involves a lot of experiment, and cancelling,
and trying again.

MY NOTEBOOK, June, 1992

I wrote 'Judith' in July 1992 during the first two days of a stay at
Annaghmakerrig, a retreat for artists in Ireland. The poem came out
of one of those serendipitous conjunctions that seem to happen if you
give time to writing poems and are open to anything that presents
itself. To read it now is almost like reading a poem by someone else.
It seems fluent, as if it was written straight out. Going back to my
notebook, however, it's possible to see the chaotic material out of
which it was born: the personal story that combined with the story
of Judith. My notebook, I should state, is at the centre of my writing.
The process that for many other poets goes on in the unconscious is
recorded in the jottings made about dreams, places, things I've read
and thought, as well as in the actual drafts of poems.

Pre-poem: Gathering of Themes

'Judith' is a dramatic monologue – written in Judith's voice. But even
before I discovered the story of Judith I had begun to think about the
idea of 'speaking for women'. Scrawled with my left hand, just before
I left for Ireland, is 'a letter to myself as a child', which ends:

> I am glad that you are a female child. You will have
> all the potential that a woman has; and more and
> more coming into this world now. You'll have a view
> of the world as a woman that is a neglected view. You
> will be able to speak for women.

Key themes in the poem – grief being transformed into anger into
action, action versus passivity, separateness versus merging of
identity – were also already emerging. 'IRELAND', I wrote,

> just the name I love . . . IRE means anger – land of
> anger – but it isn't – land of freedom/and limitation.
> I'm not going to be so rigid – I'm going to be more
> flexible, more experimental.

I had been reading Camille Paglia's *Sexual Personae* and had begun
to apply her distinction, in a chapter on Spenser's *The Faerie Queen*,
between the 'embowered woman' who is always merging and the
self-definition of the 'armoured woman' to my obsessive mourning
for a relationship that had ended more than a year previously. Freeing
myself as a writer, I was beginning to see, was part of the same
process as freeing myself from this relationship: being open to
change, moving from grief to anger, using anger positively to find a
strong, independent voice. Sitting by the Conway Falls, on the drive
to the ferry, I saw the journey as a metaphor for this:

> The motorway round Birmingham a sort of hell –
> industry, pylons, wires – and within an hour I'm

here. Things do change; more quickly in a car. But the moral is you could stay on the M42 in that hell – and to leave it you have to move. As I did on the journey and I'm doing in my life by going to Ireland. It's different; it will change things. Allow the possibility of changing in my head – moving from clinging to loss of R. A lot of that still in my head – journeys always make me think of him – although what I must remember is that although I was mostly very happy on our journeys together, I couldn't find the separateness to write. I experienced through R too much.

Day One: Monday, 21st July

Writing in my notebook on the first morning, I'm partly the writer, identifying myself with the tradition of women poets, partly still the wounded woman, trying to conduct a kind of self-therapy. One of the first entries is about my writing space:

> Disappointed with room at first: quite small and no bathroom – but now I like it – still the wonderful view over the lake and in exactly the same place – over the entrance hall – as Emily Brontë's room at Haworth.

Then, I'm back with the relationship, describing the deer I startled with my headlights the night before on the way up the drive and watched struggling to free itself from a fence:

> I must define myself more clearly. I merged with R like that deer caught in the barbed wire and then I panicked and hurt myself so much in trying to extricate myself. If the deer could have been calm and thought about what was happening. . . .

Then the writer surfaces again, prefacing a list of poems from *Perdido*, by the American poet Chase Twichell, that I want to reread with a declaration that resembles Keats's idea of the 'voyage of conception' as 'delicious diligent indolence':

> I am going to write here – but I have to come at it slowly – read poems – let ideas gather in my head like clouds.

The Discovery of Judith

Just before I went to bed the previous night, my first night in Ireland, I picked a book out of the bookcase in my room because it had a postcard sticking out of it that I thought might give me inspiration. It turned out to be written to a Miss Foster to reassure her that 'we are all well except that I have a cold', but the book was a King James Bible and the card was 'inserted at the story of Judith'. Why I didn't write about this immediately that morning – considering the impact it was to have – is very odd. All I can think of is that the delay was a necessary part of the incubation process.

The first mention of Judith in the notebook is the title, 'Judith/ dream', written above an account of a dream that again connects with the idea of speaking for women:

> Another of the dreams when I wake in my room. I wake because there are 3 (then 2) women/girls sitting on my bed and talking. I think at first they are women who are staying here. But when I sit up and talk to them I discover they are ghosts of people who used to live in the house. One takes a tiny chair and goes to work in a very small cupboard – because she's a ghost it is no problem to her. They suggest (I think) that I might write poems about them.

This is followed by a transcription of the whole of the dull message on the postcard. Then, at last, there is the key passage where finally, excitedly, I decide:

> Judith is what interests me: the card is in the story about her cutting off Holofernes' head. Surely that is a subject for me. I mean to have a go at writing it very directly with a lot of physical and sensual detail. There's quite a lot there already. Now H. rested upon his bed under a canopy, which was woven with purple, and gold, and emeralds, and precious stones.
>   (I could tell the story in her voice, or his – I must check out more of the background.)

The Story of Judith

Judith was one of the Bible heroines pictured on the stamps I collected at Sunday School. I must also have seen some of the many paintings of Judith cutting off Holofernes' head. But I hadn't previously read the story. As I discovered when I searched later, the Apocrypha, from which it comes, is omitted from most Bibles. Briefly, the Jews are holed up in a hillside town by the Assyrian army who have cut off their water supplies. The people, as summarized in my notebook, 'are ready to submit'. The priests want to 'leave it to God'. Judith, who has spent the last four years grieving for a husband who died of sunstroke in the barley harvest, 'uses her intelligence – does something'. She dresses up as a prostitute and goes to the tent of the enemy general and, as is described in the poem, cuts off his head while he is in a drunken stupor.

The Book of Judith consists of sixteen chapters and is full of details that could easily have clogged the poem. Sleeping on it gave my unconscious the opportunity to sift out the elements that were important to me. The narrative of the poem derives essentially from three verses in Chapter 13:

> 6 Then she came to the pillar of the bed, which was

275

at Holofernes' head, and took down his fauchion
from thence,

7 And approached to his bed, and took hold of the
hair of his head, and said, Strengthen me, O Lord
God of Israel, this day.

8 And she smote twice upon his neck with all her
might, and took away his head from him.

The difference in the poem is that I omit Judith's prayer and insert
instead her interior thoughts as she contemplates the murder. This
wasn't a conscious decision but, as subsequent notebook entries
reveal, a process of imagining myself in Judith's position and asking
questions – rather like an actress trying to get into a part.

Identification with Judith

Judith rouses herself from a long period of protracted grief and
inaction – I suppose we would call it depression – to carry out an
extraordinary and courageous act. My situation was not that
different. I was also in a state of grief. I wanted to rouse myself to
write. A great chunk of Judith's story consists of a description of her
preparatory rituals – prayers and penances, as well as dressing in
beautiful clothes. The rituals I was employing were not dissimilar:

> I love this room: the red paint on the outside of the
> windows, echoing the red of my blouse hung over
> the chair.

But, unlike Judith, who exhibits unambiguous confidence and conviction, I was full of twentieth-century indecisiveness:

> I feel good/together/strong/that I can find language.
> But is that a good state to write in?
> Maybe I should feel that I'm falling apart – that
> words are the glue that will hold everything together.

Asking Questions

The first fragment of what looks like poetry begins as a kind of invocation to myself to become one of Paglia's 'armoured' women but ends up recognizing how difficult this is:

> Squeeze myself into the armour
> draw a hard line
> but I am always sprawling
> trying to join
> In the armour – absence – nothing but air –
> suck you into myself.

I obviously felt ambivalent about writing in a way that was so exposing of my emotional weakness. On the next page, under the title 'Judith', the lyric 'I' is abandoned for a more distanced and objective third person:

Judith
knew what she had to do
Beauty had got her nowhere
Her beauty was waste.
Use it/the parable of the talents
At that moment she could have loved him –
the choice in her mind
Sex
Passivity is what she hates . . .
Blaming
Had she blamed god when her husband died
dying of boredom no sex
does it for the excitement of it –
violence/how can a woman be capable of violence?
how be the opposite of everything she's been brought up to be?
what is the motive?
rage? what rage? the rage of grief?

This isn't poetry, but it had got me thinking about Judith's motives and the question that propelled the poem: how can a woman be capable of violence? By investigating my own grief and anger I put myself in Judith's position:

> She has to keep him believing that she's fallen in love with him, that she's going to let him sleep with her – she has to bring out his best instincts; and in that moment when she does, she almost falls in love with him.

> Excitement/like before her marriage/as if she was going to bridal bed.
> Softness, hardness/armour that must seem soft . . .

The danger is that in the act of seduction Judith will be seduced. She has to appear soft on the outside (Paglia's 'embowered' woman') but inside retain her hardness (the 'armoured woman'). 'Armoured woman opposed to embowered woman (Paglia, p. 92),' I wrote in my notebook. Earlier I had copied out an aphorism from the story: 'For ye cannot find the depth of the heart of a man, neither can you perceive the things that he thinketh' (Judith 10: 14). Pages of theological debate, I now know, are devoted to the question of whether this virtuous woman actually slept with Holofernes.

Renewing the Attachment to the Sensual

At this point my inspiration and resolve seemed to slip away:

> I'm so afraid I won't write anything. Nothing today – and I'm so tired. It might help to look back at last year's notebooks – to see how poems come.
> Matthew said, 'Nothing comes out of nothing'.
> He doesn't write poems straight out. He makes notes. Thinks about something.

Maybe I can write the Judith poem – begin with the field, the heat, her husband dying. She told him not to go out that day, so her anger defied her, the clinging woman he was trying to separate from.

Scenes (1) barley field
(2) cut to idea
(3) cut to Holofernes' tent

Why do I want to write it?

'Matthew' was the poet Matthew Sweeney, a friend whom I have always found full of good advice on writing. Making notes is often a good idea. Also changing tack when you get stuck. It didn't matter that I changed the structure of the poem later. Just the concept of writing it as a series of scenes gave me the impetus to continue, to renew the excitement of the story and its sensual details.

I began immediately, with a fragment that links the death of the husband in the barley field and the murder, as in the final poem:

When they carried him in
he was already stiffening.
They carried him in from the heat
at that moment she raised the knife
she loved him more . . . the husband they carried in
from the barley field
already stiffening
whose frothing lips
she turned away from in revulsion
pleaded in dreams
to be kissed . . .

That last image came from a dream about her husband a widowed friend had told me. But it was too melodramatic for the poem and with it I lost the momentum of the story.

Day Two: Wednesday, 22nd July

> Went into the lake – poem MAKING LOVE TO A
> LAKE – I displace my own weight – keep my
> separateness, the lake moves to make way for me,
> folds around me, sun on it – like being hit by bright
> stones that emit light.
> I feel so much better/more alive.

Braced by the dip in the icy lake, I began work on Judith again: a
lyric poem in the first person. Again, the voice was both mine and
Judith's:

> It was the only place
> I felt safe in your arms . . .
> was the most dangerous,
> bits of me dissolving
> like a watercolour
> held under running water,
> the ideas in my head I thought were stone
> so strong and clearly defined
> like statues made of jelly
> sucked on your tongue
> until they were nothing
> but a sweet taste.

All the time I was mixing my experience with Judith's. I was in
Judith's story but writing about my emotions, trying to turn Paglia's
ideas about self-definition and merging of identity into sensuous
images.

In the following pages – filled with attempts to write the barley-
field scene – I again reverted to a third-person voice. But the memory
of walking across a field of stubble in open sandals is mine, from the
previous summer:

They'd called to her from the white heat
of the barley field, and she'd run out
without shoes, the sharp stubble
puncturing the soles of her feet . . .

'. . . like the emptiness of a temple with the doors kicked in . . .'

Then, there's another attempt to begin the poem:

>Judith.
>Grieving widow,
>life no meaning,
>she has sucked him into her
>when he died he's left empty space
>and now there was nothing inside
>but a roaring wind . . .
>the white hot
>furnace of grief

Again, I'm in Judith's story but using my experience, both literally and metaphorically. Once, on holiday in Crete, I climbed with R to the chapel on a hill top. The doors were off their hinges and a ferocious wind was filling the chapel with its fury. There was a smashed oil jar on the floor and a white muslin curtain that billowed as if alive. It was so desolate and terrifying that we left immediately. This was the origin of Judith's 'emptiness' as 'like the emptiness of a temple with the doors kicked in'. Initially, I tried to find images that expressed ideas about the loss of identity involved in a woman's longing to have her emptiness filled by a man. For instance, 'She wanted to take him into her, / the peace of not being, / of the man filling her / like an ocean with his tides / and moods'. I rejected these as attempts to convey my experience rather than Judith's, besides, the ocean didn't connect with her story.

I brought together the *image* of the chapel with a detail of Judith's actual mourning ritual from the Bible – 'she set up a tent for herself on the roof of her house' – to create a sense of both her literal space (on the roof) and her interior emotional space:

> At night she lay on the roof
> like a temple with the door
> kicked in, open to the roaring winds.

'Chapel' was transposed to 'temple' because of the context. It took a few more drafts before I finally made explicit the connection, hinted at earlier (now there was nothing inside/but a roaring wind), between Judith's 'emptiness' and the 'emptiness' of the desecrated chapel.

The Murder

There are pages of drafts before I finally got round to tackling the murder. The bones of the final version are there in my first attempt:

> As she held his hair in one hand
> and his
> > innocent
> she gazed into his sleeping face
> and felt the tenderness
> of a mother
>
> and she raised the curved sword
> & with two blows
> the bone cut off his head . . .

What had to be added was the fleshing out.
  In the next draft this is already happening:

> In one hand she held his oiled hair
> in the other his curved blade,
> and what she felt was tenderness,
> the old longing to be sheltered and safe,
> to melt like a sweet on his tongue
> to nothing.

The images from the previous draft of 'dissolving like a watercolour' and 'statues made of jelly' that are 'sucked on your tongue / until they were nothing / but a sweet taste' (I must have been thinking of jelly babies!) have become much more simply and evocatively 'melt like a sweet on his tongue to nothing'. Finally, the Paglia ideas of 'embowerment' have been integrated into a sensual image. A picture of Judith is emerging that juxtaposes violence and tenderness.

The Transition to 'I'

The voice of the first day's drafts wavers between a first and third person, but is predominantly in the third person. This is also true at the beginning of the second day. Then there is a break in the notebook – two blank pages that probably coincide with a lunch break. Back at my desk, I write:

> I've just been talking to Paula and Janet. I get such
> strength from women now. They think I look lovely
> with grey hair.

This input of female solidarity and confidence boosting obviously had a beneficial effect. From this point on the voice becomes unequivocally 'I', and much stronger. The fragments begin to come together into a cohesive narrative, and gradually the whole scene with all its sensual details begins to unfold. This is the final manuscript draft in the notebook:

> In one hand I hold his oiled hair,
> in the other raised above his wine-flushed,
> simple face, a curved blade. He's my enemy
> and what I feel is tenderness, what I most
> long for is the weakness to put down
> my weapon, to press myself
> to the warmth of his warrior's
> body, to lie under the green jewels,

the purple and gold silk
of his canopy, sheltered
and safe until dawn. And I remember
the men's shouts from the barley field,
running out into its golden heat
without my shoes, the sharp stubble
puncturing my soles, feeling
the inside sucked out of me, knowing
my husband was dead even before
I flung myself on his already cooling
corpse. And then the nights
when I lay on the roof – my emptiness
like the emptiness of a chapel
with the door kicked in, open
to a roaring wind. And the mornings
when I rolled in the fire's grey ashes . . .

In a few respects this draft marked a backwards step. Some previous sections of the poem that get into the final version have been omitted: 'the longing to be sheltered and safe', for instance. There's another earlier draft where I referred to 'the fumey (sic) warmth of his body', and this has disappeared, too. Fortunately, because I had kept the earlier drafts I could go back and recover the lost bits. However, I must have felt some confidence in the draft because at this point I began to work on a typewriter borrowed from the library.

The Opening

All the later manuscript versions of the poem begin:

In one hand I hold his oiled hair . . .

This plunges the poem right into the action – but offers no explain of who 'he' is and no sense of place. Among the typed pages, though, there's one that begins prosaically:

I am Judith about to murder Holofernes . . .

It shows the advantage, if the right words won't come, of writing anything, even if it's a statement of banal fact, because further down the same page the poem begins for the first time:

> Wondering how a good woman can murder
> I enter the tent of Holofernes,
> holding in one hand his oiled hair . . .

Somehow I had to go through the process of taking on being Judith – 'I am Judith about to murder Holofernes' – before I could properly begin the poem. Once I had done this a much better opening line flowed from my early questions about Judith's motives. 'Wondering how a good woman can murder' establishes that the voice is both mine and Judith's. The juxtaposition of 'good woman' and 'murder' establishes the central paradox of the story. The first three lines are satisfying, too, for the verbal echoes of 'wonder' and 'murder' and the alliteration of 'Holofernes' and 'holding' and 'hand' and hair'.

I wrote out draft after draft of the opening, the details building gradually. The adjective 'long' was added to the hair, not just adding a detail to the picture but the repeated 'l's and the three stressed single-syllable words ('long oiled hair') lengthening and slowing up the line. Holofernes' 'drunken little boy's face' of an earlier draft became the more sensual and visually evocative 'his sleeping, wine-flushed face', the repeated 's' sounds emphasizing his stupor. The 'little boy' went with the idea of 'a mother's tenderness'. I wanted to emphasize Judith's sexual longings, not her motherliness. I decided to use the actual name of the weapon from the biblical text, 'fauchion'. This wasn't in the COD so I later changed it to 'falchion', which was. I added 'unsheathed' both for the repeated 'sh' sound and because I wanted another precise detail for the picture as well as to create a sense of danger.

285

'. . . I rolled in the ash of the fire just to be touched and dirtied by something.'

The detail of rolling in the ash of the fire doesn't enter the poem until the final written draft in the notebook (see above, p. 284). In the Bible story ashes are part of Judith's penitential rite in preparation for the murder: 'Then Judith fell upon her face, and put ashes upon her head, and uncovered the sackcloth wherewith she was clothed.' The 'rolling' in ash was my addition. Because the typed drafts aren't numbered, it's difficult to work out precisely how it developed. Ashes are very resonant in terms of spiritual experience. On Ash Wednesday, at the beginning of Lent, churchgoers are marked with ash on their foreheads. It also connects with female rites of passage. Cinderella works and sleeps in the ashes. There is a connection with carnal experience and with death.

There are several drafts of the poem that break off at 'the ash of the fire', as if I didn't know where I was going next. As previously mentioned, there is a version that continues: 'And now I want to (be) filled again, filled with my enemies moods and tides'. The phrase in the poem that I am most pleased with, that seems most to embody Judith's loneliness and longing – 'just to be touched and dirtied by something' – seems to have grown suddenly out of the voice of the poem, as if it had written itself.

The Ending

The final manuscript draft of the poem broke off at 'the fire's grey ashes'. The ending didn't arrive until the typed drafts. Again, I had to fumble my way towards it. For instance, there's a version that reads:

> And I bring the knife
> down on his neck, and it's easy
> like slicing through fish,
> and down again, splintering
> the bone like a bullock's.

In the final version 'the knife' becomes 'my blade', emphasizing both the function of the knife and its appropriation by Judith. Also, 'like a bullock's' has gone. I might have liked the alliteration, but 'fish' is enough. The added simile weakens rather than reinforces it. The double blow comes from the Bible – 'And she smote twice upon his neck with all her might, and took away his head from him'.

In an almost final draft, the last two lines read:

> And I bring it down again,
> splintering the bone.

I know one reason why I changed 'splintering' to 'cleaving' ('cleaving the bone'). My ex-husband brought me back a cleaver from China. It was a fearsome weapon and, as he also came back with a mistress, my children hid it. I've seen fishmongers using a cleaver to chop straight through an eel, cutting through the spine. 'Cleaving' is a much more forceful word than 'splintering'. It adds to the effect of an act that is both shocking and violent and connected with a woman's domestic life, with cooking.

Final Tinkering

By the end of day two I had a typed draft of the poem that is very close to the final draft. It is titled 'Judith & Holofernes/Murder'. Before I settled for the direct and simple title 'Judith', I toyed with the idea of calling the poem 'Murder', but rejected it as unnecessarily sensational as well as redundant, as the word 'murder' is in the first line. 'Holofernes' went because I wanted to stress that the poem is Judith's story.

> Wondering how a good woman can murder
> I enter the tent of Holofernes,
> holding in one hand his long oiled hair
> and in the other, raised above
> his sleeping, wine-flushed face,

his falchion with its unsheathed
curved blade. And I feel a rush
of tenderness, a longing
to put down my weapon, to lie
sheltered and safe in a warrior's
fumy sweat, under the emerald stars
of his purple and gold canopy,
to melt like a sweet on his tongue
to nothing. And I remember
the golden heat of the barley field,
the shouts of the men, the sharp stubble
puncturing my feet as I ran,
flinging myself on a body
that was already cooling
and stiffening; and the nights
when I lay out on the roof –
my emptiness like the emptiness
of a temple with the doors kicked in,
open to the roaring wind; and the mornings
when I rolled in the ash of the fire
just to be touched and dirtied
by something. And I bring my blade
down on his neck, and it's easy
like slicing through fish.
And I bring it down again,
cleaving the bone.

The main change between this draft and the final poem comes in the barley-field section. I kept coming back to it until about six weeks later and it is still probably the weakest part. I changed 'golden heat of the barley field' to 'glare of the barley field' because 'glare' was more threatening and more suggestive of the effect of bright heat and therefore the probable cause of the husband's death. It also helps the poem's rhythm and sound: 'glare' forms a sort of half rhyme with 'stars' and enables the line to run on instead of ending dully and abruptly with 'I remember'. I inserted 'my husband pushing away the sponge I pressed to his burning head' because I wanted an image of Judith with her husband that would show her as nurturing and at the same time give her a motive for her anger.

There is one other change. At the point that I moved 'my emptiness' to the end of a line to give it more emphasis, I edited out 'open to a roaring wind'. I wanted to connect 'nights' and 'emptiness' and 'mornings' – all now at the end of lines. I also wanted the poem to move more swiftly to its conclusion. I now wonder if this was the right decision. By rearranging the line breaks I could retain 'open to a roaring wind', producing an assonance between 'in' and 'wind' that would slow the poem down before the image of rolling in the ash and maybe create a stronger, because even more physical, impression of emotional and sexual loneliness:

> and the nights
> when I lay on the roof – my emptiness
> like the emptiness of a temple
> with the doors kicked in, open
> to a roaring wind; and the mornings
> when I rolled in the ash of the fire
> just to be touched and dirtied
> by something.

It must be true what Auden said: that a poem is never finished, only abandoned.

Feeling the Burn
Julia Bell

Well, you've finished it. The manuscript sits on your desk, a wad of paper. Months and months of work. Done.

Or is it?

The best thing to do when you've finished something is to leave it for a while to stew. Do something else. Start a new story, toy with some ideas for your next novel, take a few days, a few weeks, a few months, away from your desk. Don't read it. Forget about it. This is the most important part of the writing process.

However good you might think your work is, in the endorphin-filled moments of finally crossing the finishing line, you will be sure to look at it a few weeks later and see mistakes. To revise your own work you need to be able to look at it as if you were not the writer. And this takes a crucial, critical distance.

The final edit is always the most difficult and, often, the most boring. When something is 90 per cent done, the last 10 per cent can feel like purgatory. As an idea the work has run its course, there is nothing much new to say so the excitement can often fizzle away. Only hard work lies ahead, correcting sentences, altering paragraphs, tightening the structure and making sure that all the elements of your story are intact. This work is vital. It is the final layer of polish and pizzazz that will make the narrative or poem seem tight, right, complete.

Raymond Carver wrote and rewrote his stories obsessively. In his introduction to his selected stories *Where I'm Calling From*, he writes passionately about how he had to learn to 'write fast when I had the time, writing stories when the spirit was with me and letting them pile up in a drawer, and then going back to look at them carefully and coldly later on, from a remove, after things had calmed down, after things had, all too regrettably, gone back to "normal"'.

It is the cold light of day that a writer needs to be able to revise their own writing. The heat of the moment robs us of critical distance and it is the editorial side of the brain that needs to engage when revising. It's a hard balance to strike. Too much editorial work will freeze up the flow essential to fluid writing, not enough editorial consciousness and the writing will suffer, by being uncontrolled, unwieldy.

Never be tempted to think 'that's good enough' when you know there are still mistakes to correct. The bad sentence that you just couldn't be bothered to fix will haunt you later if the work is published, spoiling a whole paragraph, a whole page, a whole scene in the story.

Conversely, you have to know when to stop. When it is really as good as it is going to be. If you are stuck with something that just doesn't seem right, put it away for a while and write something new.

I have a few dozen unfinished stories that I am constantly working on. Every now and then I go back and redraft them. Eventually I finish one or two. New ideas replace the finished pieces so I always have a pool of ideas to work with. Frustratingly, I can't seem to hurry this process. The insight or inspiration I am searching for can't be forced. I just have to sit tight and wait.

Revising is about asking yourself what you were trying to achieve in the first place. You have to trace back to the initial moment of inspiration, to the emotion that drove you to the page. I find with my stories that after a long and convoluted process of harrying and worrying over an idea, it is only 'finished' when it elicits the same feeling from me that I had when I was inspired to write it. A story is a moment of capture for me. Pinning down a moment, an idea, an abstract in a tangible, concrete way.

Here are ten questions to ask yourself if you think your piece of work is finished:

Are you happy with your characters? Can you see them in your imagination?
Is there enough setting and background detail?
Have you cut all the dead description and unnecessary adjectives?
Is your dialogue convincing? Do your characters talk like people?
Is the point of view consistent?
Have you checked for unqualified abstract words?
Are the events of the plot logical to the story?
Have you checked for clichéd words or phrases?
Are you showing and not telling?
Are you happy with it?

If the answer is yes to all these questions then it is time you found someone else to read your work.

11 Workshops

Introduction
Julia Bell

'The most essential gift for a good writer is a built-in, shock-proof, shit detector. This is the writer's radar and all great writers have had it.'

ERNEST HEMINGWAY, interview in *Paris Review*

At some point, whether you are part of a writing group or taking a writing course, the chances are you will encounter a workshop situation. In the initial stages, workshops can be a terrifying experience for the writer. You've got all the words that you have worked so hard to knock into some kind of shape, now you are offering your efforts to a group of people, sometimes strangers, for their appraisal. A good workshop will leave the writer feeling buoyant, feeling that they know more about their own work than they did before they went; a bad workshop, the writer might well end up flinging all the pages in the bin and never writing again. How can you find a workshop that will suit your needs and experience? How can you get the most out of having your work critiqued?

First of all, you need to assess your level of experience. What kind of workshop are you looking for? Would you be better off with a taught course, which offers some step-by-step suggestions to get you writing, or a more experienced group, which offers a serious appraisal of your work?

The proliferation of writing courses means there are plenty to choose from at undergraduate, postgraduate and extramural levels. An MA workshop is usually aimed at the writer who has already produced a body of work. On the UEA MA the workshops revolve around discussion of work submitted for each week's class. Usually three pieces a week in an intense three-hour session. At under-graduate level workshops are more 'taught', taking the writers through a process of exercises to encourage them to generate text for workshops. Extramural courses often follow a similar pattern to the undergraduate classes, but find out what's available in your area, some departments might offer more intermediate courses.

Off campus, the Arvon Foundation and the Taliesin Trust in Wales offer week-long residential courses tutored by professional writers. These weeks away are intended to give people who have been writing but have yet to really test their mettle a chance to take themselves seriously and receive some advice and feedback. I went on one in Tŷ Newydd in 1993, thanks to a bursary from the Taliesin Trust. I was unemployed at the time and dithering about whether or not to pursue my writing. I went there with a rucksack full of questions. Am I good enough? Is this really what I want to do? I can't make sense of the 40,000 words of the novel that I've just written. Is it any good? I came back, a week later, elated, resolved, more sure of myself than I'd felt for ages. I don't really know why: the course tutor had told me to throw my novel in the fire and start writing another, better one. Being taken seriously had a profound effect on me; there were other writers talking to me as if I had something to say. It was the point at which something that I had dreamt about for years became tangible.

It is likely that there are small local writing groups in your area, who meet to swap and discuss work. Your local arts board will have all the information. There are now several quite famous writers' groups that have nurtured a lot of new talent in the UK, for example the Lindsay Clarke Workshops in London and Tindal Street Fiction Group in Birmingham. If there isn't a group in your area, start one: all you need is a few like-minded writers and somewhere to meet.

I joined Tindal Street Fiction Group in 1993. Just before my visit to Wales. I had been living in the house next to Tindal Street School for over six months and still hadn't noticed the strange collection of cars that parked outside my house every fortnight. It was a closed group so I had to apply to join and send them some work. I had been told they had high standards and I was worried that they wouldn't take me seriously. When I got the letter back telling me that I had been accepted I was delighted, but there was one big drawback, as a new member, my first meeting would be about my work.

I suppose it's like standing on the edge of a high diving board just before you jump off: a mixture of nerves, vertigo, exhilaration. You so want the work to be good, but by submitting it to criticism you are accepting that there is still something not right about it. A workshop is an acknowledgement of a reader's perspective, an admission that you are trying to communicate and that you might not be the best person to judge the effectiveness of your own work.

When I got to the meeting I felt ill. I was about to allow a group of strangers free rein with my work and, oh horror, they expected me to read it aloud to them. I could hear the bad sentences as I read them. I cringed at some of the dialogue. I remember being pleased with very little of it by the time I'd struggled through thirteen pages of badly printed typescript. I was going to be eaten alive.

But the discussion that followed was gentle, pragmatic, encouraging. I was reading not just to other readers but to other writers who understood the struggle of creating fictions.

A workshop is a demanding environment both intellectually and emotionally. To get the best out of a writer, the workshop has to look for what the text is trying to achieve and push the writer towards what they do well and away from the mistakes and jumbled sentences and stillborn ideas.

But the writer still needs to protect themselves. Ultimately, a workshop is only as good as its members. A top-heavy group with one or two leading spokespeople runs the risk of splitting into factions and becoming too personality driven. The other members of the group may not be sympathetic to your type of writing, they may push you away from your original intentions. A good rule of thumb with workshop appraisals is to acknowledge the criticism that articulates a weakness in the work you had already feared to be true but hadn't quite expressed to yourself. If the comments seem irrelevant or off the wall or excessively negative, ignore them, steel yourself against them, not everyone is going to get what you are trying to do.

A constructive group will leave their egos at the door in pursuit of a co-operative goal. Some groups may even have a written policy that outlines how they will try to achieve excellence and develop writers' work. The workshop is not a competition, it's a place to have free and frank debate about what makes writing successful. Good workshop practice involves not only good writers but good readers, who like fiction for its own sake and are prepared to see through their own bias to what the work is trying to do.

Much of this is about luck. I know I was lucky with Tindal Street, other workshops haven't always been so kind or so instrumental. The vagaries of group bonding can mean that while one workshop will be spectacular, another can dissolve into reticence and competition. Bad workshops can be damaging to a writer, making them defensive and underconfident. If this happens to you, you are better to cut your losses and try somewhere else. It may take a few attempts to find a workshop that suits you.

Taught classes are a different matter altogether. Much like the structure of this book, they take the writer through a series of exercises and topics. They offer the writer a chance to practise their skills and learn a few crucial dos and don'ts. They suit people who have little or no previous writing experience and are designed to ease you gently into the practice and process of becoming a writer.

Courses like these vary according to the tutors who are teaching them. Check them out before you sign up. Read some of the tutors' work to give you an idea of what their bias might be. Again, these classes aren't free of the problems encountered on the more experienced courses, and if you are aspiring to write romantic fiction it may not be sensible to choose a tutor well known for writing hard-boiled crime novels. Because there is no set curriculum, every writer will have – much like this book – their own methodologies and obsessions.

In some ways the point of workshops is to socialize the practice of writing. The image of a writer scribbling away in a lonely garret is far from true. Writers coming together for their own and each other's benefit has magical effects. Discussion and debate generate ideas, provoke the imagination, sharpen the writing and extend the writer's critical and editorial vocabulary.

A Brief History of Workshops
Jon Cook

Writing workshops come in different shapes and sizes. They can last for a week, meeting each day, or meet once a week for ten or twelve weeks as part of a university course, or be a smaller part of something else, a critical course on twentieth-century fiction, for example, or a lesson in secondary-school English class. Workshops also come with a history as an educational form. Something of that history is embedded in the shifting contexts of the word's use.

The slogan that identified 'Britain as the workshop of the world' reminds us that nineteenth-century uses of the word were concerned with a world of industrial or artisan labour and the activity of shaping materials by technological means into artefacts or commodities. The idea that workshops might be something to do with cultural activity is a later invention. Two notable examples from this country are Joan Littlewood's Theatre Workshop, started in the London East End in the 1950s and, a little later, the History Workshop movement, shaped by the work and invention of Raphael Samuel. Both these uses evoke cultural and intellectual politics. In Joan Littlewood's case the Theatre Workshop had its roots in the agitprop theatre of the 1930s. The basic idea was to give working-class people the opportunity to make theatre, and a similar impulse lay behind the History Workshop, giving people customarily thought of as outside or beneath what counted as significant history a chance to become the writers of their own individual and collective pasts. In both cases experts in theatre or history made their knowledge available for the purposes of further invention and discovery. Even if that idea might be complicated by the presence of charismatic personalities, a basic assumption about culture persisted. Workshops of this kind were places where cultures were made as well as interpreted. They carried on an artisan tradition of learning by doing, but applied this to the making of plays and histories rather than steam engines or turbines.

Some, at least, of this history is inherited by writing workshops. Although not necessarily named as such, writing workshops have existed in primary and secondary schools for years. In the 1950s and '60s the idea that writing might be extended to creative writing assumed a new prominence. One result was the publication of numerous books about the teaching of creative writing. David Holbrook's work is one example. Frank Whitehead's book *Creative Experiment* is another. Running through this work is a sense of children's entitlement to creative experience. Literature was the model and the stimulus for this creativity. The tone of these books is earnest but dedicated. Whatever their cultural or class background, all children have within them a history and an experience that can be discovered through creative writing. As Whitehead puts it:

> The real problem the teacher of English has to face is not how to supply his pupils with 'matter' to write about; it is rather how to develop within the classroom a climate of personal relationships within which it becomes possible for them to write about the concerns which already matter to them intensely.

Whitehead's book reminds us of the obvious: writing workshops are always also reading workshops, although the place and purpose of reading are not necessarily the same as they might be in a seminar on literary theory or when reading a novel in an armchair. I want to return to the relation between reading and writing later in this piece. For the moment, something else that is obvious needs to be noted:

that, as so often in the history of education, what is developed in schools is later taken up by universities.

But this transposition is by no means simple, both for historical and cultural reasons. The writing workshop in a university is an American invention. It was the bearer of a democratic confidence. The workshop provided a means for creating a literary culture where none had existed before. The University of Iowa is the exemplary case. The Iowa writing workshop became nationally and then internationally famous. Other universities in the US created their own variants, some focused around the work of charismatic writers like Robert Lowell, some were more explicitly concerned with using the workshop as a means of learning the craft of writing through writing exercises.

The American precedent did play a formative role in the growth of writing workshops in universities in this country. This, at least, was the case when the Creative Writing MA was started at the University of East Anglia in 1970. Malcolm Bradbury and Angus Wilson, its two founders, both drew on their experience of creative writing in American universities when they established the course. Both saw the writing workshop as a means of educating writers to be writers rather than teachers, academics or pub bores. This belief was intimately connected to another: whoever led a workshop should themselves be a professional, published writer. They might, in addition, be critics or teachers or journalists, but the workshop was essentially a place where an experienced writer might help others less experienced. The analogy was with a masterclass. Dedicated writers learnt from other equally dedicated but more experienced writers about their limits and potentials. The focus of the writing workshop was not the writing exercise, but the exposure of an individual writer's work to detailed scrutiny. The purpose was to help a particular work to evolve through a process of rewriting, to challenge writers to find their own distinctive voice. But this purpose could only be realized when there was an equally dedicated critical seriousness about contemporary writing. Writers became the critics both of their own work and the work of their immediate contemporaries.

This brief history may seem to labour the obvious. It acts at least as a reminder that writing workshops do have a history and that what can and cannot be done in them will be affected by the context in which they are devised. On the one hand, writing workshops are micro-cultures. They establish communities of writers and readers, the means for writing to be circulated, and explicit or unconscious rules for how work is to be valued. They combine the work of creation, publishing and criticism within the confines of a small group. Yet these micro-cultures also reflect or enact tensions within the wider culture. The ideal of democratic participation, of entitlement to imaginative creativity, can brush up against the ideal of the masterclass, the workshop as the place where a new generation of significant writers finds its voice. Or, in the context of the university writing workshop, institutions that have historically devoted themselves to the criticism of literature find themselves awkwardly harbouring the practice of its creation. And then there is the fantasy and the fact, always closely intertwined, of writing itself. In workshops people write together. Different imaginations inform, provoke or do battle with each other. The writing workshop is clearly a collective activity, although how that collective is defined will vary from one context to another, and is never an entirely conscious act. Yet this temporary collective draws upon what many people regard as the epitome of privacy and solitude, the act of imaginative writing. Workshops exist in a transitional space between the public and private worlds of writing. Public facts about genre, technique, verse form or the meanings of words can be as creative in writing as private worlds of fantasy and memory. Workshops that work display the truth of this. And they do so by showing that the relation between public facts and private worlds is far from being a zero-sum game.

All this suggests that what happens in a workshop is going to be decided by something more than a statement of its purpose and a selection of techniques appropriate to that purpose. But that 'something more' does not diminish the importance of clarity about purpose and technique. Workshops don't happen because a group of people get together, read each other's writing and then talk about what they've read. Some agreement about purpose is necessary. Is the purpose of a workshop to help its participants become better critical readers of literature? Is it for writers who are just beginning to write or for those who have already built up a portfolio of work? Is this work going to be subject to a formal or informal assessment? Does the workshop claim that it will help writers get their work published? And, even if it doesn't, do they still come to the workshop expecting that publication will be one of its outcomes? This last question can serve as a reminder that statements of purpose and agreements about them are not at all the same thing.

Agreements about purpose – including the agreement to have more than one – inform the relation between reading and writing in a workshop. For example, writing sonnets is a way of learning how to read them. The sonnet form can be built up, one step at a time, by exercises in rhyme and metre. The purpose of the exercise is to begin to discern the deep skill that is required to write sonnets well, but also to realize that this is not necessarily the result of introspection or emotion. Sonnets are, amongst other things, performances and their writers can be like actors who perform highly stylized roles. Testing this out first-hand can give an insight into how the form worked, which no amount of enquiry into discourses of power in Elizabethan England can provide. The main purpose of the exercise is not to write a brilliant sonnet, although that may happen, but to complement critical enquiry with some creative experiment, to understand a literary form in terms of craft and technique, both compositional act and cultural process.

This example gives a brief illustration of how creative writing can help with critical reading. Like genetic codes, writing workshops can be spliced into courses on criticism. The same exercise could be put to different use in a poetry workshop. Here the sonnet would become one of a series of forms, each one like a test and something to be tested. Successful imitation, not originality of expression, is the primary goal. Success here means taking a writerly pleasure in discovering what forms can do. There can be a craft satisfaction in this, a pleasure in something well made. But something else can be at work as well, another kind of discovery. Attention to form or technique can allow powerful subject matter to emerge by indirection.

The relevant distinction is made by Seamus Heaney in his essay 'Feeling into Words', where he proposes a distinction between craft and technique. The former is what can be learnt from example. It is the 'skill of making' and can be 'deployed without reference to the feelings or the self'. This sense of craft is close to what we also think of as technique, a set of instruments for getting something done. But there is another kind of technique, one 'that involves the discovery of ways to go out of . . . normal cognitive bounds', 'a watermarking of your essential patterns of perception, voice and thought into the touch and texture of your lines'. Imitation or absorption in a moment of craft precipitates the discovery of a subject. Nothing guarantees this transition, but it can mark a threshold in what kind of writing gets done in a workshop.

What applies to poetry can be translated into the requirements of prose. The emphasis can be on a piece of writing that returns to an act of reading, or on the use of reading to exemplify an aspect of technique: point of view, first-person narrative, dialogue, character and place. In the latter case, a technique can be developed into a writing exercise, and writing exercises, in turn, can lead on to something more sustained. This gives one identity to a workshop, a kind of gymnasium for producing writing. The emphasis here is on routine: learning a technique through example and application, testing its pertinence to whatever you might want to write, realizing the relations between writing and rewriting. These are the collective exercises and disciplines of the workshop; everybody starting from a shared example and task. Then there is the possibility of that movement described by Heaney, technique in an inward sense. Here writing becomes another kind of discovery, the realization and remaking of experience or the invention of an imaginary world. This could be the goal of a workshop or its starting point. This distinction between an exercise-driven workshop and one that starts with the writers' own work may lend itself to a further distinction about 'levels'. These, in turn, can be embedded in the requirements of degree programmes. Creative writing workshops become routine in another sense: another element in a large bureaucratically driven education process whose primary requirement is not that anything good or useful might happen but that whatever happens can be measured and reported. How this will affect what happens in writing workshops remains to be seen. But it would be wrong simply to assume that standardization must come at the expense of vitality.

An important element of vitality in a writing workshop is its double nature as a place of instruction and a process of discovery, a collective and individual endeavour. Which brings me to one further and final relation between reading and writing. We usually read in the absence of authors. That absence is filled with their ghostly spirits, and much literary criticism has been devoted to the task of thinking about how the ghosts get into the page and whether they call for celebration or exorcism. But in a writing workshop writers are physically present as their work is read; they are poised to hear, ignore, be upset or delighted by what others think about their latest chapter, short story, poem or script. This can produce anxieties about the trade-offs between face-saving and honest appraisal. Some workshops are set up with a rule that positive comment must come first, critical reservations second. In most it seems important that the work should be circulated and read before the workshop meets to discuss it. These are important details in the planning of any writing workshop. They contribute to another central process: alongside the invention of writing there is also the creation of value. A workshop is a place where different pieces of writing are inevitably compared and, out of these comparisons, evaluations of however provisional a kind emerge. Sometimes these evaluations emerge in the difficult recognition that a piece of work is failing. Mostly evaluation is to do with how a story, poem or script can be improved. It is the kind of conversation that might occur amongst technicians concerned to get an engine to work better. Occasionally there is the euphoric or envious moment when something is written which everyone knows is good. The process of evaluation calls for a commitment to creative reading, sympathetic to a writer's intentions but attentive to a work's success or failure. It is hard to see a workshop succeeding without it.

Collective Works:
Tindal Street Fiction Group
Alan Mahar

Tindal Street Fiction Group is remarkable as a nexus of fiction-writing activity. Every fortnight since 1983 there has been a group meeting in a community room in Balsall Heath in Birmingham, focused solely on the reading and discussion of the member-writers' fiction. The pattern of meeting – reading, discussion, support, criticism and mutual self-help – has been unusually consistent over that period. Though there have been fallow periods, the group has remained ambitious and productive, and notched up a fine tally of publication credits. Somehow, a small provincial group, burdened with all the usual dark suspicions about literary London con-spiracies, has managed to achieve a measure of national success without becoming bitter, inward looking or complacent. How come?

The recently acclaimed anthology *Hard Shoulder* (published by Tindal Street Press) was not intended as a showcase for the fiction group; indeed most of the contributors are not members. However, one of the most gratifying spin-offs from publication has been the spotlight of publicity on a generation of new writers who are members: Julia Bell, Jackie Gay, Steve Bishop and Gemma Blackshaw. Of course, they are 'new' only in a limited sense; each of these individual writers has had stories published in anthologies and literary magazines elsewhere, under their own steam, independently of the fiction group. They all have books-in-progress and literary agents now. Naturally, they were ambitious for a writing career before; but Tindal might have helped.

When I asked Gemma Blackshaw, now teaching Creative Writing at Birmingham University, how Tindal might have helped, she singled out the importance of deadlines in aiding productivity. 'Booking a story ahead for reading means you have to work very hard to have it ready for discussion. And I find the detailed feedback from people whose writing I respect extremely valuable.' Jackie Gay, whose first novel *Scapegrace* has recently appeared under the Tindal Street Press imprint, emphasized the 'valuable interaction with other writers and the genuine critical feedback from members'. The writers in the group, as Steve Bishop, a story writer with an active interest in film, remarked, are 'sympathetic to the creative process. Their comments can help you see your story in a new light, and smooth off its rough edges.' Clearly the development of each writer benefits from working closely with his or her peers, which is a kind of collaboration requiring a proper attention to the craft and detail of fiction writing.

These individual talents are just the younger generation of a continuum of activity stretching back more than a decade. Think of the writers whose first books have only in recent years appeared: Alan Beard (*Taking Doreen out of the Sky*, Picador), Alan Mahar (*Flight Patterns*, Gollancz), Joel Lane (*From Blue to Black*, Serpent's Tail). They were following a lead shown by Annie Murray, who, after winning a national story competition, signed a five-figure contract with Macmillan (for *Birmingham Rose* and *Birmingham Friends*). Inevitably, there are others whose time will come. This litany is just by way of explaining the background of achievement, which is by no means sudden.

Tindal Street Fiction Group has helped writers in Birmingham to write their stories or chapters, bring them along for scrutiny, rewrite and submit to editors with a better than hopeless chance of publication. The system has worked. But not without a lot of graft from many people. How did it all get started?

The name first: *Tindal Street* was the inner-city terraced street I worked in, as a writer in the community, back in 1982. Tindal Street is also the name of the Victorian junior school with a community room where we meet. My brief there was to initiate writing work with children at the school and any other groups. I bonded with pensioners in reminiscence work, met local writers, tried to start classes, workshops and actually began the fiction group. The area of Balsall Heath, once a red-light area, still a touch risky, overlooks one of the best panoramas of Birmingham at night: twinkly lights against an uncompromising mass of tall city buildings, vibrant, unlovely; well, quite lovely in its own way, really. This talismanic scene graced the cover of one of our earlier anthologies, *The View from Tindal Street*.

Fiction, and definitely not poetry. This was just a prejudice on my part. I'd witnessed some of the internecine warfare at the scrappier local poetry readings. Fine for performance, but in group anthology publications and magazines this writing was nearly always dead on the page. Why not poetry for TSFG? For practical purposes and for group discussion, it is over too quickly. And it is difficult to develop into helpful discussion. A poem might be read and met with silence. It might require too much pre-existing technical literary knowledge, and discussion too often tends to be exclusive and divisive. At least stories allow for inclusive discussion of narrative authenticity and plausibility. In fact, some of the group members also write verse, but the rule was that they should not bring poems to the group.

Group: Why not write alone? Like many another in the eighties I was carrying around a heavy bag of collective political ideals. I later joined a workers co-operative and learned some of the practical problems in group working – democracy, equality being all very nice, yes, but skills and productivity can be much more important. I believed writers – especially in the provinces – deserved support. They're so isolated. Nobody wants to know. So in some ways this started as a support group for embarrassed writers, who were nonetheless serious and ambitious about their writing. But the co-operative political spirit was real enough. Although there was never any group dogma, there are some broadly political principles, some well-intentioned ideals on which there is basic agreement. We try to have an equal number of men and women within the limit of twelve in the group. Enshrined in our constitution are democratic procedures, equality of opportunity, and a certain cussed local patriotism about Birmingham. So, not just a support group.

I have to admit that some awareness of Philip Hobsbaum's practice, with the Group poets in London, the Belfast poets and most especially in Glasgow, had filtered through to me in Birmingham. When Alasdair Gray's and James Kelman's books started appearing in the eighties, their success seemed sufficient vindication of the principle of writing groups – especially for proud non-Londoners like us, voicing 'a provincial sense of locality'. A recent Radio 3 feature on Hobsbaum (*Hobsbaum's Choice*) reminded me that his emphasis on 'the presence of the text', and the requirement of the text to stand alone, without the author's intervening explication or justification, was implicit, too, in Tindal's group practice. A close, 'disinterested' critical-reading approach was favoured over newer continental theoretical models. I wonder if I am right to detect a difference of emphasis: according to the radio programme, Hobsbaum was a charismatic and supportive teacher, a leader in the critical process. Whereas at Tindal, there was no bible, no guru, no teacher, just writers acting as facilitators for other writers.

I promise this is the end of the history lesson. TSFG was formed as a fortnightly (weekly was too frequent) meeting for local writers. I happened to have good access to local writing because I was reviewing local books for a regional arts newspaper, teaching creative writing classes at the local arts centre and editing a newspaper anthology for West Midlands Arts. In its first year the group produced a small collection, economically printed, but struggled to sell it. The next year (1985) it was *Six Caribbean Stories* by Leon Blades. A professionally produced collection called *The View from Tindal Street* benefited from proximity to the Birmingham Readers and Writers Festival, which was then in full swing. We could command a local audience, but no more. The book still stands up as a decent collection; sales, however, were disappointing. For years after, we shied away from further anthologies until an influx of enthusiasm, from Penny Rendall and Julia Bell in particular, drove the production of *Mouth: Stories from Tindal Street* (1996), which was shortlisted for the Raymond Williams Community Publishing Prize 1997. This effort was to lead, eventually, to the establishment of the Lottery-funded Tindal Street Press.

Now down to practical matters: a neutral room, not especially comfortable, not too far from the pub. Not someone's house where they have to jump up and answer the phone and make cups of tea. No smoking or drinking inside. Members' subscriptions pay for the room hire and photocopying. We have a treasurer for subs and a secretary for correspondence and arranging photocopying and distribution. Constitutional meetings are kept to a minimum.

You need access to photocopying because you have to have hymn sheets at the service. And the sheets have to be sent out in good time so that people can read beforehand and comment at the meeting. Everyone has to have exactly the same copy, otherwise it can be confusing. There's some pressure on the writer to finish a story in good time for photocopying, in good time for being sent out by post, though this pressure is easing as more members have email. If someone forgets, or doesn't complete their story in time, or the photocopier breaks down, or there's a postal strike, or everyone's experiencing a barren patch at the same time, well, there's no story at the meeting. And believe me, that is always disappointing. It rarely happens. I remember us devising talks instead: on V. S. Naipaul, B. S. Johnson, on endings. Dire. No, all the writer wants is the close study of stories.

Reading aloud is always a must. It helps situate the story in the reader's mind. It shows up weaknesses. This isn't performance art. And only one member treated it as something essentially dramatic. But the intention was never an exercise to see who could read the best – though some do beautifully. Audible and clear is sufficient, since we have the words in front of us. Reading aloud ensures the story gets the closest, most detailed attention from the audience. This is how an evening goes: 8.00; easy chairs in a circle, magazine gossip, competition deadlines, success stories, encouraging letters from editors. Books borrowed and recommended, a fruitful exchange of enthusiasms. Issues of magazines passed round, editors' addresses. Then, 8.30, 8.40, down to business. We owe it to the writer to give proper time to the work under discussion. A long piece can take half an hour to be read out loud.

As a participating member, you've already read it quickly once and again in more detail; you might have made notes. There might be a bit that doesn't quite work. Because when it's read you notice such things. You notice spellings and anachronisms and tone problems and duff dialogue; and you have to say so. And you think of new things as the piece is being read. After the silence following the reading, the talk starts round the room. I liked this and this. I had a problem with that. Top of page four lost a bit of continuity. Everyone to have their six pennyworth. No one person to dominate. Won't be more than forty minutes, maybe even half an hour for discussion. Some disagreement on key points; three-way discussion can blossom. Lively debate; consensus sometimes. The talk could go on. We get thrown out of the hired room by the grumpy caretaker at ten. The writer, meanwhile, takes all these comments away and decides who to agree with, who touched a nerve, who spotted something they thought they could get away with. They have to decide whether to alter the piece before sending it off to a magazine, whether to abandon it. Hurt feelings? Probably, but the comments are always well intentioned. Which isn't to say that for the evening's writer it hasn't been anything but daunting, bracing, exhilarating and instructive.

Did we actively recruit new members? Yes. For instance, I had come across Alan Beard's first published story – it later appeared in *South West Review*. By the time he joined the group his story 'Taking Doreen out of the Sky' had been accepted by Alan Ross at *London Magazine*, which impressed everyone and gave us all a target to set our sights on. Joel Lane was spotted in the pages of *Panurge*. (Would he like to join?) Mike Coverson made enquiries at a library reading we gave. Others simply sent their stories with a covering letter. Whether from recommendation or unsolicited enquiry, everyone was asked to send a couple of stories for scrutiny. Photocopied, passed round, commented on in the group, voted on: in or out, by majority. Entry depended on spaces available; maximum twelve, six men, six women. The membership was stable for a time, too stable; and there were always plenty of ambitious poets and assorted scribblers queuing up, eager to join. But we didn't have space. For a number of years we had difficulty attracting women writers into the group. Later, the constitution was amended to allow an influx of promising younger writers who had shone at a university group; perhaps, yes, we had been in danger of going stale.

Writers left for the best of reasons: having babies, change of job, starting university courses, writing a novel and for the worst, too: not writing, pique. Some weren't writing fiction any more, only drama, only verse. Fine, no place in the group then. But we did our best to keep the numbers stable at six and six. There were times when we had too many constitutional meetings. And a couple of our sixties' politicos excelled more at debating the constitution than writing stories for consideration by the group. The writers got restive because we weren't engaging in our main activity: writing, reading and discussing stories.

The group is 'closed', because we, none of us, have time to waste on time-wasters – people in town to impress and then off again to the next fascinating project in their career. Well, we have all taken the trouble to carve out from busy lives, as librarians, gardeners, teachers, administrators, students, unemployed somethings, a time every fortnight, a night when we discuss a story or chapter seriously. This was all hard won. No one is a full-time writer, no one imagines they are a genius. There is no room for anyone who only wants to impress or to prove we are a sinister clique. Waste of everybody's time. The production and fortnightly processing of stories is far too precious to be wasted on bullshit artists. Membership is earned by making helpful (not sycophantic) comments and by bringing a piece along at decent intervals. Average would be two per year. Reading them is like subscribing to a fortnightly literary magazine.

This process certainly improves the chances of magazine publication. I had stories published by *London Magazine, Bête Noire* and *Critical Quarterly* and by Heinemann. Beard had them published everywhere – *Panurge, Sunk Island Review, London Magazine, Critical Quarterly* and *Bête Noire*. One of Annie Murray's stories won the *She* short story competition; she had others in *London Magazine* and *Bête Noire*. Penny Rendall had stories in the *European* and *Metropolitan*; Jackie Gay in *London Magazine*; Joel Lane in countless mags, literary and horror. Every one of these stories and more of similar quality were read out at the group. They're all in our archives. And we all knew they would be published; and others should have been. Which is some kind of proof of our collective critical assessments. Success in little magazines started many of us on the rocky road to agents and publishers.

TSFG has always been finely focused on the main task in hand – writing quality fiction. But some opportunities can take the effort of the group away from the writing. It's the writing of stories, and not performances, not anthologies, which is our raison d'être.

But the publishing impulse was always there. Anthologies were produced in 1984, 1985, 1986 and 1996; notice the gap. But it wasn't the main thrust of the group. The possibility of appearing with peers in a group anthology in a self-published anthology was undoubtedly an incentive to many. Why not? The readership for this is limited, however. Distribution and collection of sales income are a drain on members' time. Time that could be resented. Precious time from reading stories, the real job of the group.

Whether to give readings and performances. At times we had the opportunity to read as part of a festival. There was interest from other writing groups and some supporters. Readings in the Midlands Arts Centre and Library Theatre. All of which call upon organizing abilities, publicity skills – which is a different thing again from writing. Because we happened to have those skills in the group – people who had worked in publishing, design and print, and publicity – we were able to set up a publishing arm.

This isn't the place to explain the aims of Tindal Street Press. Except to say the group as a whole wanted Alan Beard's collection *Taking Doreen out of the Sky* to be published. The stories deserved national recognition. In spite of his magazine publication track record, three London publishers had turned the book down as being uneconomical. A sub-committee within the group (only those so minded) made sure that this materialized to the highest quality, with the support of a small Lottery grant. The fact that the book was reviewed splendidly right across the national press was pure, sweet vindication for all of us. That it was then bought up by Picador was a neat irony. But this first venture was so successful that a larger grant support led to the establishment of Tindal Street Press, to *Hard Shoulder* and to novels by Jackie Gay, and by non-members Michael Richardson and Gul Davis; with more to come.

How collective are we in the fiction group? Twelve egos in a room: What do you think? Healthy rivalry, but not bitter competitiveness. We've got to know each other well, but we're not in each other's pockets. There've been tiffs, divisions, high dudgeon; and friendships, phone calls, correspondences. Support, definitely. Commitment; no point otherwise. Easy networking. Prima donnas not tolerated. Ah, but don't go thinking the group mentality causes atrophy in the talent of the individual writer. It doesn't follow. This was only for writers with the good sense to want to improve their craft.

Tindal Street Fiction Group is a simple system set up for developing members' short and long fiction. There's no doubt it works much better with short than long fiction, though all our novelists have tested at least some of their chapters on fellow writers. Most helpful, as I can attest. But whatever the length – and this pleases me as much as it salves some of the hurts to my idealism – the activity of close reading and discussion happens somehow to be for the mutual benefit of *all* members. The group has run for nearly twenty years. Collective works; don't think it needs fixing yet.

Listening to Criticism
Richard Aczel

Offering criticism of another's writing can be a precarious affair; listening to criticism can be downright disastrous. Many first-time participants in writing workshops clam up, or even stop writing altogether, because of the criticism of tutors and fellow writers, even if this criticism happens to be to the point, constructive and carefully delivered. Listening too reverently to misguided criticism, on the other hand, can lead to the jettisoning of a perfectly good idea. This chapter starts out from the premise that good, constructive criticism is an absolute gift to the writer; the problem lies in knowing how to take it and what to do with it.

Because in most of what follows I'll be assuming that the criticism we're being asked to listen to is well founded and constructive, it may be worth beginning with three short tips on giving criticism, before looking more closely at ways of listening to it. Firstly, constructive criticism should always recognize the integrity of the piece of writing under discussion, and therefore seek to improve it in its own terms. Secondly, good criticism is always part and parcel of the recognition and acknowledgement of the interest and value of the writing it addresses. The clearer it is that criticism stems from the recognition of value, the easier it will be to listen to. It is one thing to say, 'There are too many adjectives in this poem,' and quite another to say, 'I really like the way the poem builds up a powerful atmosphere of bleakness, but I wonder whether the doubling of adjectives in line four doesn't actually work against this atmosphere.' Thirdly, criticism needs to be local, particular and above all – when it comes to responding to it – practicable. Two of the greatest obstacles to listening to criticism are the feeling that it constitutes a rejection of our writing (and person) as a whole, and that we can't anyway do anything to make the writing better.

Thus the first important thing about listening to criticism is recognizing just what is being criticized and being confident that it is not us or our writing as a whole. In order to do this, we need to be able to establish a certain distance between our writing and ourselves. This often means 'letting go' of experiences, ideas and words which may be very precious to us. One good way of fostering this kind of distance in a writing workshop is to experiment with writing practices that involve exchanging texts and working with the ideas and words of others. One writer begins a story and passes it to the next, who rewrites it from a different perspective and then passes it on in turn. The same exercise can be done with rewriting the same scene in different voices or styles. Alternatively, the same story can be passed around and continued by a group of writers. In each case our own writing is seen as part of something larger, and we get into the habit of (quite physically) letting go of our work and seeing how our own ideas can be developed by others. One project that proved particularly effective in my seminar at the University of Cologne was to get a group of writers to invent a common town. They drew maps, shared locations and developed a pool of characters and histories, then went away and wrote their own short stories, each of which would contain links of character, event and place with all the others. At first, some of the writers actually got quite annoyed and possessive about how others were taking 'their' characters in directions quite different from their own. Then they increasingly began to thrive on one another's imaginations, changing their own storylines to take in events and characteristics suggested by others. Characters started taking on lives of their own and making new demands of the texts in which they first appeared. Everyone's writing was forced to make sallies into unforeseen territory charted by somebody else. The result was that each writer produced a story that was more than just his or her own work, and the whole collection belonged to everyone.

The point of exercises like these is to encourage writers to feel that their writing is not theirs alone. A piece of writing is always 'bigger' than we are. As soon as we put pen to paper we set in motion possibilities and echoes that resonate way beyond the confines of the idea that originally got us writing. Others will see and hear our words differently. Often, and especially when we are feeling defensive about our work, we take this 'hearing differently' for misunderstanding. Some writers will spend the best part of a workshop session defending what they 'actually meant'. Such argument has its proper place; critics, to be sure, are not incapable of misunderstanding. More often than not, however, the problem stems from our own failure to see that what we meant and what we have written are not one and the same thing. We tend to be so sure of what we ourselves mean that we take it for granted that our words will say it for us. Again, what is needed is a degree of detachment, critical distance from our work. In order to 'hear' the criticism of others, we need to be able to listen critically to our own work in the first place. I've often found it helpful in a workshop to get writers to criticize their texts themselves. To get that necessary detachment, the writer needs to imagine that he/she is someone else: to step into the shoes of another critic, or at least of a familiar critical style. He/she can write a scathing review of her work for the *TLS*, or a nuts-and-bolts deconstruction for the *Journal of Literary Mechanics*.

One way of opening ourselves and our writing to the different ways in which others hear our work is to imagine ourselves as translators. When we translate, we are trying to find and project in our own writing the voice of another. Our own voice, together with all the voices we know and can 'do', will not usually be enough to cover the idiomatic range of another's style. When I show working translations to friends, they almost invariably suggest alternative words and phrases that are not in my active vocabulary. If I can imaginatively 'hear' them in the vocabulary of the voice I'm translating, however, these suggestions are of enormous value. It is the same with our own writing, especially when it involves the projection of several voices, as in spoken dialogue. In this way, listening to criticism becomes a listening to voices with spans and inflections different from our own. What more could a writer ask for?

Another way in which workshops can help us make the best possible use of criticism is by encouraging the vital habit of rewriting. The challenge of changing what we've written should not merely be a reluctant response to the criticism of others, but needs to be incorporated into our everyday writing practices as a source of inspiration and pleasure. When we ourselves get into the habit of recognizing that there is always another way of doing what we've done, it becomes easier to take on board the suggestions of others. There is an endless number of exercises to encourage the habit of rewriting. Try rewriting a poem by replacing all natural images with mechanical ones, or by altering rhythm and line length, by substituting metonymy for metaphor, abstract for concrete, or by imitating the style of various writers in your group. You may find that some of the ideas you produce will feed back into your original poem and open up new possibilities for another. In rewriting a story from the point of view of a different character, you may come up with new insights into your main character or plot that are worth incorporating. In reworking the order of events or images or information in a piece of writing you may discover new possibilities of suspense, anticipation, surprise. Above all: once you get into the habit of trying out alternatives, you will be more likely to take the criticism of others as a further source of inspiration, rather than a reason for stopping writing altogether.

I don't think anyone would deny that when we show our writing to others, we do so at least partly in search of affirmation. But we also show our work to get new ideas, stimulation, practical feedback. We want to be told that it is fine to write as we do and to be who we are, but that we can also discover ways of being more, or less, or other. Criticism belongs to the very fabric of a writing workshop, and we need from the outset to think of our participation as an openness to, and appetite for, the exciting possibilities of change. But for all our openness to the suggestions of others and willingness to try again, in 'listening to criticism' the final benchmark or court of appeal has to rest with our own ears. When we have done all we can to detach ourselves from our words, to hear ourselves as others hear us, and still can't help feeling what they are telling us sounds wrong, it's time to turn the other ear. We've tried the third person, we've tried cutting the adjectives and making the farewell scene a smooch less sentimental . . . but the first version still sounds best. For the most important, and hardest and least teachable, part of listening to criticism is, of course, knowing how and when to ignore it.

Dynamics
Paul Magrs

You can learn an awful lot about writing from other people's work. I don't just mean published poems and novels, though of course you ought to be reading those voraciously as well. One of the most effective things to be engaging with is other people's works-in-progress.

Writers spend a long time alone, working on their own texts. Every writer, I think, needs at some point to belong to a supportive group. You need to have a whole set of people reading your drafts and giving good, constructive feedback. You need it to improve the work, but also as a morale boost, in the sense that you need your work to be out there, being read and being inside other people's minds. The reactions to your writing can be illuminating, stimulating and sometimes frustrating. But the reactions are also fascinating and often useful.

When you come to publish your writing, if that's what you want to do, all sorts of people will read it. People you've never met and never will. They will have all sorts of reactions to what you have written – some of which you would never have guessed in a million years. You can't anticipate or control the multiplicity of readings that your work will get. A writing workshop is this kind of diverse readership in microcosm. It's a training ground for letting go of your work; for learning the confidence to push your work out there, into the world, and standing back. When your workshop group has read and discussed your writing, that's when you see if it can stand up on its own two feet and be quite separate from you as a person.

Say you've found yourself a writing group, a local group that meets once a fortnight, or you've enrolled yourself in a class at a college or university, or gone on a week-long residential writing course. There you will meet people from all kinds of backgrounds and, at first glance, they won't appear to have much in common. There could well be the retired bank manager who's always thought he had a novel inside him, the mother of four who's at last got herself some time away from home to spend on her writing (which she's kept hidden from everyone for years), and there's the sensitive-looking young man, the youngest in the group, who says he wants to write an epic fantasy quest novel.

If you go to enough workshops, you are bound to meet all of these people at one time or another. And you are thinking – who in the group will be able to make sense of what I'm on about? At this stage you can feel helpless, scared, belligerent and quite protective of your work. Especially in that crippling, silent moment when the group leafs through their own copies of your pages. You look around and see that they've written comments all over the margins. They've evidently got things to say about your writing, so why aren't they saying anything? Why this horrendous silence?

I think the silence is because the other members of the group are waiting for someone to take the bold step of making the first comment. They want to say the right thing.

In the worst kind of workshop there would be this kind of charged silence and then, eventually, someone would say something mild and complimentary. Then someone would hesitantly back them up. Then someone else would burst out suddenly and say he thought it was a rotten piece of writing, but he can't exactly explain why. At this point you, the writer, start defending yourself and take over the workshop with a long, boring explanation of where you are coming from and how the whole class are idiots for not understanding any of it. You have to explain every bit of what you've handed in. The whole thing ends in recriminations, and maybe a punch-up, and no one has learned a single thing.

That's the nightmare scenario.

What a workshop needs is a set of rules and a shared vocabulary. Any assertion or criticism made by any member of the group needs to be backed up by close examination of the text and specific examples. No one can boldly state that a piece of writing is the greatest (or the worst) thing they've ever read, without even trying to say why. In fact, you could say that the rules of good writing apply to the art of workshop dynamics. Specify and back up your points and don't make sweeping generalizations.

If you are making constructive comments about a piece of work, you are in dialogue with a whole set of people. Don't be mystifying, pretentious or opaque; remember your audience. I once had someone tell me in a workshop that I must be a Scorpio and that I was in a typically driven mood when I wrote that particular story. I didn't quite know what to say to that (given that I am, actually, a Scorpio). It didn't seem very relevant to the discussion at hand. I'm much happier in a workshop when people are picking up on particular phrases and sections of the text and saying things like 'What I think is meant by this sentence is . . .' or 'This image is suggesting to me . . .' The group members need to question each other as to whether this plot point, this image or their character detail actually works, or whether it's relevant at this stage in the text.

There is a fine balance in workshops between being nit-picking and being too abstract. As in writing itself, the group has to find that balance. A workshop that spends two hours talking about all the commas and their placement in someone's short story is as much of a waste of time as one in which everyone debates the existence of the abominable snowman. These are conversations that you might have at some time or other, but not to the exclusion of all else in a work-shop.

A workshop is a place where you have to get a certain amount of work done. Perhaps, in one session, you have four pieces of work to discuss, allowing forty-five minutes on each. Each writer needs to feel that they're getting a decent amount of useful, critical feedback in that time. They won't feel they've had that if all they've got is a list of commas they need to take out, or if everyone's simply said that their work is 'lovely', or if they now know that 30 per cent of the group believe in the yeti and the rest of them don't.

It's up to the workshop leader to guide the conversation and make sure that the group returns to the work in hand and they are asking and answering interesting, useful questions about it. As a member of the workshop, though, you also have a responsibility to the group. Firstly, of course, you have to have read the work, given it your undivided attention, made notes on it, and arrived at the meeting ready to talk honestly and clearly about it.

Don't sit and say nothing. Sometimes people do it out of shyness, thinking they can't contribute criticism at the right level. Other people seem to be more astute. Don't let this hold you back.

Everyone's voice should be heard. Sometimes people stay silent in workshops so that they will appear to be the enigmatic and brilliant one in the corner; the one who didn't say a word. Don't do this. It's not fair on the others who are, after all, reading your work and are here prepared to talk about it. You have to be fair and take your turn. Equally, don't be the one who needs to talk all the time and butts in over everyone else's comments. That doesn't make you look more talented or brilliant either.

Workshops aren't – or shouldn't be – a competitive space. You are not there in order to look the most brilliant. You are there to present your work-in-progress and engage with other people's works-in-progress. It's by taking your responsibility as a member of a group of writers and reading, commenting and engaging with their work in a fair, reasoned, equal-handed and polite manner that you'll get the most out of the group experience.

At the end of each session, you ought to have the pages of your scribbled notes that you took down as each person spoke about your work. This is what you were doing as you listened to their comments; you were writing them down. You weren't trying to break in with excuses, rebuttals, further elucidations of your work. Listen to what the group has to say. Take the notes home with you afterwards and see what you can make of them. Some of it will be off the wall and maybe not relevant. But if a workshop's been successfully run, there will always be something you can take away from it and plough back into the next draft of your writing.

12 Off the Page

Introduction
Julia Bell

*'I could sway people with words! Strange and magic words
that welled up from within me, from some unfamiliar depth.
I wept with the joy of knowing.'*

EMMA GOLDMAN, *Living My Life*

Milan Kundera says famously in *The Book of Laughter and Forgetting*
that we are becoming a culture of writers but not a culture of readers.
As if we are becoming a society of babblers, endlessly talking at each
other without listening. The great mountains of unsold books tell us
that there is too much text in the world, and yet we keep on writing.
After all, there's gold in them there hills. It could be you.

Perhaps, as Kundera suggests, we just all have too much experience;
our urge to record ourselves has increased in accordance with the
strangeness of our times. But this proliferation of print creates new
readers as well as new writers and there is, if you want one, an
audience out there for your work. The trick is finding the right one.

Deciding what to do with what you've written depends in large
part on what you've written and why. Clearly it would make sense
not to send a horror novel to a romance publisher or sci-fi to a literary
editor. But more importantly than that, you need to be aware of your
own progression, where your own writing is *at*. The writer's 'radar'
that Hemingway refers to. It's hard to judge these things for yourself
when you feel as if your nose is squashed against the page. This is
where an audience can help give you a fair idea of the effectiveness
and coherence of your work.

When I was younger I used to think my work would become magically transformed by the Royal Mail into a work of genius. I knew in my heart it wasn't up to much, but I kind of hoped that my latent, undiscovered prodigy self would be spotted and championed by some top editor.

The world of writing is full of many valid and functional parts, and being published by a London publishing house may not be the best route to your ideal audience. If you really want people to read your work, give it to your friends, read it out loud in a pub, publish it in a small magazine. Dip your toes in the water tentatively, don't be dazzled by Lottery-like dreams of millions; the glittering prizes come to a very small percentage of writers. You think writers are glamorous? Go see them read. They're usually on the edges of poverty, badly dressed, in need of a haircut, slightly red-eyed from too many late nights and too much coffee.

If you are starting, start small. Join a local writing group, find out if there are readings, get yourself a slot, read a few pieces aloud in public. If that is too daunting, find out what magazines there are in your area and offer to write for them. Local arts boards will be able to help. They usually have details of local publications, readings, magazines, workshops, and will have a literature mailing list you can join.

Some national magazines and journals publish short fiction and poetry (for example *London Magazine*, *Rialto*, *Stand*, *Pretext*, etc.). Look in *The Writer's Handbook* for the current list. There are competitions you can enter – the Stand Short Story Competition, the Bridport Prize, for women, the Asham Award.

If you are struggling with postbags of rejection slips, perhaps it's time to get some editorial advice. If you can't attend a workshop, try one of the editorial services like The Literary Consultancy, who will be able to give you insight and feedback into what's going wrong and, of course, what you are doing right, too.

Tenacity is part of the package; John Updike famously claims to have had over 200 rejection slips. Is this a sign of his undiscovered genius or that he was still in training, still practising, still learning his craft? Two hundred editors won't have been wrong about his work. Chances are it was still pretty rough and ready.

If you've already had a few hits, some short stories, poems published here and there, it might be time to seek out an agent to develop your work further. Some of the bigger, more corporate agencies aren't particularly interested in developing new talent, so you may find a smaller agency is more suited to your needs. Again, all these are listed in *The Writer's Handbook*. Be aware that most agents will prefer you to be writing a novel. Unless you are already a high-profile story writer, publishers won't be interested. Collections of short stories don't sell. Allegedly.

Another, perhaps more radical, alternative to seeking a publisher is to become one yourself. Publishing your own work is part of a long tradition of creative production that can be traced through Virginia Woolf right back to Caxton. In the early 1990s a whole wealth of authors was brought to greater attention through magazines such as *Rebel Inc, Pulp Faction, Verbal* and Duncan McLean's Clocktower Press. Irvine Welsh, John King, Gordon Legge, Nicholas Blincoe, among others, all started out publishing in these small magazines and books.

Self-publishing forces a more rigorous critical approach to your own work and there is a real, tangible sense of achievement to a successful self-published work. Of course, you are damned by the critics because 'you're not good enough to go anywhere else' or because 'all you do is publish yourself and your friends'. But in this game, if there's a critical angle, someone will find it, and what's really important to self-publishing is the integrity of the product. If you are doing it to inflict your 1,000 page opus about aliens from Pluto on the world, then it may be doomed to collect dust on your embarrassed friends' bookshelves. If you are publishing because you are part of a group of writers that wants to reach out into the local community with its writing, then you have every chance of gathering the goodwill and support of your local reading community.

John Betjeman said that an artist should be a part of and be used by the community to which they belong. Small publishing ventures are beneficial because they offer up a written reflection of the community from which they come. Alan Mahar has described how Tindal Street Press in Birmingham is a startling example of how a local writing group turned to self-publishing out of sheer frustration with being ignored by London publishers. All it took was a Lottery grant, a computer and some stories from Alan Beard to create a literary sensation. Since then the press has produced an anthology of stories and two novels with plenty more to come. The response in Birmingham has been overwhelming, people are pleased to see their city reflected in print, to feel as if where they come from is worth writing fiction about.

If you are part of a writing group, investigate the funding possibilities in your area. Contact your local arts board for details of available grants. Technology makes the actual production of a book cheaper and easier than ever before. The laborious typesetting process Virginia Woolf struggled with is thankfully a thing of the past. Perhaps, if your writing group has enough members, you could pool your resources to pay for publication.

At this point it's vital to make a distinction between self-publishing and the vanity publishers who will produce your book for a hefty fee. Avoid these charlatans like the plague. They are interested in your money, not your welfare. You will get boxes of your books back but they will give you no help to distribute or sell your book. There are many disappointed writers who have spent money to get their work printed only to be left with stacks of books going mouldy in the garage. Not a happy ending for your hopes and dreams.

The Internet offers many exciting possibilities for writers to find an audience for their work. You might think that the Net is the poor sister of the printed page. That it only exists for the truly unreadable manuscripts or cult fiction, which has a very small audience. However, there are signs that writers are using the Internet more and more as a resource. In the US there are several web sites that promote new stories to the film industry. If you want to set up your own site, a stringent editorial policy will be the key to its success. Only publish good stuff, don't use it as a dumping ground for the stories you can't sell. Perhaps collectively your writing group can use the site to show work to prospective publishers and agents. Why not send them your URL as a calling card from your writers' group?

Genre fiction is worth mentioning here. If you are a horror freak or a sci-fi nut or a sex-and-shopping fiend, chances are you are already familiar with the market, with the publishers who print the kind of writing you admire. If not, study the market. Publishers such as Mills and Boon offer guidelines for their prospective writers to follow. Again, *The Writer's Handbook* will list the publishers who take your kind of work. If you are going commercial, really think about why someone would want to read your book. How is it different from other books in the genre? What's your angle? What makes your story fresh and exciting? Genre fiction survives on mutation, on new angles to old stories. Keep your synopsis short and sweet and highlight the elements that make your book unique. A successful synopsis will entice the agent or editor to pick up the book, a bad one will get you a rejection slip.

If you're trying for an audience for your poetry, you may find plenty of small local pamphlets and magazines that will consider your work or local reading nights that would be pleased to let you have a go on the open mic. If not, set one up. Some of our creative writing students at UEA started putting their poems on flyers and handing them out for free around the university. Poetry has a long and honourable tradition of small presses: Bloodaxe, Anvil, Carcanet all publish new work, as do Faber and Faber, and Picador. Again, for an up-to-date list of who's publishing what look at *The Writer's Handbook* for details.

The most important thing to remember when venturing towards the spotlight with your work is not to expect too much. Heady dreams of millions will only set you up for disappointment and perhaps put you off the idea of writing altogether. Despite the old clichés of writers struggling in lonely garrets, writing is a communal activity. Working collectively not only helps to smooth out the rough edges in your work, it also generates an audience. My grandma once wrote a children's story in a little black notebook that smelled of the plastic of the faux-leather cover. She read it to all her grandchildren in turn. She never even bothered to type it up. It was enough that we were entertained, that we were delighted, that we listened.

How to Cook a Book
Julian Jackson

General Ingredients:

- Content
- Equip
- Cost
- Edit
- Style
- Design
- Tweak
- Proof
- Print
- Publish

These ingredients can obviously vary, but this is a good solid recipe for a basic publication.

Content: What Do You Want to Publish?

What and why you want to print should dictate how you decide to publish. Is it text? Text and images? Text as images? Is it colour? Black and white?

How are you going to get the text? Is it ready already? Do you need to advertise for submissions? Do you need an editorial board? If you are going to advertise for submissions who is your target market? Students? Children? General Public?

Are you going to sell it? Or will it be free? (If you are going to sell it, the printing and production costs can be higher than if you are giving it away for free.) Are there going to be restrictions on word length or subject material? For example, in the UEA anthology *LAVA* we asked for submissions of between 2,000 and 5,000 words. We chose six pieces in all, amounting to 90 pages, roughly 200 words per page. Deciding on length is vital at this stage as it will dictate costs later on. Remember to allow for readability when calculating your desired length, squashed text will be unreadable, too much white space scrappy, too large and it will run to hundreds of pages. Look at other publications for ideas.

This is the planning stage of your publication. It might be useful at this point to make a timescale sheet so you know exactly how long you have to put the book together. A traditional book publication takes months, even years, from acceptance to publication. A small pamphlet can be done in a couple of days.

Equip: Do You Need to Equip Yourself?

To publish, all you need is a typewriter and access to a photocopier. Some students have produced books by gluing and sticking and photocopying. For more formal publications you will need access to a computer with desktop-publishing software, for example QuarkXpress, Pagemaker, Microsoft Word, Claris Works, etc. Any software that allows you to manipulate the layout of the words on the page. Coupled with that, image-editing software like Photoshop or Illustrator is useful for cover designs and images. Access to a scanner can prove useful for importing images and text.

This is probably one of the major costs of publishing. But a computer with DTP capability need not be that expensive. (For example you can buy a second-hand Macintosh computer with DTP facilities for under £500.) Also, you may well find plenty of people with computers that have these facilities that aren't being utilized. Any PC running Windows '95 can cope with basic DTP software.

Using the software isn't as complicated as it may seem. If you can use a basic word-processing package then you will already have some of the skills needed to use DTP software. Alternatively, we produced an anthology of work by photocopying the student type-scripts to make a fanzine.

Cost: How Much Will it Cost?

The cost of your book will depend on what you want to produce. A booklet with a card cover costs about 30p a copy if you print more than 20 of them. For a book of 250 pages with a full-colour cover you are looking at paying about £2,500 for a print run of 1,000.

Our <texts> series at UEA, small books of 12.5cm x 16cm, are cheaper because we are only doing small print runs of 250 copies. Our printer charges £450 per print run (£1,800 for a print run of four), which is a discount because we're printing four together. (To print one book would normally cost £550.)

The major cost in printing is the paper and the colour processing of the covers. If you are on a tight budget a duotone cover (black and white and one colour) will significantly reduce your costs. Recycled paper is often cheaper than dense top-grade paper. Also books cost less per copy the more you print, so if you think you can sell them, print runs of over 1,000 are more likely to allow you to make a profit, or at least cover your costs.

To produce 1,000 copies of a standard paperback book of 250 pages you will need around £3,000 and some equipment to produce it. For a small pamphlet of poetry or a single short story £50 will be enough.

Finding funding for your project is obviously the biggest headache of all, but there is money around for publishing projects. Try your regional arts board, the Lottery grants or approach local businesses for sponsorship. Do you have a local paper? They may be able to help with printing. Or you could sell advertising space. You may want to invest some of your own money if you are sure you are going to sell the end product. Don't be too ambitious, work to a budget you are sure you can manage. Our printer (Biddles Ltd) specializes in small, cheap print runs – shop around for a printer who will work to your requirements.

All of this is assuming you are going to have negligible labour costs (that you are giving up your own free time to produce the book); if you include paying for editing, layout and designing, your costs will become too high to manage on a small print run. To cover these costs and make a profit you will need to print and sell over 3,000 copies at £7.

Edit: How Are You Going to Choose and Correct the Work?

An editor should control the actual content of the book, deciding on what gets published and where. If you have a book of short stories, for example, what order will they be in?

You may want to employ a copy-editor at this point, someone who will check your manuscript for inconsistencies and grammar and help you stick to your house style.

Editing a text is a personal choice about content, grammar, style and audience. The editorial process involves allowing for proof-reading and copy-editing to ensure that the text is clean. Decisions about spelling – American or UK or intentional misspellings – need to be decided, however pedantic or petty they may seem.

Style: What Do You Want Your Book to Look Like?

Are you publishing one book or a series of books? If it's the former then you need to ensure consistency throughout the text in terms of grammar, layout, pagination, etc. If it's a series then you will find that you will need certain design consistencies, usually called the 'house' style. Style sheets allow you to double-check every publication for things such as spaces after full stops, protocol for commas and full stops and a typeface that suits your requirements. There are lots of different styles to choose from; you will want something that reflects the content and potential market of your publication. Something that is easy to read is always a good idea.

Design: What Do You Want Your Book to Look Like?

At this stage you may want to find some designers or, if you are doing it yourself, to decide what you want the whole book to look like. Cover design is all important if you are aiming your publication at the bookshops. You'll want it to stand out, look professional, have a desirable 'feel'. We use a matt laminate on some of our covers to give them a silky, tactile quality – it makes people want to pick them up and handle them. At this point it's useful to try to visualize your book as a three-dimensional object, not just two-dimensional images and text.

How big will your book be? A paperback? A hardback? A magazine? Will it be perfect bound (like most paperback books) or stapled? Will your cover be full colour, duotone, or black and white?

You will want to choose a printer who suits your requirements, too. With 1,000 copies of a 250-page book with a full-colour cover you will need to use litho printing. For pamphlets or booklets, photocopiers or design and print shops can cope with small print runs.

How your text looks on the page will be vital to the readability of the text, how the cover looks, to its potential sales. Point sizes and line spaces are vital. Look at these examples:

This is too small.

These lines are too close together
These lines are too close together

These are too far apart

These are too far apart

Consistency in your story headings and page numbers is vital, too – choose a font and a size that will match the body style of your text.

Also, you might want to choose the paper you are going to use to print the books (any printer will send you a set of stock samples).

Brilliant white paper makes text hard to read and can make the overall effect quite cheap, off-white or recycled paper often looks much better.

Tweak: Are You Happy with What You've Got?

At this stage in the production you may want another opinion on your book. If you've been looking at it for weeks it might be hard to see any mistakes in it. Pass it around your friends for an opinion, get feedback on the cover design and the layout. Once the book has gone to the printer it will be too late to change anything. If you are not happy with something, however trivial, it's always a good idea to double-check it. 'Tweaking' your cover and your layout will ensure that you get what you want.

Proof: Is it Perfect?

This is the last stage of the production process. Proofreading is boring, labour intensive work. You need to read through the text to ensure that there aren't any mistakes that have been missed at an earlier stage. Is it 100 per cent? Are you sure? Are you happy with it? It might be useful to look at a book about proofreading and copy-editing to familiarize yourself with the short-hand symbols that professional editors use.

Of course, there are always going to be mistakes in your book – there are in the books in Waterstone's – but to make something both satisfying and professional, attention to the detail of the text is vital.

Print: Who Will Print My Book?

For a big print run you will want to use a litho printer who will print on to rolls of paper. With a small print run something such as the DocuTech™ system, used by Biddles (and lots of other printers), is a brilliant development for small publishers. Basically, it means that pages are photocopied (at a very high resolution) rather than printed. Making it as easy to print one book as it is to print a hundred.

When you send your text and images to the printer, it is vital that you remember to include a disk with all your images and fonts as well as a hard copy of your cover and contents so the printer has something to refer to in the printing process. Make sure to include clear details of what paper you want and what laminate you want on the cover, etc. Most printers will help you choose and provide samples and details of how to send your work to them. Remember to choose a printer you like and who you feel will do a good job for you – ask for samples of other work they have done so you can see what kinds of book they do, an odd size or a complicated cover might need specialized equipment. If you get the book back and you are not happy with the job, and you are sure it's not your fault, the printer is legally obliged to reprint the run for you.

When you plan your publication you will need to allow at least a month for your printer to turn your book around. It is also a good idea to book your slot with the printers a few weeks ahead of delivery so you get your book back in time.

Publish: What Do I Do Now?

Now you've got your books back. They look lovely and you are really happy with them; you'll want to sell them. How are you going to distribute your book? You might want to use a distribution agency, and for this you will need an ISBN number (International Standard Book Number), which will register your book in the British Library Catalogues and allow bookshops to look your book up on their computers. A distribution agency is only useful for print runs of around 1,000, they will take 45 per cent of your cover price but they will ensure that your book goes to bookshops nationwide. They will expect you to submit an advance information sheet at least three months before publication, with a cover image for their catalogues, and to show that you are chasing some national publicity.

Publicity is really a question of try and try again. To promote your book to the national review pages is a question of sending out a press release, following that with a phone call and then, if you get some interest, a copy of your book. Don't waste precious copies on people who are only going to leave them lying around the office. Who do you know? Who do your friends know? Lean on any contacts you might have for publicity. Newspapers rely on people to make stories for them, so remember to write a press release that has some 'story' base – something that can be cannibalized to make a good article in the papers.

Organize a book launch and a reading. Invite the local papers, get someone to take pictures; your book will sell the best in its local environment first, don't expect to get national sales straight away.

One successful publication is likely to lead to others, so ensure before you print thousands of copies of your book that there's a market for what you're doing.

The Rise of Literary Consultancies
Rebecca Swift

Printing press, printer-publisher, publisher, literary agent and now the literary consultant. It is my belief that the changes in the publishing industry in the 1980s in this country, as well as the unprecedented plethora of people trying to write in various literary forms – poetic, testimonial, autobiographical, fictional and now fictional non-fiction – have helped spawn a new breed of literary interlopers, of which I became one, when I co-founded, with Hannah Griffiths, The Literary Consultancy in 1996.

We are consultants, and there are an increasing number of us, a relatively new link in the chain between author and publisher. We offer, for a fee, professional, detailed, objective attention to manuscripts before they are submitted – or resubmitted – to publishers and agents. Alternatively, if a manuscript is not ready to send out, nor ever likely to be, we will do our best to be constructively candid.

Thus we hope to help the author, either by making a link to an agent on their behalf, suggesting improvements to their work and therefore their chances of publication, or to help them face the likelihood that their work will not sell and offer constructive workshop-style advice to help their chances of improvement. We also hope to relieve the industry from the enormous amount of work it receives every day that is not suitable for publication.

What Can a Client Expect from a Consultant?

The main benefit of paying for professional advice is that an author has paid for attention to his or her work on a one-to-one basis, regardless of their relationship to the marketplace. They are paying for a consultant to assess how well a book might be working on its own terms, and they can expect the report to give their work time and energy, even if it won't make much money. A good consultant should not only have good editorial skills but also be well informed about the marketplace, as most clients are interested to know how they would fare in the commercial industry. A consultant, however, should also know a bit about, for example, the existence of small-scale publishing ventures, Internet or Arts Council-backed local publishing ventures, as well as responsible self-publishing which can certainly be a satisfying alternative to commercial publishing for a certain kind of client. If a project is worthy of some kind of publication then a consultant should help the client think about what it is sensible for them to take up.

In addition, it needs to be said that a consultant must be an empathic person who is not of the opinion that people should not write if they 'can't write'. Much of the work they will read will be of a pretty unsophisticated nature. Yet somebody has been driven to write it and a consultant, if they accept work from writers who do not have proven track records, will have to care that they have. The reports should be diplomatic and sensitive, and some may see one of the chief skills of the consultant as being more akin to those of a therapist than an editor. After all, the act of writing and showing your work to people is famously emotional and difficult. Individual consultants often judge for themselves what work they are happy to tackle and what not. And the client can try to assess, through conversations and word-of-mouth, if the consultant will have the particular skills they are looking for in relation to their work.

Of course, one person's opinion can never represent that of all possible readers and is subject to personal taste. However, as far as possible a consultant should possess the experience and imagination to see where a book might suit another person if not themselves. They are there to see if the project is working as well as it possibly can, and to advise on how to improve work if it isn't. At our consultancy, for example, we will try as much as possible to match project to reader. In other words, we would send a thriller to a reader who has an understanding of how thrillers work, as opposed to a reader whose strength may be in literary fiction or children's fiction. In the world of non-fiction a client will be best served by a reader with an under-standing of what is being written about, as well as an understanding of the market for that subject. Of course, this is setting standards high and it is not always possible to find the ideal reader; a good general editor should be able to tackle a variety of material, but in specific cases we reserve the right not to read work if we can't do it justice.

A report should be devised on a one-to-one basis depending on the work and the client. I am not a fan of editorial services that provide pre-formatted responses which address pre-configured elements, such as 'character', 'use of metaphor', 'stucture', 'language'. I remember receiving a report back from a short story competition that had several boxes ticked (or otherwise) down a pre-set list of expectations. It felt as if any detail from the work had not been attended to and that it was worse than useless, it was also insulting. I think a reader should feel free to construct a report in response to the work and client, having absorbed their covering letter and the book. They devise their own list of what might be important to think about, although there are usually questions relating to structure, characterization, writing style, use of cliché, etc. Structure is a classic problem for writers, especially first-time writers, and the shape of the work often needs addressing.

Is the story being told to best effect or are great pages of irrelevant passages that the author can't bear to let go of clogging up the works? Is a thriller giving away its plot too quickly? Is a literary work too interior to be interesting to an outside party? Has a non-fiction book been written before? Is the material well organized? A reader should address the project freshly and then have the skill to articulate that to a client. Often a report for a less well-written novel will address 'basics', such as repetition, use of clichés, lack of originality, poor spelling and grammar and so on; for a more competent manuscript it may be a question of focussing in detail on why a plot is falling down halfway through, why an ending disappoints us, why a character fails to impress. Readers also often use pencil annotations to make their points about the work, which is helpful to pick up details as you go. I should stress, however, that the work of an editorial assessor is not to re-edit the MS completely; I am suspicious of people who say they can re-edit an MS to a publishable standard, unless they have a secure offer at the end of the rainbow. After all, the marketplace is not an easy one to crack. Being clear about what is and isn't likely is important at all times in this job, as so often writers have unrealistic ideas about their own work in relation to the world of publishing.

Stigma of Paying for an Assessment?

There used to be more of a stigma attached to having to get paid editorial help with manuscripts. Indeed, people are right to be cautious about people asking them for money in exchange for services vis-à-vis their writing. Many of the vanity presses have notorious reputations for providing clients with flattering reports and taking several thousands of pounds from them to publish, only for the client to find themselves stuck with thousands of copies of their badly produced book that they don't know how to distribute or sell. I have had several clients who have either already been 'ripped off' in such a manner, and are now looking to see if their book really does stand a chance of respectable publication, or who have come for a second opinion before parting with their money. After all, most people only want their work to be published if it is working well and if at least some others may genuinely wish to read it.

Things have got so tough with commercial publishing, however, that certain responsible types of self-publishing are becoming respectable again. There are many cases of books that have built up reputations, the best-selling *Celestine Prophecy*, for example, which started with self-published volumes. Indeed, Timothy Mo and Stephen King have made their own forays into self and Internet publishing. Times are changing. The emphasis that emerged in the rationalizing 1980s, on getting the end product right before approaching agents and publishers, has meant that it makes increasing sense for a writer to invest in getting an objective opinion of their own before sending out their work. Also, as agents and publishers have less time to give any real feedback on the manuscripts they receive that aren't immediately commercial, and as they often take several months to respond to unsolicited manuscripts, it is increasingly viewed as worthwhile to pay for a one-to-one responsible assessment with a short turnaround period.

Changes in the Industry

It may be illustrative to chart my own route through publishing. In 1987 I joined Virago Press as an editorial assistant/secretary. It was there I first became acquainted with the notorious 'slush pile'. In the manner of many young editorial secretaries, I began with a sympathetic heart, often overwhelmed by the sheer effort so many people had put in to producing manuscripts. These manuscripts were, 98 per cent of the time, in harsh commercial terms, of no use whatsoever. Either they were inappropriate for the press or simply (in most cases) not well enough written. Having begun writing a long and detailed letter back to someone I was rejecting, I was told that our job was to spend time on what we were publishing, not what we would not be publishing. Indeed, being sympathetic was often more trouble than it was worth. If one did send a detailed reply back to somebody, explaining why we could not take them on, it often had the opposite of the desired effect (to let them accept the disappointing state of affairs quietly) and had them coming back for more. For more what exactly? The answer is what all writers crave: feedback and contact.

As is well known, writing a book is often a difficult and lonely experience. This remains true whether the end product is considered marketable or not. People who make the effort of trying to write tend to want to be taken seriously. At a fee-paying consultancy they can be treated with seriousness and respect, without being dismissed as being writers of nonsense. This is not to say that a reputable consultancy will soft-soap people, just to say that at least someone who has spent the time trying to write will know their work has been read from cover to cover in a considered way.

Whilst working at Virago many people called to ask where they could get an opinion about their work. At that time, in the late 1980s, I did not know what to recommend. Apart from telling them to join a writing group, or try an Arvon writing course, there was nothing I knew of at the time to suggest (although I have since learnt that private consultants did exist but weren't widely advertised). Writing groups are not always accessible and can be unpredictable and self-consoling, as well as productive and creative. Even at the excellent Arvon courses you can't get what a consultant offers: a full, detailed read of a complete manuscript, whatever shape it is in. This is partly because such a read is an extremely time-consuming, and often laborious, job to do well. It is far easier to say something is 'boring' or 'rubbish' than it is to try to work out why something is not effective, and then explain that to the writer. The work of detailed feedback needs to be properly rewarded for time taken and expertise. Enter: the literary consultant with a professional background in editing.

Redundancies of editors from publishing houses in the 1980s and 1990s left a pool of strong editorial talent freelancing for a living. An increasing number of ex-commissioning editors offered their services in the back of writing magazines. They offered a knowledge of the industry with strong editorial skills. It was this also that The Literary Consultancy hoped to offer. In addition, we wanted to have access to a range of editors to suit different projects and to stick to tight turnaround times and good links with agents and publishers. Such we did. Another excellent source of readers has proved to be the creative writing MAs, such as those at UEA or Sheffield. There, students who are good writers learn much about writing technique and novel structure; they learn about the pitfalls common to all inexperienced writers and also learn from the inside about how those pitfalls can be best avoided or amended.

It is worth noting that the arts boards in Great Britain sometimes offer reading services at subsidized rates. A drawback may be that turnaround time is slow, and readers are not as up to date with the industry as may be useful. As from April 2001, in fact The Literary Consultancy will benefit from an Arts Council grant themselves, with which to help low-income writers of quality.

Editorial consultants at best help good writers make serious links with the agenting/publishing industry. Whilst, of course, many clients must receive a report on their work and be disappointed, such close attention, when responsibly and ably done, has also helped people to think more realistically about their work in relation to a demanding, commercial marketplace.

Agents and How to Get One
Candi Miller

What do agents do?

Essentially, they sell rights related to your manuscript, and take a 10 to 20 per cent commission for doing so.

They begin by touting it around all the likely UK publishers. With their credentials they can bypass the mouldering slush piles, go straight to an editor and make the excited, 'Didn't you just love it?' follow-up call. (If they don't make that call, they don't believe in the work, one editor reckons.) Or an agent might decide on a multiple submission to several suitable publishers and an auction of your manuscript. Thrilling for you. For a publisher, 'always nerve-racking; always energizing; always shrouded in query and secrecy even after the event . . .' according to Philip Gwyn Jones, Editorial Director of Flamingo.

Next, the paperback rights to your manuscript must be sold, then, with luck, the audio rights and foreign rights, and, with a lot of luck, the film or television rights, and the ones causing current consternation, e-book rights. All along the way an agent must advise the author about the best deal, bearing in mind their client's career plan, i.e. two-book wonder or a long-term literary career that builds up a devoted readership. While a six-figure, two-book deal sounds seducing, agent Lisanne Radice, a crime fiction specialist, believes it can prevent an agent from negotiating for more money if the first book does better than expected. Agent for twenty-something writers of literary fiction Victoria Hobbs believes that putting novelists under the pressure of a big advance can sink a career. 'One must be allowed to make mistakes as a first-time novelist.'

If you are wondering how you'll have the nous to push away the honeypot when your turn comes, relax. Only 1 per cent of literary deals involve a figure of over £100,000, an aspect of literary reality an agent should point out to a new client, along with the pros and cons of every contract they are asked to sign.

Nowadays, most literary agents do more than look after a writer's commercial interests. They might support an author through a sticky professional or even personal patch; they might come up with that missing bit of plot or make suggestions for revision. Good agents bawl out (not too loudly) a publisher who's not fulfilling their marketing obligations – lack of promotional effort is the biggest gripe authors have about their publishers. Jane Bradish-Ellames of Curtis Brown says, 'My job's a constant mix of nannying and bullying.' From Philip Gwyn Jones's point of view, a good agent is one who knows 'when to rein in an author's unrealistic or misguided apprehension of an aspect of publication.'

Once your book has been launched and royalties start coming in, your agent should check the statements, query them with the publisher if necessary, and chase up any outstanding amounts.

Handy, then, having a literary agent. But how to get one?

Unfortunately, finding an agent can be more difficult than finding a publisher. The sheer volume of the competition is one reason; subjectivity is another. One agent's 'To die for' is another's 'No thanks'.

Increase your chances of success by keeping a file on likely agents before you are ready to submit. Watch the press, national and trade, for leads. You'll come across reports that make you think you or your work stands some chance of interesting a particular agent. Personal introductions are valuable too. Jonathan Lloyd, Managing Director of Curtis Brown, who specializes in popular women's fiction, gets new clients from the recommendations of existing ones.

Save yourself a lot of time and postage by ensuring you are applying to the right person. Don't send your literary, self-conscious-new-man masterpiece to Jonathan Lloyd or your children's book to agents listed as adults only. And you must address your submission to someone specific, not to Mr Curtis Brown or Mr A. P. Watt. Call up the agency and check that your preferred agent is still there. If not, ask the receptionist or some other initiate which of their agents deals with your type of work. Ask, too, if there are any new or junior agents. They're usually the hungriest for new authors. Now, ascertain the specific submission requirements. It's usually three chapters only or the first one hundred pages. Some agents want a synopsis; others can't bear them. But everyone wants a succinct but appealing covering letter from you, containing a paragraph of pitch about the manuscript and another about you and why you are qualified to write the novel. Don't forget the presentation basics – for all the finer details see Penny Rendall's chapter on how to submit your work for publication – and remember an SAE.

If your pitch works, the agent will ask to see the whole MS. If they're still impressed, you'll be invited to meet.

By this stage, most not-yet-published (NYP) writers, bruised by years of rejection, are so grateful for the agent's attention, the last thing they'll think about is whether the person buying them lunch is right for their careers. But take a long cool sip of the Perrier and summon up the chutzpah to ask the person offering to represent you at least some of these questions:

Why are you an agent?

Which aspect of your job do you like/dislike the most?

Which recent publication would you compare with my manuscript?

If you were a publisher, how would you publish my manuscript?

Does your agency handle foreign rights? If not, what arrangements do you make?

What will you be doing to secure film/TV/radio reading rights?

How involved will you be in my book? Will you attend publicity meetings, jacket design sessions, etc?

How do you see my literary career developing if all goes well?

How do you work on your backlist – i.e. what strategy do you employ for keeping publishers active on past books?

Do you charge for incidentals – photocopying, couriering, etc.?

How long do you keep trying to sell a manuscript?

Interview several agents, if you are lucky enough to have a choice, and choose someone you are not afraid of. In many ways, an author–agent relationship is like a marriage. But while you don't want to snuggle up to your agent, you do want someone you can call and talk to.

Be suspicious of an agent who tries to make you agree to a three- to four-year contract. It's vital to choose an agent who is evangelically enthusiastic about your manuscript. Only that sort of faith and conviction will keep them making the huge effort required to sell a manuscript in an over-supplied market.

But before you get to the happy place – having an agent who believes in you – there'll be rejection, a lot of it, probably justified. Even solicited manuscripts are rejected. The sheer volume of submissions – two man-sized postbags a day at the biggest literary agent, Curtis Brown – means agents are looking for a reason to reject your typescript. Don't let it be because it wasn't ready in the first place. Most NYP writers reach a point, prematurely, where they want professional input. Understandable. But don't scupper your chances with an agent. Most keep records of submissions and their rejections. Instead, use an editorial service, who can provide a much more comprehensive report. You'll find these services advertised in the classified section of writing magazines.

A subscription to a trade publication is a good idea for keeping abreast of the literary business. Main libraries keep the *Bookseller* and the *Author*, and magazines like *Writers' News* and *Publishing News* are useful for updates on who's moved where. And did you know, there are now agencies which find NYPs an agent? Helen Corner (ex-Hamish Hamilton and Penguin) of Cornerstones undertakes to place good manuscripts with an agent. No place, no pay. There is a rub: if Helen judges the manuscript needs editorial polish, she will engage professional readers to do page-by-page nit-picking or give a more general report, depending upon what you are willing to pay.

Bear in mind, aside from China, the UK publishes the most novels of any country in the world every year. With a good literary agent, yours could be one of them. But when you've just received your sixth, twelfth or twentieth rejection letter from an agency and are beginning to feel hopeless, remember: agents don't write, you do. And they admire you for it. Genuinely.

You'll see.

Final Revisions and Submission
Penny Rendall

Your novel is finished: written, rewritten, revised again. It's the very best you can do, possibly a masterpiece. Now put yourself in the position of the agent or the publisher's slush-pile reader who has to judge it.

Agents receive, on average, thirty to fifty unsolicited manuscripts every month, publishers even more. They have to wade through these to find the 2 per cent (that's the usual figure given) with any spark – not necessarily good enough to be rushed into print, just those with some potential. If agents are to spend any time on their real work, representing the authors they do decide to take on, they're not going to waste more than a few minutes on each MS. Nor is the slush-pile reader, whether a youngster starting out, who wants to be a hot-shot publisher making the million-dollar deals, or an experienced old hand, perhaps semi-retired. In either case he/she'll have a very low tolerance of badly presented scripts.

Later in this chapter I'll give some dos and don'ts about submitting your work, but first I'm going to take you back to basics. In general, the better the appearance of your manuscript and the fewer obvious howlers, the easier it is to read and, something writers often seem to forget, the less work there will be in preparing it for publication.

By now everyone must have heard the complaints that the publishing industry has been taken over by accountants. Make the logical next step, whether your book is a potential blockbuster or a beautifully crafted work of contemporary literary fiction with a likely readership of a few thousand: don't burden the people you hope will champion your baby with extra editorial costs. Every change made to your manuscript, whether it's to structure, content, style, spelling, punctuation, grammar or layout, takes time and costs money. Get it right from the start and you'll give yourself a much better chance.

The idea is to keep your manuscript clean, clear, simple, without distractions.

1 Text Layout

Open any book of fiction and what do you find?

- The first line of almost every paragraph is indented
- There is no space between paragraphs
- A line space between paragraphs indicates a section break – a change of scene, of viewpoint or to show that time has passed

- The first paragraph of a chapter or after a section break is full out (not indented)
- There are no asterisks, except to draw attention to a section break that has fallen unavoidably at the top or bottom of a page and might be missed by the reader.

There are exceptions, of course, but this is the standard format.

Now look at your manuscript. The chances are, especially if you are inexperienced, that your paragraphs are full out, with a line space between them. You typed to the end of the paragraph, pressed return twice, then started typing the next paragraph. Except, perhaps, sections of dialogue, where the paragraphs might have no space between them and even be indented – but you may well have typed a random number of spaces for the indent instead of a tab.

When you wanted to indicate a section break – probably more often than you really need; remember that too many create difficulties with the page layout of the book – you either typed a row of asterisks or several paragraph returns to distinguish it from the single line spaces between your other paragraphs. Or you might not have made it any different at all, and then you'll complain that the copy-editor has closed up all the paragraphs when the section breaks you wanted would have been obvious to any intelligent ten-year-old.

✐ *Exercise*

Find out how paragraph formatting and setting tabs work in your word-processing program.

- For maximum readability, set your font to an 11- or 12-point serif font (e.g. Times New Roman not Arial).
- Set your line spacing to double (easier for agent/editor to read, for the person who has to work out the extent, i.e. the number of pages when the book is set in a given format, and leaves room for the editor and copy-editor to write suggested changes above each line).
- Choose alignment left (you may prefer the look of justified alignment, but it's harder for the copy-editor to spot inconsistent

spacing between words; alignment left also means the word processor will not introduce hyphens; it is also a good idea to turn off the automatic hyphenation).

- Make sure your page has generous margins (at least 3cm each side: space for editorial comments and queries).
- Set a single tab stop at 0.5cm or 1cm from the left margin.
- Unclick widow and orphan control (which prevents very short lines at the beginning or end of a paragraph at the bottom or top of a page; they don't matter in manuscripts, but preventing them can leave unexplained gaps at the bottom of pages – more headaches for the extent calculator and copy-editor). And turn off 'keep with next' and 'keep lines together'.
- Put 'this page number' in header, top right (it's surprising how many people forget; then someone has to number every page by hand and if the manuscript is dropped first all the pages are mixed up . . .). Don't number pages from nought to whatever in each chapter, because someone will still have to number the script by hand.
- Put your name and the title of the book in the header or footer, in a different place from the page number (this isn't essential but will save your work from abandonment in despair if a whole pile of manuscripts slides off the prospective agent's or publisher's overcrowded desk; it happens).
- Make sure the text is presented on one side of A4 paper only.

Now set these up as your standard document format for all your creative writing. If you can copy your finished novel into it before you send it out, do so.

2 Dialogue

After general layout, this is the next most obvious thing that inexperienced writers seem to have difficulty with.

In general, each person's speech should start a new paragraph – indented, of course. That does not mean you can't have some narrative text before, between or after a single speaker's quoted words, as in the following extracts from *Scapegrace* by Jackie Gay (Tindal Street Press, 2000):

> Cora stopped and whipped round. 'I'm not going,' she said. 'You lot can do what you like.'
> 'Where are you going then?' said Gina.
> 'To the park.'
> 'Someone'll see you.'
> 'Well, I'll go and walk the streets then.' She said it with peculiar vehemence.
> Ellie fluttered around next to her. 'Come on, Cora,' she pleaded. 'Don't let it get to you.'

In certain cases it's quite acceptable to have more than one speaker within the same paragraph:

> 'Maybe that's what we need.' Gina started jogging.
> 'What? To get mean?' I swung round a lamp post and dodged in front of her.
> 'No, a lovelife, prat.' She was running fast, hair streaming back, body a fuzz of moving denim. An old man she was closing in on shouted, 'Oi, watch it, you,' and Gina sidestepped him just in time. 'Soz,' she said. Someone clapped.

Use single quotation marks for all speech and quoted words within the text; double when they fall within another pair. Keep closing punctuation within the quotation marks, except occasional words or phrases, where punctuation follows quotation marks:

> *'I despise you. You're a pitiful creep,' she said.*

> *'She said she despised me,' said Peter, 'and called me "a pitiful creep".'*

He couldn't get it out of his head: 'creep', 'pitiful creep'.

He booked into what The Times *had called 'the best "aparthotel" in Greece'.*

Put a comma before question tags ('isn't it?', 'don't you?', 'shouldn't they?', etc.) and before (or after) the name or title of someone being addressed:

'Hello, sailor.'

'Well, Richard, that's a fine mess you've landed us in, isn't it?'

Many of these rules for commas that young writers are determined to disregard as old-fashioned are there for good reasons.

✍ *Exercise*

Consider the following pairs of sentences. Are their meanings different? Is the same person being addressed in each version? Write short dialogues including each sentence.

'Do you know John?'
'Do you know, John?'

'Never mind Julia. This is about us.'
'Never mind, Julia. This is about us.'

'What do you think about Louise?'
'What do you think about, Louise?'

'I'm not daft Pam.'
'I'm not daft, Pam.'

If you habitually omit the comma before the name, you'll find it hard to make these sorts of subtle distinction when you need them.

If the narrative following speech describes actions other than speaking, the speech should end with a full stop (or question or exclamation mark), not a comma:

'Brilliant!' He grinned. (Not: 'Brilliant,' he grinned.)

The alternatives are:

'Brilliant,' he said, grinning.
'Brilliant,' he said with a grin.
'Brilliant,' he said, and grinned.

There's a reason: you can't grin, smile, laugh or grimace words. Your characters can – if they must – gush, sigh, sing, sob, splutter and yell them. It's also okay to use a comma before exclaim, plead, beg, whine, retort, demand, etc. Remember, too, that anything more than he said/she said, with an occasional she told him, he replied, is irritating and distracting for the reader, so restrict yourself to a judicious sprinkling of the rest.

If narrative not describing the act of speaking interrupts continuing speech, the punctuation should normally be parenthetical en-dashes around the narrative (see Dashes and Ellipses, under House Style, below, for the difference between hyphens and dashes):

'Oh, Liz –' he was smiling '– that's such a relief.'

She peeked round the corner. 'It's Ricky,' she hissed. 'Shit, and'
– ducking back and grabbing my arm – 'Joe.'

Note that since the speech in the first example requires punctuation ('Oh, Liz, that's such a relief.') the en-dashes go inside the quote marks. Where no punctuation is needed at the point of the narrative interruption ('Shit, and Joe.') the en-dashes go outside the quote marks.

Use closed-up em-dashes (double the length of an en-dash) for interrupted speech; ellipses for speech that tails off:

'I was just thinking—' Alison began, but Catherine interrupted her.

'I wonder . . .' She was gazing out of the window. 'No, probably not. But then again, maybe . . .'

There is a trend among writers of contemporary fiction to dispense with quotation marks in dialogue. This can be very effective but is trickier to pull off than many people realize. Make sure you know exactly what you are doing before you take this step. Think through your alternative system – there has to be one – carefully.

If you use em-dashes instead of quotation marks, open every new bit of speech after narrative that ends with a full stop (or question or exclamation mark) with an em-dash. If, on the other hand, the narrative ends with a comma or semicolon, don't put an em-dash:

> *—You still here? she said. —I thought you'd gone ages ago.*

> *—Here, he said with a leer, get this down you.*

This allows at least the possibility of narrative text enclosed in its own pair of dashes as in the earlier example:

> *She peeked round the corner. —It's Ricky, she hissed. —Shit, and – ducking back and grabbing my arm – Joe.*

If your main narrative is in the present tense, the reader has to work even harder to distinguish speech from narrative. It makes your job, and your copy-editor's, much more difficult.

✍ *Exercise*

Consider the following dialogue:

> *—Oh, Tom, I'm sorry. Jim thinks it's all your fault. He—*
> *—What do I care? He's smiling but he's hurting inside.*

Can you tell whether it's Tom who's smiling but hurting inside (narrative) or Jim, according to Tom (speech)? Write out the dialogue with quotation marks, twice, to show the two different versions.

✍ *Exercise*

Read the two versions of the same dialogue, below, from 'Grey' by Mark Newton in *Hard Shoulder*, edited by Jackie Gay and Julia Bell

(Tindal Street Press, 1999). Ignore the ellipses in square brackets, which are there to show where narrative in the published story has been left out. Find and underline those parts that are clearly narrative in the second version but might be mistaken for speech in the first.

Phil looks around, knowing what to expect, sighs and lights a cigarette.

—Can you crash us one of those?

[. . .] —Yeah, sure.

I light it and begin to fill my mouth with the old and new stains of today. [. . .]

—You look like a fuckin' corpse.

—No, I don't. I look like River Phoenix, I say. I do. I bought a jacket just like the one he wore in *My Own Private Idaho*. [. . .]

—Can you see the remote anywhere? I ask.

—Yeah, it's over there by the bin. Phil points.

—Which bit? The whole room is a bin; it just happens to start with a plastic container in the corner. [. . .] It's a fucking jungle in there.

—Phil, I can't see it anywhere. I can never find remote controls in the jungle.

Phil looks around, knowing what to expect, sighs and lights a cigarette.

'Can you crash us one of those?'

[. . .] 'Yeah, sure.'

I light it and begin to fill my mouth with the old and new stains of today. [. . .]

'You look like a fuckin' corpse.'

'No, I don't. I look like River Phoenix,' I say. I do. I bought a jacket just like the one he wore in *My Own Private Idaho*. [. . .]

'Can you see the remote anywhere?' I ask.

'Yeah, it's over there by the bin.' Phil points.

'Which bit?' The whole room is a bin; it just happens to start with a plastic container in the corner. [. . .] It's a fucking jungle in there.

'Phil, I can't see it anywhere.' I can never find remote controls in the jungle.

It's worth bearing in mind these extra difficulties before you decide not to use quotation marks in dialogue.

3 Commas

Many writers like to reduce their use of commas to the minimum. There are, however, some instances where their use is crucial to convey the meaning you intend. Commas in modern English have a grammatical and syntactical purpose, and are no longer there to indicate breathing and natural rhythm.

Clauses, phrases or single words that are clearly parenthetic – i.e. they could be enclosed in parentheses or a pair of dashes, as here, without changing the basic sense of the sentence – require commas before *and after* them:

> *He saw,* a moment later, *that the game was up.*

> *I watch them,* the people who still live here, *as I go back in.*

> *They failed,* astonishingly, *to grasp the obvious distinction.*

Many writers leave out the comma marking the end of the parenthetical phrase or clause. Sometimes they mistakenly enclose with commas phrases or clauses that are integral to the main sentence. Some also begin the parenthesis with a dash and end with a comma and vice versa. This can produce absurd results, such as:

> *A small girl, hair scraped tight into many little bunches pointed excitedly at the helicopter.* (The bunches did the pointing?)

> *If you grow up, in the shadow of war, it damages your sense of security.* (Growing up itself does the damage.)

> *I flung open the curtains – bright sunlight streaked under heavy purple clouds, and recoiled sharply.* (The sunlight recoiled.)

✍ *Exercise*

Compare the three following sentences, each using a phrase with 'under':

> *Her face, under its thick make-up, was tired and lined.*

> *His life, even under the dictatorship was becoming worth living at last.*

> *Many people were happy to spend their whole lives, under this intolerant system, without ever saying a word.*

Show where one comma should be added. Find a pair that is clearly wrong. Could one pair of commas be left to personal preference?

Relative clauses using who or which follow the same rules when it comes to commas. Non-defining relative clauses, i.e. those that supply extra, non-essential information, must have commas, while defining relative clauses, which are essential to the meaning of the main sentence, must not:

> *The lass who lived upstairs always seemed to have money.* (Defining)

> *Janice, who lived upstairs, always seemed to have money.* (Non-defining)

> *This is the book which, for me, best captures the mood of pre-millennial tension.* (Defining)

> *He ruffled her hair, which was unexpectedly coarse, and stroked her cheek, which was as soft as it looked.* (Non-defining)

Again, the second comma in the pair is often mistakenly omitted, especially when it is followed by 'and'. You should not be confused by the common preference, in British English, against a comma before 'and'. In cases like the last sentence above this is overridden by the need for a closing comma for the non-defining relative clause. Similarly, while the subject of a sentence should not usually be separated by a comma from its verb, any clause or phrase requiring a pair of commas takes precedence.

Sometimes a comma is needed to avoid ambiguity:

> *Tea, bread and butter, and cake were laid out on the table.*

> *Way down below, the river reflects the midday sun.*

> *He'd tried Milletts, Marks and Spencer, and Oswald Bailey, before finally finding the sort of walking socks he needed in, of all places, C & A.*

> *The MP admitted that she had hunted, herself, when she was younger.*

Or for emphasis:

> *The rich, and white, citizens are pulling up the drawbridge to the sound of classical music.* (Justin Cartwright, *Leading the Cheers*, Sceptre, 1999)

✍ *Exercise*

Consider the following two pairs of sentences:

> *You can't blame your dad, because he's nice.*
> *You can't blame your dad because he's nice.*

> *I stepped out of the phone box into the still, smoky night air.*
> *I stepped out of the phone box into the still smoky night air.*

How does the comma or its absence in each case change the meaning? Construct other sentences in which a single comma can make a real difference to the sense.

The following sentence appeared in Jackie Kay's *Trumpet* (Picador, 1998):

They are in a big bright yellow field.

This apparently simple sentence, part of a dream sequence, is open to a number of subtly different interpretations, any one of which could have been given priority, if the author had wished.

✍ Exercise

Consider the variations below.

They are in a big, bright, yellow field.
They are in a big bright-yellow field.
They are in a big, bright yellow field.

How does the deployment of comma and hyphen affect the image you see? Focus on the word 'bright'. Is it describing the field, the yellowness, the air, the quality of the light enveloping the scene (remember it's a dream)?

Here are some other examples where the placing of a comma changes the meaning:

My first, prize-winning novel (I won a prize for my very first novel.)
My first prize-winning novel (The first of several for which I won a prize.)

My son, Nick (I have one son and he's called Nick.)
My son Nick (I have more than one, but he's the one I want to talk about now.)

The humble and much maligned comma can thus work two ways: if you use it inappropriately you can find yourself creating ludicrous scenarios in the mind of the reader (including the agent or publisher you are hoping to impress), as in some of the examples above; or, with proper understanding of its power, you can imbue your writing with great subtlety.

Finally, watch out for examples in your work of what is called the 'comma splice' – separate sentences joined by commas, where full stops (or, in some cases, semicolons) should be used. This is one of the most common punctuation errors. It is still frowned on by educated readers. In the following examples the commas should be replaced by full stops or semicolons:

> *The cars slow down as they pass me, I can hear their engines pausing.*

> *Retailers are complaining of poor figures in the run-up to Christmas, many are slashing prices already.*

> *Matthew worked in the city centre, it was a long commute.*

4 Semicolons

A series of simple sentences joined by full stops can be abrupt; a string joined by co-ordinating conjunctions (and, but, then) is tedious to read. This is where the semicolon comes into its own. Two simple sentences on the same subject joined with a semicolon carry extra force.

> *Annemieke is multilingual; she speaks Dutch, English, German and French.*

> *Annemieke is multilingual; Karen speaks only English.*

But note that the following two sentences should not be joined by a semicolon because their subjects, though related, are actually different (Annemieke's skill, Karen's ambitions):

> *Annemieke is multilingual. Karen has ambitions as a writer.*

Put like this, they can:

> *Annemieke is looking for work as a translator; Karen has ambitions as a writer.*

✍ *Exercise*

In the following, can you replace the conjunction or full stop with a semicolon?

> *Stephen did love her for her mind. He also wanted her body.*

> *Stephen did love her for her mind but she had a beautiful body.*

> *Barry was a train anorak. His flat was comfortable.*

> *Barry was a train anorak and his flat was full of memorabilia.*

> *Jude hated science at school. Her parents were strict.*

> *The stairs creaked and Tony froze.*

> *The actress had a stalker. He made her life a misery.*

5 Dangling Participles (and Similar Constructions)

These are also called hanging, misrelated and unattached participles. They refer to sentences in which the subject of a participle ('being', 'given') is not the same as the subject of the main verb. They jar on educated readers (including, we hope, your potential agent) or create ridiculous pictures in their minds, distracting them from what you intend to convey. Like the comma splices explained above, they are seen as markers of careless thinking and writing. Some of the examples below are quoted in *Fowler's Modern English Usage* (OUP, 1996):

> *Being unique, I am not going in any way to imitate him.* (Willie Whitelaw, who did not intend to imply that he himself was unique.)

> *After inspecting a guard of honour, President Reagan's motorcade moved into the centre of Moscow.* (Reagan himself, not his motorcade, inspected the guard of honour.)

> *Now demolished, I can call it to mind in almost perfect detail.* (Richard Ingrams on the house he grew up in. We are not

supposed to think that he is demolished, but that's the picture that comes to mind.)

Running down the road, the cherry trees were in blossom. (Energetic trees.)

Shrieking with laughter, chewing gum falls out of our mouths. (Exuberant chewing gum.)

A similar type of construction, called misrelated construction, produces equally unintended results:

Fluent in German, his position at the university was professor in ... (A position can't be fluent.)

John lived with an aunt after the death of his mother at age nine. (A very young mother.)

A Yugoslav woman married to a Kuwaiti and about twenty Asians were among those fleeing. (Notable example of polygamy.)

6 Apostrophes

Apostrophes seem to cause all sorts of problems. Once you know, it is easy to get them right.

There are two main uses of apostrophes:

- to indicate missing letters, as in isn't (is not), they're (they are), 'cause (short for because; note that bus, cello, flu and phone no longer take apostrophes as they are considered words in their own right these days);
- to indicate possession, as in Donna's book (the book of/ belonging to/written by Donna), the committee's decision (the decision of/made by the committee).

The worst culprit, which everyone knows about, is the so-called greengrocers' apostrophe: peach's, banana's, etc. Many people who

357

would never dream of putting an apostrophe before an 's' to make fruit or veg plural, still think it right to do so with abbreviations or numbers: the apostrophes in (plural) MP's or the 1990's are equally wrong.

The other most common misuse is the inappropriate appearance of an apostrophe in 'it's'. It couldn't be simpler to determine the correct use here: if 'its' is short for 'it is', you need an apostrophe, which stands for the missing 'i' in 'is'. If you can't replace the 'its' in your sentence with 'it is', you don't need an apostrophe:

> *It's a beautiful day.*

> *The sun spread its magic over the day.*

The same basic approach will also stop you putting apostrophes wrongly in words such as 'hers', 'ours', 'yours', 'theirs', since you can't expand the words to 'her is', 'our is', 'your is' or 'their is' (though of course you can write 'there is' and therefore 'there's'). The confusion comes from the fact that 'its', 'hers', 'ours', etc. carry the sense of possession. Another way to remember that they shouldn't have an apostrophe is to think of the words missing from that series, 'his' and 'mine'. If an apostrophe were needed, 'his' would have to become 'his's', 'mine' 'mine's', and it would never cross your mind to write that (except in the construction 'Mine's a beer, thanks'; the equivalents with the others would be 'Hers *is* a gin and tonic', 'Yours *is* a whisky').

Watch out for this tricky one: one's [one is] tired of grammar; one might say one's mind is blown. Ones and zeros are the only numbers used in binary code.

Another common difficulty is the difference between 'whose' and 'who's'. Again, it's simple: 'who's' is short for 'who is'; 'whose' is the equivalent here of 'its', 'his', 'hers':

> *Peter, who's an accountant, has a surprisingly rich cultural life.*

> *Peter, whose work is not very fulfilling, goes to the theatre regularly.*

With straightforward possessive apostrophes the apostrophe comes before the 's' when the owner is singular, after the 's' when they are plural: Peter's work, the solicitors' offices (a practice with more than one solicitor), the grocer's ('shop' is understood).

There are five areas people have difficulty with:

- Irregular plurals in which no 's' is required to make the plural: women, men, children, people. The possessive apostrophe naturally has to come before the 's': women's jobs, men's families, children's games, people's houses.
- Collective nouns such as flock, herd, pack, crowd, and people when used as a singular entity: the people's choice, the crowd's excitement, the pack's leader (but note also peoples' movement in prehistory, for the movement of whole peoples).
- Words, usually names, ending in 's': Charles, James, Dickens, Zacharias, Mrs Bridges, Mr Richards. The apostrophe obviously has to come after the 's', which is an integral part of the name; the difficulty is whether to add an extra 's' or not. The rules here are not hard and fast, but the general preference is related to how we say the word: we say James's, Gladys's, Elvis's, Charles's, Dickens's, Zacharias's, Mr Jones's lifestyle, but Mrs Bridges' kitchen, Mr Richards' car. These names ending with 's' become even more tricky in the plural: the Jones family; the Joneses; the Joneses' car; the Jones car, used adjectivally; never the Jones' car.
- Constructions such as each other's books, someone else's fault. The confusion arises particularly when what is possessed is plural as in the first example: the books belong to more than one person, but the apostrophe is connected to each of them in the singular, the book(s) of each other, so use apostrophe 's', not 's' apostrophe.
- Constructions such as four weeks' holiday a year, six months pregnant, two days' consultancy work, three weeks ago, in fifty years' time. It's not always easy to make the distinction in these cases, as they're not obviously owned by anyone and don't

always lend themselves easily to conversion into the full form with 'of': holiday (entitlement, say) of four weeks. My trick is to reduce the number to one: one week's holiday, one month pregnant, one day's work, one week ago. If you still find yourself pronouncing an 's', you need the apostrophe (after the 's' when you return to the plural); if not, you don't.

🕮 *Exercise*

Put in apostrophes, with or without an extra 's', as appropriate:

> *'Are these socks yours or Tessas? Its so hard to tell.'*
> *'Theyre mine. Hers havent got reinforced toes.'*
> *'For heavens sake. Thats the only difference?'*
> *'Fraid so. At least the boys are easy to tell apart. James are much bigger than Charles, arent they?'*

> *The judges decision, after only five hours deliberation, came as a surprise. Theyd been expected to rule three to two the other way. If the womens case had come up three weeks earlier, before the publics awareness of the issues had been so dramatically raised, the court would have reached its verdict in a much more hostile atmosphere. The Williams sisters held a press conference immediately after the announcement. Mary Williams son, John, was not present.*

7 I/Me: My Husband and I

A word here about when to use 'I' and when 'me'. There seems to be a misconception that it is somehow posh to use 'I' rather than 'me' whenever it is linked with 'and' to another name or person – Sally and I, my friends and I. In fact, it is correct when the 'I' and other person(s) are the subject of the verb, quite wrong when they are the object. To work out which you should use, simply excise the other person(s) mentally; whether you find yourself then using 'I' or 'me', that form is correct when you restore your companions to their rightful place:

[My husband and] I wish you all a very happy new year.

They wished [my husband and] me a very happy new year.

You would never say, 'They wished I a very happy new year.' Nor should you say, 'They wished my husband and I a very happy new year.' It's as simple as that.

I noted down the headline that appeared above a review in the *Guardian* of Jane Hawking's account of her life with the famous scientist: 'A Brief History of Stephen and I'. Checking the Internet archives, I see that at some stage the headline has been changed to 'The Physics of Love and Loss'. Aah. They must have been very embarrassed. They needed only to change 'I' to 'me' and it would have been fine.

8 Capitalization

The preference among publishers is for fewer capitals than used to be the norm. I'll mention only two particular types of use that raise difficulties for inexperienced writers.

* When referring to my mum, his father, their aunt, etc., you should use lower case. When addressing them or referring to them using the title as a name, use upper case for the first letter:

    Since he lost his job, Dad's always moping around the house.
    Since he lost his job, my dad's always moping around the house.

    I've been staying with my aunt Alice.
    I've been staying with Aunt Alice.

    Is Gran feeling better, Mum?

- Names of pubs, hotels, etc., should have initial capitals on the main words, but not for the 't' in the: the Dog and Duck, the Crown Hotel, the Three Tuns.

9 House Style

Publishers provide their copy-editors, typesetters and proofreaders with their house style, which is a list of spellings, guidelines on hyphenation, capitalization, layout and forms of punctuation they prefer. Sometimes they send it to authors as well, but by that time the book is often already written.

The details differ slightly between publishers (e.g. elite or élite, gaol or jail, okay or OK), and some impose their house style more rigidly than others, but I can give a flavour, listing some preferences that are shared by nearly all UK fiction publishers. There are considerable differences between UK and US standards in style as well as spelling, such as the US preference for double quotes as against single in the UK, for closed-up em-dashes over spaced en-dashes, but these need not concern us here. It is, however, worth pointing out that most house styles are based on particular dictionaries, and writers should aim to use an up-to-date one.

Spelling

all right (not alright)
any more (two words)
blond (hair, man; but she is a blonde)
biased
focused
for ever (but forever young)
goodbye
guerrilla
judgement
kerb (stone; curb = restrain)
MPs (no apostrophe)

no one
thank you
till (not 'til)
1990s or the nineties (some insist on one or the other, but never
    1990's, '90s or 'nineties)

Nearly all prefer -ize endings in words such as recognize, realize, theorize, but note the many exceptions: advertise, advise, apprise, compromise, despise, enterprise, exercise, improvise, promise, revise, supervise, televise, etc., as well as analyse, catalyse, paralyse.

It is sensible to use your spellcheck program for basic spelling errors, but make sure it is an English not an American one. Bear in mind, too, that it won't distinguish between words such as tire/tyre, curb/kerb, licence/license, their/there/they're; it's up to you to use the right spelling according to context.

There are general rules for contractions, abbreviations and acronyms. Contractions, in which the middle of the word is cut out, such as Dr, Ltd, Mr, Mrs, Ms, Revd, St, have no point. On the other hand, abbreviations that do not retain the final letter of the original word, such as Co., etc., No., and other lower-case abbreviations, a.m., e.g., i.e., p.m., pp., do have points.

Acronyms, which are words formed from the initial letters of other words, such as radar and NATO, have no points, nor do upper-case abbreviations such as BBC, EU, ITV, UN, USA.

Dashes and Ellipses

When you want a parenthetical dash, use en-dashes – which are like these, longer than hyphens – with a space before and after, as here. (En is a printer's term, used for measuring space. It is half the width of an em, which is based on the size of the letter 'm' in a 12-point font.) Also use en-dashes with a space before but none between the dash and the closing quote mark when continuous speech is interrupted by narrative, as described under Dialogue, above. See Numbers, below, for other uses of en-dashes. To show broken-off speech and to introduce dialogue when no quotation marks are used, use the longer em-dash, as shown previously.

> *I was driving home from work when – guess what? – they pulled me over again.*

> *—Let's go to the beach, she said. —I want to see the sea.*

> *'I think, no, I know –' she pounded the table '– I know what they'll say. They'll go on about—'*
> *'You're so paranoid, Lou,' said Viv, hoping to stop her before she got into her stride.*

In Word you can find the en-dash and em-dash at Insert/ Symbol/Special characters, where it will also tell you the keyboard shortcut. If you press the Shortcut Key button on the same screen you can change it to something easier (my en-dash is simply Ctrl+-, which I stole from something else). Some programs automatically convert two hyphens to an en-dash.

An ellipsis is three (never four) points used to indicate missing words in quoted material and for speech that trails off or fades away. Publishers hate to see a lot of ellipses on a page, so use them sparingly. It is best to type a space plus a full stop, three times.

Hyphens, One Word or Two

There is a trend towards fewer hyphens.

Avoid over-hyphenation of compound nouns, such as dressing gown, dining room, washing machine, phone box, tablecloth. Try to be consistent in your spelling and hyphenation: street lamp or street-lamp but not both; ear ring, ear-ring or earring, phone call or phonecall; letter box or letterbox, door knob or doorknob, table top or tabletop, window sill or windowsill, etc. (Your copy-editor has to note every instance of every word whose spelling you are likely to vary, then choose one version and change all the others. If you are consistent, you'll save her a lot of time. She's likely to show her gratitude by doing a better job on everything else.)

Hyphens are, however, very useful and sometimes essential. Note the difference in meaning:

> *thirty-odd people* (about thirty people) *and thirty odd people* (the people are odd)
>
> *extra-territorial rights and extra territorial rights*
>
> *more-important people and more important people*

This use, to avoid ambiguity, also applies to some words with prefixes:

> *recover* (get better) *and re-cover* (put a new cover on)
>
> *recreation* (having fun) *and re-creation* (creating again)
>
> *resign and re-sign* (e.g. a footballer)

Compound adjectives (and compound nouns used as adjectives) usually need hyphens when they are placed before the noun but not when they stand alone:

> *half-open eyes, eyes were half open*
>
> *a well-known fact, the fact was well known*
>
> *a greenish-grey colour, it was greenish grey in colour*
>
> *nineteenth-century values, in the nineteenth century*
>
> *ten-year-old girl, who is ten years old today*
>
> *second-hand clothes, she bought them second hand* (*or secondhand in both positions*)
>
> *dressing-gown cord, dining-room table, washing-machine drum*

Omit hyphens in compounds with adverbs ending in -ly:

> *an easily learned lesson; a wholly satisfactory conclusion; badly dressed men*

Numbers

In fiction, most publishers prefer numbers up to and including a hundred, as well as round hundreds and thousands, to be spelt out in words, not figures. Also spell out:

- any number that begins a sentence (but try to avoid 'Nineteen seventy-nine, when Margaret Thatcher became prime minister . . .')
- centuries: the nineteenth century, twentieth-century wars
- ages: Darren was five years old, the twenty-six-year-old novelist (though some allow you discretion if you find this latter too cumbersome, so you can put 26-year-old, but she was twenty-six)
- numbers used in dialogue unless this is clearly impractical.

Use figures for:

- exact numbers of three or more digits: 365 (but three hundred); 22,148 (but twenty-two thousand)
- weights and measures (though some prefer, e.g. he was six foot two)
- exact sums of money: £6.99 (but five thousand pounds)
- sets or lists of numbers, e.g. the guerrillas had 10 rifles, 2 Uzis and 5 SAM missiles
- percentages: 50 per cent (not fifty per cent or 50%)
- inclusive pairs of page numbers, years and house numbers, separated by an en-dash without spaces: 11–18, 230–32; 1939–45, 1998–9, 1999–2001. Note that teens, and those following round tens, hundreds and thousands appear in full: 1914–18, 40–48, 500–502; otherwise as short as possible: 46–8, 236–9. This is how we would say the numbers out loud: nineteen fourteen to eighteen, forty to forty-eight, five hundred to five hundred and two, but forty-six to eight, two [hundred and] thirty-six to nine.

Dates and Times

Use 14 July 2000; Wednesday 14 July, 2000; on 14 July; on the fourteenth; July 2000. AD precedes and BC follows the year: AD 85; 54 BC.

There's little agreement on times. Use five-thirty, 5.30 or half past five; five thirty-five, 5.35 a.m.; quarter to two, 1.45 p.m.; ten o'clock. Try to be consistent, at least in the narrative, throughout the book, and spell out the words in dialogue however your character would say them.

If your publisher sends you their house style, study it carefully and follow it, if not in the book you've already written, at least in the next. It will be appreciated.

10 Agents, Editors and Copy-editors

I've mentioned agents and, in passing, copy-editors, but not editors. It may be useful to clarify their different roles.

As you already know, the agent's job is to find writers whose work they think they can sell to publishers and represent them as well as they can in all their subsequent dealings.

The editor, who works in-house at the publisher that has bought your manuscript, helps you to knock the book into the best possible shape, bearing in mind the market they are aiming to pitch it at. He/she may ask you to cut several thousand words if the book is too long, sort out problems with the plot, strengthen the characterization of a particular character, join chapters together or split them into shorter ones, change the tone of the ending. He/she may find irritating a particular stylistic quirk that recurs throughout the book, or think the name of one of your characters has misleading overtones and ask you to change it.

Once the structural matters have been attended to, your script will be passed to a copy-editor. Copy-editing is done either by a freelance, paid by the publisher at an hourly rate, or by an in-house desk editor. Her job is to correct errors and inconsistencies in spelling, punctuation and grammar, to impose the publisher's house style and to make sure that the plot fits together properly after editing (which often creates new problems with chronology, for instance, over-looked when changes are made elsewhere in the text). She marks all these changes, as well as technical details to do with the layout, on the manuscript for the typesetter.

As publishing has become more of an industry and less of an art, however, the roles of these three people, who are so important in the process by which your manuscript becomes a book on the shelves of your local bookshop, have changed, too. Some publishers seem to object to spending time (and money) on editing. As a result, many good editors have left their jobs at publishers and set themselves up as agents. This means they may concentrate more on editing your work, but not be so good at representing you. On the other hand, your agent may be a brilliant representative, but sell your work to a publishing house that puts little emphasis on editing. In that case, the editing of your book may be left to the copy-editor, who acts as a (much cheaper) editor, but one trained to put right details rather than the bigger picture.

The worst case result of all these changes is a poorly edited book, bad reviews, disappointed readers, poor sales, lower royalties and a lower advance next time round. All the more reason to make the best job you can of revising your own work.

The publisher may send you the manuscript the copy-editor has marked up so you can check it before it is typeset. Now that so much copy-editing is done on screen, many only send proofs, at which stage very few if any corrections can be made (and they may ask you to pay for them). If you're lucky enough to get to see the marked-up script, do check it carefully: it's your last chance to get it right. The copy-editor will have looked out for mistakes such as hawthorn blossoming in August or weeks with eight days. She will have done her best, in the time available, to check that factual details are correct – that *La Bohème* isn't attributed to Verdi, dates of historical events, the spelling of real people's names and of trademarks, such as Coca-Cola, Hi-Tec. All this is very time-consuming and it is your respon-sibility to try to get things right yourself. She also suggests ways to avoid unnecessary repetition or to improve awkward phrasing.

With – or without – the manuscript, she may send a list of queries: for you to check facts she's doubtful about but hasn't been able to track down, to come up with a solution to some inconsistency in the narrative, or to rephrase a sentence that clearly doesn't express what you want it to. You have the right to accept or reject her suggestions, though your publisher will generally insist on its own house style in questions of spelling, punctuation, etc. But it is important that you take the job seriously and answer queries rigorously; it's a painful and time-consuming business for the desk editor (who might not be the person who copy-edited the book, might not even have read it) to have to follow up things that you haven't addressed adequately, and sometimes these details may be sacrificed. Some authors feel, understandably, that their job is over, and resent having to do yet more work on their manuscript. But dealing with these final details thoroughly is important and worthwhile.

11 Submitting to an Agent or Publisher

Remember, they are looking for good, original writing, but they can easily be put off. They're all in it to make money, probably more now than ever before. Poor understanding of such basics as how paragraphs work, basic rules of sentence structure and punctuation all take time to put right, add costs and reduce any chance of profitability and therefore of your chances of acceptance. So never send a draft.

There should be three components to your submission:

- Covering letter
- Synopsis
- Stamped addressed envelope.

Some, but not all, agents and publishers are happy to receive sample chapters as well. Check in the current *Writer's Handbook* or *Writers' and Artists' Yearbook*.

Covering Letter

This should be typed and short. Point out intelligently what is unusual about the book – not 'it's like X'. Publishers may have a tendency to leap on to bandwagons, but they'd rather be offered the next new thing than yet another imitation of the last. If your work does fall into an obvious tradition, make sure you have – and point up – a new slant on it. Show a sense of the genre you are writing in and awareness of the market. Include some biography, and mention anything you've had published already. If you can't keep it short, add a separate CV. If you can convey something of your personality wittily, do so, but don't try too hard and fall flat. Don't boast. Avoid gimmicks. Include daytime and evening phone numbers if you can and an email address if you have one. If you can't take calls at work, get an answerphone or answering service.

Synopsis

No more than two sides of A4. This needs to be at least as well written as the book itself – if the synopsis is poorly written, what agent or publisher will bother to read or ask for sample chapters?

Stamped Addressed Envelope

Big enough to hold your work unfolded. Ideally a self-sealing A4, folded once.

Sample Chapters

Whether you are sending on first approach or later, these should be the first two or three chapters *and no more* (which will at least save you postage). This should be quite enough for the agent or publisher to get a good feel for your writing style and the content. Often the first chapters are clunkiest, though. If you find you want to send later chapters, which you feel better represent the quality of your writing, you haven't finished revising: if you don't think the first chapters are good enough, you are not ready to send them out. You have to grab the reader in the first paragraph, whether that person is an agent, a publisher or someone who pays good money in a bookshop.

Follow the advice on layout, numbering pages, etc., at the beginning of this chapter. Finally, keep the pages together with a paperclip or rubber band, perhaps in a flat folder. Don't staple them or use any sort of binder.

Good luck.

Useful Reference Books

The Oxford Dictionary for Writers and Editors, ed. Robert Ritter, OUP
Hart's Rules, ed. Horace Hart, OUP
The Oxford Writers' Dictionary, ed. R. E. Allen, OUP
Mind the Stop: A Brief Guide to Punctuation, Gordon Vero Carey, Penguin Books
The New Fowler's Modern English Usage, ed. R. W. Burchfield, OUP
The Good English Guide, Godfrey Howard, Macmillan
Complete Plain Words, Sir Ernest Gowers, David R. Godine
Copy-editing: The Cambridge Handbook for Editors, Authors and Publishers, Judith Butcher, CUP

Carrying On
Paul Magrs

As we've seen in the preceding essays, there are a great many things to do once you've got a manuscript you are happy with. As if it's not hard enough working with actual words on pages, you've got a whole lot of other jobs to do afterwards.

As Penny Rendall makes clear, you really have to get your work into proper order. It's a bit like tidying and cleaning your house up before you try to sell it. The best thing is to put yourself in the position of the people popping round to have a look. Would you buy a house that was strewn with empty coffee cups and old newspapers? You have to do justice to yourself.

In her essay, Penny is offering good, commonsensical advice about how to make your manuscript legible to whoever you are presenting it to. As she says, editors and agents receive a great many and they get through these things often at a rate of knots. Don't make it easy for them to thrust your piece of work aside. The rules are just conventions that everyone has to abide by. Yours could be the most avant-garde piece of work the world has ever seen, but people still have to be able to read it. You need the standard rules of grammar and laying out.

Even when you have a manuscript that is immaculately set out and edited and, as far as you are concerned, completed, the choices of what to do next seem endless. You could submit it to a workshop and receive further criticism. You could revise it again. And again. You could go on a course at a college or university, you could attend a residential course and submit it for comments from another class or another tutor.

In the end, only you know when you are ready and prepared, and when your work is ready and prepared, to take it further.

You might not want to publish it. People sometimes write only for themselves, or for a few others. Even so, if they are calling themselves a writer, they will still be working their text up into a finished, polished state. Something they can be proud of. Something only they could write. A finished something, in which they have done justice to and got the greatest potential out of the material they began with. Some of the most precise and beautifully finished writing I have ever read is in the journals of the novelist Denton Welch. They weren't published until after his death. Similarly with the letters of Katherine Mansfield, which she had ordered destroyed, but which were published in volume after volume in the decades following her death.

On the one hand, I'm saying that not everyone is writing with publication (and profit and reviews and awards and prizes) in mind. On the other, I am also saying that you ought to bring all your learned skills and techniques for writing to bear upon everything you write. The benefits of good writing practice help expression and clear thought in all kinds of ways, all parts of life.

However, if you do want to publish your writing, the real work starts here.

When it's just a case of you and the manuscript, you only have to answer to yourself. Even if you are in a workshop or on a course, you can still ignore all of the comments you receive from others. You'd be daft to, but you still could. At that stage nothing need come between you and your work.

When you box it and parcel it up into brown envelopes and send it off to an editor, an agent or a competition, you are offering it up for public consumption. Here you have to learn to be brave. Of course you'll get knocked back and the letters you receive won't always be sensitive appraisals of your talent and worth. Learn to cope with getting your work sent back to you. Whoever is sending it back isn't the be-all and end-all. However powerful they are in the publishing world, theirs is only one opinion. Buy yourself lots of brown envelopes and lots of stamps. Look in the *Writers' and Artists' Yearbook*. Just see how many editors, agents and publishers there are. Enough to be going on with, at any rate.

If someone writes to you and says that though they don't want to publish or represent what you've sent them, they'd like to see what you write next, don't throw up your hands in resignation and give up. In my experience, if someone says this, they actually mean it. People in publishing or agenting don't often have time to solicit work. If they ask to see the next thing, take it as a good sign. In all likelihood they mean it. Get back to work. Don't rush it. Keep records of who you've been in correspondence with, who has what work. When you've got the next book or story or collection of poems finished, send it to that person.

Just keep going. There's a lot of writing out there already

published, and there are a lot of writers out there still writing and either being published or trying to be. Sometimes, as someone who teaches them, it seems there are a limitless number of people with books they are working on. When you go into bookshops or on courses, don't let that fact depress you. Sometimes it will make you think 'What's it all about?', when everyone seems to be writing like this. Sometimes it will make you wonder why you want, so keenly, to get your work out there into the world.

This is good. We all need to think about why we're writing and why we set such store by it. It's obviously important to all of us in different ways. The thing to remember is that we all have our own reasons for doing this and our own means of doing it. Writing itself would go on without your contribution, but it would be without your own unique contribution. If you feel you want to offer that, then go for it.

Conclusion

A Good Thing
Paul Magrs

The first creative writing course I ever taught was for the WEA (Worker's Educational Association) in Grange-Over-Sands in Cumbria. At that point, in 1991, I was twenty-one and fresh from my own MA in Writing at the University of Lancaster. During that course I had written the very earliest draft of my novel *Does it Show?*, which was later to be published by Chatto and Windus. Teaching creative writing alongside English literature seemed a natural thing to do, as I embarked on the endless revisions of my novel. It was also a necessary thing to do, in terms of earning a bit of money. It has been said in this book that writing courses need to be taught by practising, published writers, who understand what their students are going through, who have been there and are still learning new things about their craft. For my first teaching job, at twenty-one, I had a lot to say about how to set about writing, but I also wanted to learn from my students. In teaching, I've never gone in with a whole set of incorrigible propositions about writing. From the start I've wanted the students to tell me what they want to write and I've tried to nudge them into a position where they can accomplish that. The impetus, the need to write, comes from them – and so should the subject matter. As teacher, what I need to do is show them the forms, the precedents, and enable them to investigate the possibilities.

Writing courses are a place for conversation. Tutors can set out ideas, examples, suggestions, but they also need to be in conversation with their students. The exercises couched within the chapters of this book are where its authors expect you, the reader, to step in with your own contribution. This book is an attempt to distil the teaching practice of a whole range of practitioners and tutors, and re-enact the experience of a creative writing course.

It's a book for starting you off. But it's also a book for keeping you going. A book for returning to and finding the exercise or the word of encouragement to turn you back to writing.

The voices in all of the preceding essays are distinct. We wanted a book in which each contributor spoke from their own specific position as writer and teacher. There's a lot of experience here to draw upon and to learn from; a smorgasbord of expertise. Conversations are carried on between the essays in this book. I've found, through my teaching, that writers of all kinds enjoy this kind of conversation as much as they enjoy the act of writing itself.

Every week during the gloomy autumn of 1991 my first teaching group and I would meet in the foyer of a grand hotel in Grange-Over-Sands. There we would talk about the novels being written by group members who were mostly women and mostly over fifty years of age. They were writing romances, memoirs, historical fiction and one, rather alarming, gothic fantasy. Soon I realized that they had been writing these books for years and only one or two seriously entertained the idea of submitting their work for publication. The real point was the communality of the exercise. What the group's members relished was the chance to sit for hours, each week, sharing the experience of making their inventions and memories readable.

I've always thought that the main purpose of doing a creative writing course was to make sense of your life; to find some way of making your private world public. Tutoring on Arvon residential courses or for the Open College of the Arts, I've seen people tackling their raw materials and I've tried to help them to craft something that will push their thoughts and ideas 'out there', into the world. Their poems, plays, stories and novels become independent artefacts that anyone can appreciate and understand on their own terms. The main point is always communication and the accent is on language skills. Learning to write is about making connections, so that your work is tight and weatherproof and ready to create links with the outside world, with other people.

This has been the underlying idea behind the courses I've taught in night classes, residentials, by correspondence, and in formal university structures: you are creating something that only you can create, something that people you have never met before can appreciate.

In 1999 we had a creative writing conference at the University of East Anglia, where I now lecture in English literature and writing. Teachers from various institutions, agents, academics and editors met to discuss issues such as purposes, assessment and the practicalities of the discipline. Malcolm Bradbury, who, with Angus Wilson, began the MA in fiction writing at UEA in 1970, spoke about the genesis of the subject in the UK and the difficulties its supporters faced in the early days. Its subsequent success isn't hard to miss; a whole generation of writers have found their voices and places through courses such as UEA's or Lancaster's. During the conference, participants talked about the issues to do with training people to engage with the marketplace and become professional writers. But this, of course, wasn't the whole story.

What I particularly enjoyed about that weekend conference was that no one seemed to feel that fame and success and the huge advance was the whole story. Bradbury talked about the course's initial premise being the dismissal of the concept of 'genius' and the idea that students can be taught to write like they might be taught to mend a car. I was reminded of my earliest writing workshops at Lancaster with David Craig, who approached the whole business with the same level-headedness, the same common sense. 'Does anyone get a meaning for this?' he would ask the whole class, after peering at some opaque and overwrought phrase in a work-in-progress. Every part of every manuscript would be held up for scrutiny and taken into account.

Workshops and writing courses are great levellers. There is no genius, no fame, no glittering prizes. The success you are after is writing something you are pleased with, that has communicated itself to those who read it.

In the pieces collected here there is a gratifying degree of assent over the opinion that learning to write well is a good thing in and of itself. This isn't one of those books that tells you how to earn millions from writing blockbusters. It isn't a recipe for instant Booker Prize-winning success. It's a book, hopefully, that shows you how to sustain yourself and nourish yourself as an ongoing, practising writer.

I've heard the novelist and teacher Fred D'Agiar speak very movingly about the fact that writing courses which produce good writers are also producing good readers and therefore good citizens. To him, a good citizen is one who can engage sympathetically with the world. I've always thought that good writing opens you up to other points of views and alerts you to worlds, issues, lives, whose existence you'd never have suspected before. The improved articulacy that you gain from learning to write well enables you to better negotiate an ever-increasingly complex textual world. Writing well allows you to feel at home in language; to have a place in culture.

At the 1999 conference Maureen Freely described her teaching experiences in the UK and the US. She said that people can get 'ground down' by popular mass culture, and she stated plainly that writing courses enable and empower people to engage with culture in a way they had never expected to do. She was talking about issues of race and class and the point was clear: if you are learning to write well, writing from your own experience and imagination, then you are engaging in a massive, cross-cultural conversation in which every voice has equal validity. Freely said when you first teach people to write, you are sometimes watching them discover for the first time that they are allowed to have opinions about their culture.

This is certainly my experience as both writer and teacher. I come from a working-class background; the first member of my family to go to university and engage in that wider culture. It's hard. It's also easy to lose sight of where you came from, what informed you in the first place; to lose your accent and your roots and your very language. Doing an English literature degree back then, I was meant to cleave to standard English, received opinion, orthodox thinking.

Learning to write fiction at the same time, I managed to remind myself continuously of my own particular voice and background, and to start to make for myself a place where that could fit in.

As a teacher, whether of students finishing their first novels in a university environment or of those broaching their first poems in a starting-to-write course, I hope to inculcate an atmosphere in which people can find the confidence to write about where they are coming from. I don't want them to pretend to be something they aren't, something they think they ought to be. I want them to learn that what they set down actually counts for something in the wider culture. I'll help them craft their work into something as good as it can possibly be; but I want to respect its integrity, their integrity.

Writing courses are sometimes accused of producing writers like clones, through workshops that prune the distinctiveness and oddities out of their work. If the courses are good, I think they make writers who are entirely distinct. They enable voices to respect their own integrity and grow accordingly towards articulacy. They are, in the end, about the vital importance of learning to frame the questions we all still need to ask about the world.

Bibliography

Non-fiction

Barthes, Roland; *A Lover's Discourse* (Penguin Books, London, 1990)
– *Camera Lucida* (Vintage, London, 1993)
Bennett, Alan; *Writing Home* (Faber and Faber, London, 1994)
Berger, John; *Ways of Seeing* (Penguin Books, London, 1990)
Bradbury, Malcolm; *The Modern British Novel* (Penguin Books, London, 1994)

Cixous, Hélène; *Three Steps on the Ladder of Writing* (Columbia University Press, Columbia, 1994)
Cuddon, J. A., and C. F. Preston (eds.), *A Penguin Dictionary of Literary Terms and Literary Theory* (Penguin Books, London, 1999)

Eagleton, Terry; *Literary Theory* (University of Manchester Press, Manchester, 1996)

Feather, John; *A History of British Publishing* (Routledge, London, 1988)

Gardner, John; *The Art of Fiction* (Vintage, New York, 1979)
Goldberg, Natalie; *Wild Mind* (Rider, London, 1991)
– *Writing Down the Bones* (Shambala, New York, 1988)
Goldman, Emma; *Living My Life* (Dover, London, 1930)

Lawrence, D. H.; *Selected Letters* (Penguin Books, London, 1958)
Lee, Hermione; *Virginia Woolf* (Chatto and Windus, London, 1996)
Lodge, David; *The Art of Fiction* (Penguin Books, London, 1992)

Nin, Anaïs; *A Woman Speaks* (Penguin Books, London, 1992)

O'Connor, Flannery; *Mystery and Manners* (Faber and Faber, London, 1972)

Paglia, Camille; *Sexual Personae* (Penguin Books, London, 1992)

Redhead, Steve; *Repetitive Beat Generation* (Rebel Inc, Edinburgh, 1999)

Sansom, Peter; *Writing Poems* (Bloodaxe Books, Newcastle, 1993)
Sellers, Susan (ed.); *Taking Reality by Surprise* (Women's Press, London, 1986)
Singleton, J., and M. Luckhurst (eds.); *The Creative Writing Handbook* (Macmillan, London, 1986)
Sontag, Susan; *A Susan Sontag Reader* (Penguin Books, London, 1983)

Thurman, Judith; *Secrets of the Flesh: a Life of Colette* (Bloomsbury, London, 1999)
Turner, Barry (ed.); *The Writer's Handbook* (Macmillan, London, annual publication)

Vogler, Christopher; *The Writer's Journey: Mythic Structure for Storytellers and Screenwriters* (second revised edition) (Boxtree, London, 1996)

Whitehead, Frank; *Creative Experiment* (Chatto and Windus, London, 1970)
Woolf, Virginia; *A Room of One's Own* (Penguin Books, London, 1992)

Fiction

Amis, Kingsley; *The Old Devils* (Penguin Books, London, 1987)
Arnott, Jake; *The Long Firm* (Sceptre, London, 1999)
Atwood, Margaret; *Alias Grace* (Virago, London, 1997)
Austen, Jane; *Emma* (Penguin Books, London, 1994)

Banks, Iain; *Complicity* (Abacus, London, 1994)
Brontë, Emily; *Wuthering Heights* (Penguin Books, London, 1995)

Carey, Peter; *Oscar and Lucinda* (Faber and Faber, London, 1989)
Carter, Angela; *Wise Children* (Vintage, London, 1992)
Carver, Raymond; *Fires: Essays, Poems, Stories* (Harvill, London, 1985)
– *Where I'm Calling From* (Harvill, London, 1993)
Chekhov, Anton; *The Kiss and Other Stories* (Penguin Books, London, 1982)
Conrad, Joseph; *Heart of Darkness* (Penguin Books, London, 1999)

Defoe, Daniel; *Moll Flanders* (Penguin Books, London, 1994)
Dickens, Charles; *Great Expectations* (Penguin Books, London, 1996)

Fitzgerald, F. Scott; *The Great Gatsby* (Penguin Books, London, 1998)
Forster, E. M.; *A Room with a View* (Penguin Books, London, 1998)

Golding, William; *Lord of the Flies* (Faber and Faber, London, 1997)

Hemingway, Ernest; *For Whom the Bell Tolls* (Vintage, London, 1999)
Hornby, Nick; *High Fidelity* (Victor Gollancz, London, 1996)

Irving, John; *The World According to Garp* (Black Swan, London, 1986)
Irwin, Robert; *Satan Wants Me* (Bloomsbury, London, 2000)

James, Henry; *Portrait of a Lady* (Penguin Books, London, 1997)
Joyce, James; *Ulysses* (Penguin Books, London, 1992)

Kennedy, Pagan; *The Exes* (Scribner, London, 1999)

Mansfield, Katherine; *Collected Stories* (Penguin Books, London, 1989)
McDonagh, Martin; *The Beauty Queen of Leenane* (Heinemann, London, 1996)
Minghella, Anthony; *The Talented Mr Ripley* (Methuen, London, 1999)
Morrisson, Tony; *Beloved* (Vintage, London, 1997)
Munro, Alice; *Open Secrets* (Vintage, London, 1997)

Nabokov, Vladimir; *Lolita* (Penguin Books, London, 2000)

Proulx, E. Annie; *Close Range* (Fourth Estate, London, 2000)

Roth, Philip; *Portnoy's Complaint* (Vintage, London, 1995)
Rushdie, Salman; *Midnight's Children* (Vintage, London, 1995)

Smith, Ali; *Other Stories and Other Stories* (Granta, London, 1999)

Tolstoy, Leo; *Anna Karenina* (Oxford University Press, Oxford, 1999)

Winterson, Jeanette; *Oranges Are Not the Only Fruit* (Vintage, London, 1991)
Wolff, Tobias; *Back in the World: Stories* (Vintage, New York, 1996)
Woolf, Virginia; *Mrs Dalloway* (Vintage, London, 1992)

Zola, Émile, *Germinal* (Penguin Books, London, 1969)

Poetry

Armitage, Simon; *All Points North* (Penguin Books, London, 1999)
– *Book of Matches* (Faber and Faber, London, 1993)
Dooley, Maura; *Explaining Magnetism* (Bloodaxe, Newcastle, 1991)
Doty, Mark; *Atlantis* (Jonathan Cape, London, 1996)
Duffy, Carol Ann; *Meeting Midnight* (Faber and Faber, London, 1999)
– *The World's Wife* (Picador, London, 2000)
Feaver, Vicki; *The Handless Maiden* (Jonathan Cape, London, 1994)

Hughes, Ted; *New Selected Poems 1957–94* (Faber and Faber, London, 1995)

Motion, Andrew; *Selected Poems 1976–97* (Faber and Faber, London, 1999)

Plath, Sylvia; *Collected Poems* (Faber and Faber, London, 1981)

Biographies

RICHARD ACZEL teaches English and American Literature and Creative Writing at the University of Cologne. His translations from Hungarian include Dezsó Kosztolányi's *Skylark* (Chatto and Windus, 1993) and Pétér Esterházy's *The Glance of Countess Hahn-Hahn* (Weidenfeld and Nicolson, 1994). He is currently writing a book on voice and ventriloquism in Henry James.

DAVID ALMOND writes for children and adults. His novels are *Skellig*, *Kit's Wilderness*, *Heaven Eyes* and *Secret Heart*. His story collection *Counting Stars* is set in his home town, Felling-on-Tyne. His many awards include the Carnegie Medal and the Whitbread Children's Book of the Year. His work is translated into over twenty languages. He lives in Newcastle with his family.

ELLEKE BOEHMER is the author of the novels *Screens Against the Sky* (Bloomsbury, 1990), *An Immaculate Figure* (Bloomsbury, 1993) and *Bloodlines* (2001), as well as many short stories. She has published several works of criticism, including the well-known *Colonial and Postcolonial Literature* (Oxford, 1995). She is the new Professor of Postcolonial Studies at Nottingham Trent University.

(PROFESSOR SIR) MALCOLM BRADBURY founded, with Sir Angus Wilson, the UEA MA course in Creative Writing in 1980, the first such course in Britain. At the time of his death in 2000, he was Professor of American Studies, a leading novelist and scriptwriter. His eight novels include *Eating People is Wrong* (1959), *The History Man* (1975, made into a major television series), *Rates of Exchange* (1983, shortlisted for the Booker Prize) and, most recently, *To the Hermitage* (2000). For film and television he adapted *Porterhouse Blue*, *Cold Comfort Farm* and many other works, and wrote episodes of *Inspector*

Morse, A Touch of Frost and *Dalziel and Pascoe*. Critical works include *The Modern British Novel* (1994), *The Atlas of Literature* (1996) and *Dangerous Pilgrimages* (1996). He was knighted in 2000.

RUSSELL CELYN JONES is the author of the novels *Soldiers and Innocents, Small Times, An Interference of Light, The Eros Hunter* and *Surface Tension*. He is a lecturer at Warwick University and a regular reviewer for *The Times*.

LINDSAY CLARKE is the author of three novels, *Sunday Whiteman, The Chymical Wedding* (which won the Whitbread Fiction Prize in 1989) and *Alice's Masque*, all published by Picador. A new book, *Parzival and the Stone from Heaven* appears in 2001. He has also written several plays for Radio 4. As well as running his own writing workshops in Bath and London, he is currently Associate Lecturer in Creative Writing at the University of Wales, Cardiff.

JON COOK is currently Dean of the School of English and American Studies at UEA. He has published critical books and articles on Romantic and post-Romantic writing, cultural theory, and contemporary poetry. Convenor of the Creative Writing MA at UEA from 1986 to 1994, he is writing a book on poetry and modernity, and editing, for Blackwell, an anthology on poetry in theory. He is also Director of the Centre for the Creative and Performing Arts, UEA.

DAVID CRAIG was born in Aberdeen in 1932. He is married to the writer Anne Spillard and lives in Cumbria. He has taught for thirty-seven years at Lancaster University, where he is Professor (Emeritus) of Creative Writing. His novel *King Cameron* is in print with Carcanet and his trilogy of prose books, *Native Stones, On the Crofters' Trail* and *Landmarks*, with Pimlico.

AMANDA DALTON has worked as a deputy head teacher, a centre director for the Arvon Foundation at Lumb Bank, and is currently Education Director at the Royal Exchange Theatre in Manchester. She is a prize-winning poet whose first collection, *How to Disappear* (Bloodaxe Books, 1999), was shortlisted for the 1999 Forward Prize. Her radio plays, including *Room of*

Leaves and *Desire Lines*, have been broadcast on BBC Radio 4.

PATRICIA DUNCKER is Senior Lecturer in the Department of English at the University of Wales, Aberystwyth, where she teaches writing. Her first novel, *Hallucinating Foucault* (Serpent's Tail, 1996), won the Dillons First Fiction Award and the McKitterick Prize and has been translated into nine languages. She has also published a collection of short fiction, *Monsieur Shoushana's Lemon Trees* (Serpent's Tail, 1997), and her second novel, *James Miranda Barry* (Serpent's Tail, 1999).

NELL DUNN was born in London in 1936. Her first book, *Up the Junction* (1963), was filmed by Ken Loach for the BBC. Her second novel, *Poor Cow*, was also filmed by Loach, with Nell jointly writing the screenplay. Her book *Talking to Women*, published in 1965, was an early exploration of what women wanted and cared about. A book of poetry written jointly with Adrian Henri, *I Want*, was published in 1972. Her first play, *Steaming*, opened in 1981. Her latest novel is *My Silver Shoes* (Bloomsbury, 1996). She continues to write and to teach a summer course on Skyros in Greece.

VICKI FEAVER has published two collections of poetry, *Close Relatives* (Secker, 1981) and *The Handless Maiden* (Jonathan Cape, 1994), which was awarded a Heinemann Prize and shortlisted for the Forward Prize. Her poem 'Judith' won the 1993 Forward Prize for the Best Single Poem. A selection of her work is included in volume two of the new *Penguin Modern Poets*. She recently received a Cholmondeley Award and is Professor of Poetry at University College, Chichester.

ALISON FELL is a prize-winning novelist and poet. Her most recent poetry collection is *Dreams, Like Heretics*, and her six novels include *Mer de Glace*, *The Pillow Boy of the Lady Onogoro* and *The Mistress of Lilliput*. She tutors regularly for the City Lit. in London and for the Arvon Foundation, and was the 1998 Writing Fellow at UEA.

MAUREEN FREELY was born in Neptune, New Jersey, and grew up in Istanbul, Turkey. Since graduating from Harvard in 1974, she has lived mostly in England. She is the author of five novels – *Mother's Helper* (Cape, 1979), *The Life of the Party* (Cape, 1985), *The Stork Club* (Bloomsbury, 1992), *Under the Vulcania* (Bloomsbury, 1993), and *The Other Rebecca* (Bloomsbury, 1996) – and three works of non-fiction. The most recent of these is *The Parent Trap: Families, Children and the New Morality* (Virago, 2000). She teaches creative writing at the University of Warwick and is a regular contributor to the *Guardian, Observer, Sunday Times, Daily Mail* and *Independent*.

JAMES FRIEL is the author of *Left of North, Taking the Veil* and *Careless Talk*. He is currently redrafting what might be his fourth novel.

ANNA GARRY teaches creative writing at the University of East Anglia. At Manchester University she studied Biology, and then completed a PhD in Political Science. She is a graduate of the MA in Creative Writing at UEA. She has been published in *Critical Quarterly, Pretext* and *Reactions*.

LESLEY GLAISTER is the author of nine novels, including *Honour Thy Father* (which won a Somerset Maugham Award), *Easy Peasy* (shortlisted for the *Guardian* Fiction Prize), and, most recently, *Now You See Me*. She also reviews regularly and writes short stories and radio drama. She teaches on Sheffield Hallam University's Writing MA.

JULIAN JACKSON lives and works in Norwich. By day he designs and typesets books for the Creative Writing department of the University of East Anglia. He is the co-founder of aztec-culture.co.uk, an online gallery for artists and writers. He also works in collaboration on a number of different ventures: installation art, live robotic poetry, techno-treasure hunts, gallery art spoofs, web sites, teaching, and many paper publishing projects for regional organizations.

JOHN LATHAM was formerly Professor of Physics at Manchester University and President of the International Commission on Atmospheric Electricity. He has published four volumes of poetry with Harry Chambers, Peterloo Poets, most recently *The Unbearable Weight of Mercury*, 1996. He has won first prize in about twenty national poetry competitions, has had numerous stories broadcast or anthologized, and three plays broadcast on BBC radio.

DAVID LODGE has published ten novels, including *Small World*, *Nice Work* and *Therapy*, and a novella, *Home Truths*. He has also written stage plays, screenplays and a great deal of literary criticism, including *The Practice of Writing*. He is Honorary Professor of Modern English Literature at the University of Birmingham, where he taught from 1960 to 1987.

ALAN MAHAR is Chair of Tindal Street Fiction Group (which he founded in 1983) and Publishing Director of Birmingham's fiction imprint, Tindal Street Press. He has contributed short stories and reviews to numerous national literary magazines. His first novel, *Flight Patterns* was published by Gollancz.

SARA MAITLAND is a feminist. Her first novel, *Daughter of Jerusalem*, won the Somerset Maugham Award in 1979. Since then she has published across a range of genres, and taught creative writing in a range of contexts. She has recently moved to Co. Durham to think and perhaps write about silence.

CANDI MILLER spent her MA years infiltrating literary agencies and writing a manuscript that's proved resistible. One day she'll take her own best advice and write an irresistible one.

ESTHER MORGAN completed an MA in Creative Writing at the University of East Anglia in 1997, where she is currently teaching. She received an Eric Gregory award in 1998 and a bursary from Eastern Arts in 1999. She is the editor of an anthology of new poetry, *Reactions*, published by UEA in October 2000. Her first collection of poetry, *Beyond Calling Distance*, will be published by Bloodaxe Books in 2001.

GRAHAM MORT lives in North Yorkshire and works as a freelance writer and writing tutor. His first collection of poems won a major Eric Gregory Award and his latest, *Circular Breathing* (Dangeroo Press), was a Poetry Book Society Recommendation. He has also published short fiction and writes for BBC radio.

JENNY NEWMAN is the author of two novels, *Going In* (Penguin Books, 1995) and *Life Class* (Chatto and Windus, 1999). She is also the editor of *The Faber Book of Seductions* (1988) and co-editor of *Women Talk Sex: autobiographical writing on sex, sexuality and sexual identity* (Scarlet Press, 1992) and *The Writer's Workbook* (Arnold, 2000).

SUSAN PERABO is Writer in Residence and Assistant Professor of English at Dickinson College in Carlisle, PA. Her first collection of short fiction, *Who I Was Supposed to Be*, was published in the summer of 1999 by Simon and Schuster; the same collection was published in the UK by Bloomsbury under the title *Explaining Death to the Dog*. Her novel *The Broken Places*, also from Simon and Schuster, is due out in August 2001.

PENNY RENDALL is the founding publisher of Tindal Street Press and a member of Tindal Street Fiction Group. Previously she worked as a free-lance proofreader, copy-editor, editor and translator, and taught English in Iran and Venezuela. She lives in Birmingham with her family and a stream of visitors.

CAROL RUMENS has published eleven collections of poetry, including *Thinking of Skins: New and Selected Poems* (Bloodaxe Books, 1993), *Best China Sky* (Bloodaxe Books, 1996) and *Holding Pattern* (Blackstaff Press, 1998). She has held writing fellowships at several universities, and was instrumental in establishing the creative writing modules at Queen's University, Belfast. She now teaches at the University of Bangor.

VICTOR SAGE is Reader in English Literature in the School of English and American Studies at the University of East Anglia. He is the author of a collection of shorter fiction, *Dividing Lines* (Chatto and Windus, 1984), and the novels *A Mirror for Larks* (Secker, 1993) and *Black Shawl* (Secker, 1995). He is currently working on a collection of short fiction.

ALI SMITH was born in Inverness and lives in Cambridge. She published *Free Love and Other Stories* (Virago) in 1995, *Like* (Virago) in 1997 and *Other Stories and other stories* (Granta) in 1999. *Hotel World* (Hamish Hamilton) will be published early 2001. She was UEA Creative Writing Fellow in 1999.

ASHLEY STOKES was born in 1970 in Carshalton, Surrey, and educated at St Anne's College, Oxford, and the University of East Anglia. His writing has appeared in various journals and anthologies. He teaches creative writing at UEA and reviews paperbacks in the *Daily Telegraph*. He is currently writing a novel.

ALICIA STUBBERSFIELD has an MA in Creative Writing from Lancaster. For ten years she tutored for the Open College of the Arts and was Course Leader for Creative Writing until recently. She tutors extensively for the Arvon Foundation and Taliesin Trust at Tŷ Newydd. Her first collection, *The Magician's Assistant*, is published by Flambard Press, her second, *Unsuitable Shoes*, by the Collective Press.

REBECCA SWIFT was born in 1964 and read English at Oxford University. For several years she worked as an editor at Virago Press, after which she co-founded The Literary Consultancy. She has edited a volume of letters between Bernard Shaw and a woman who had her baby swapped in a nursing home, called *Letters from Margaret* (Chatto and Windus, 1992), and edited a volume of conversations between A. S. Byatt and psychoanalyst Ignês Sodré, called *Six Conversations about Women Writers* (Chatto and Windus, 1995). She has had poetry published in *Virago New Poets* (1993) and *Vintage New Writing* vol. 6 (1996), and has recently completed a libretto for a forthcoming opera, *Spirit Child*.

VAL TAYLOR is a director/producer, writer and script adviser, with production credits in Britain, America and Europe. She is Director of the UEA Drama Studio, and convenes the Scriptwriting stream of the Creative Writing MA. Val is a consultant to Playwrights East (funded by Eastern Arts), and is preparing *Stage Writing: A Practical Manual* (due 2002).

NICOLE WARD JOUVE was born and grew up in Provence and has spent most of her adult life in the UK. She writes both in French and in English, both fiction and essays. Among her books are short stories, *Shades of Grey*

(Virago), a novel, *L'Entremise* (Éditions des femmes), a study of the Yorkshire Ripper Case, *The Streetcleaner* (Marion Boyars), and *White Woman Speaks with Forked Tongue: Criticism as Autobiography* (Routledge), and *Female Genesis: Creativity, Self and Gender* (Polity Press). Her latest story to appear, 'Narcissus and Echo', is in Phillip Terry, ed., *Ovid Metamorphosed* (Chatto and Windus, 2000).